PRIVATISATION OF STATE LEVEL PUBLIC ENTERPRISES IN INDIA: SECTORAL APPROACH

PRIVATISATION OF STATE LEVEL PUBLIC ENTERPRISES IN INDIA

SECTORAL APPROACH

By

Prof. R.K. Mishra
Ch. Lakshmi Kumari

ANMOL PUBLICATIONS PVT. LTD.
NEW DELHI - 110 002 (INDIA)

ANMOL PUBLICATIONS PVT. LTD.
4374/4B, Ansari Road, Daryaganj
New Delhi - 110 002
Ph.: 23261597, 23278000
Visit us at: www.anmolpublications.com

Privatisation of State Level Public Enterprises in India: Sectoral Approach

First Published 2004
ISBN 81-261-1738-9

PRINTED IN INDIA

Published by J.L. Kumar for Anmol Publications Pvt. Ltd., New Delhi - 110 002 and Printed at Mehra Offset Press, Delhi.

To

Prof. T. Navaneeth Rao

President, Institute of Public Enterprise
Chairman, Swami Ramananda Theertha Institute for
Rural Development
Former Vice-Chancellor of Osmania University
Who is a Constant Source of
Inspiration to Researchers in Social Sciences.

CONTENTS

PREFACE

The Planning Commission started investigating into the performance of the State Level Public Enterprises (SLPEs) in the middle of 1980s. The Commission launched a study on the financial performance of the SLPEs during 1986 the findings of which were discussed in July 1989 at New Delhi. In order to have a reliable assessment of financial resources generated by the public sector, the Commission organised a Seminar on the performance of these enterprises in collaboration with the Institute of Public Enterprise in January 1992 at New Delhi. The Commission intended to continue with this exercise and sponsored a research study in 1994. The Institute of Public Enterprise was identified to take up the study which, among other things, was required to highlight the sectoral and the state-wise financial performance of the SLPEs. The study was completed in 1997 and modified in 1998 in the light of the suggestions offered by the Commission. The present work is an attempt to bring out to the readers the Planning Commission's approach to deal with the problem of efficiency concerning the SLPEs.

The present Volume depicts the performance of the SLPEs into three categories: Manufacturing, Commercial, Commercial-cum-Promotional. This is followed by a presentation of the financial performance of the SLPEs state-wise. The information contained in the Volume has been collected through a data sheet circulated to all the SLPEs. The response rate has been about 50 per cent. This was supplemented by interactions with the policy makers, public enterprise managers and the visits to select SLPEs.

We hope that the Volume would be of immense research interest to the Central and the various state governments in their task of policy making. The research community involved in studying the efficiency of the use of economic resources would also find the Volume of considerable interest to them. The students of post-graduate courses and the first level doctoral programmes in economics, commerce, management, public administration would find the book very useful from the point of view of understanding the fiscal dimension of the financial performance of SLPEs.

We thank Prof. T. Navaneeth Rao, President, Institute of Public Enterprise and the former Vice-Chancellor, Osmania University for encouraging us to complete this study. He is a constant source of inspiration for researchers engaged in the study of social sciences. His support has fuelled our interest in research at the Institute which provides vital inputs to its consulting, training and teaching activities. We therefore, dedicate this volume to him.

R.K. Mishra
Ch. Lakshmi Kumari

CHAPTER 1

SECTORAL PERFORMANCE OF STATE LEVEL PUBLIC ENTERPRISES: AN OVERVIEW

The purpose of this chapter is to discuss the overall performance of the state level public enterprises (SLPEs) in terms of their sectoral groupings. At the outset, an attempt has been made to bring out the importance of taking up such an exercise. This is followed by the presentation of certain macro economic and financial dimensions of the sectoral groupings. The question of an optimum rate of return for the SLPEs pertaining to different groups is discussed in depth thereafter. Finally, the status of the financial performance of the various groups of SLPEs has been discussed, and the broad reasons for their under performance have been narrated to help the policymakers to bridge the gap.

Importance

The major problem in analysing and understanding the performance of the SLPEs is that it is viewed in totality. Such an approach does not help the policymakers in finding out the causes responsible for the sub-optimal performance of these enterprises. It is, therefore, necessary that the SLPEs are unbundled and divided into certain homogeneous groups in order to research whether all sorts of SLPEs have been incurring losses/earning profits, or the problem of loss-making/earning profits has different dimensions in the case of the various groups of the SLPEs. An unbundling of SLPEs in this manner is likely to help the policymakers further in prioritising a plan of action for the restructuring of these enterprises. It is likely to help in segregating the more important SLPEs from the less important ones, and provide a signal as to which groups of SLPEs deserve the attention of the policymakers on the basis of immediacy and their socio-economic and political relevance.

Classification of Enterprises

The policy writings on the SLPEs and the research efforts originating in academic quarters and policymaking organs, sadly lack the rigour of classifying the SLPEs into certain cognate groups. One of the reasons responsible for this phenomenon is that these efforts have been problem-specific and, therefore, did not make any attempt to classify the SLPEs to comprehend the dynamics of their performance as influenced by the internal and external factors. There may have been certain other associated valid factors which might have impeded a sound conceptualisation with regard to developing a framework for the classification of the SLPEs. These include, among others, their varying size, nature, product mix, and divergence of objectives.

The State Bureaus of Public Enterprise have exhibited their awareness of the problem of classification. However, the stand taken by these Bureaus has not been consistent, as they have categorised the SLPEs in their respective states in terms of their location under the various State Ministries/ Departments, soci-economic functions, and the nature of activities performed by them. The policymakers made the first effort in this direction in the Capoor Committee Report on the SLPEs submitted to the Ministry of Home Affairs in 1974. H.K.L. Capoor, the then Chief Secretary, Government of Gujarat, headed the Committee, which had nominees of the Government and some chiefs of SLPEs. The report took a broad sweep of the SLPEs into consideration and categorised them into 13 divisions, which hardly made any sense in so far as the problem of dissecting the performance of these enterprises was concerned. B.L. Maheshwari, in his paper in the Economic and Political Weekly, Special Issue on Industry, May, 1984, discussed the problems of these enterprises, and to comment on their financial performance, adopted the approach enlisted in the Capoor Committee Report and was, therefore, not able to suggest a financial goal for the SLPEs, and also the varying rates of return that should be earned by the various groups of these enterprises. The Seventh Finance Commission mentioned, for the first time, the need for the SLPEs to earn a rate of return. It categorised these enterprises as departmental and non-departmental, and studied their profit-earning record. It was not satisfied with the suggested optimal rates of return that the SLPEs should have earned as part and parcel of the various categories. The Eighth and Ninth Finance Commissions devoted their mind to this complex problem. They suggested a five-fold categorisation of these enterprises to develop the targeted rates of return which these enterprises to develop the targeted rates of return which these enterprises should have earned. They divided the SLPEs into five categories, namely, manufacturing, service and trading, financial, promotional, and welfare SLPEs. The reports submitted by the Eighth and Ninth Finance Commissions observed that the SLPEs, like any enterprise, should have a financial goal and suggested optimal rates of return of 12%, 10%, 9%, 8%, and 5% per annum to be earned on capital employed by these enterprises, based on a matrix of financial parameters as given in Table 1.1. There was a broad consensus among the policymakers and SLPE chiefs about earning the suggested rates of return. However, the implementation of the suggestion fell short of expectations in view of certain practical constraints, such as a watertight compartmentalisation of the SLPEs, as suggested by the Eighth and Ninth Finance Commissions, for a clear-cut division of the SLPEs in terms of the various categories was just not fit from the

Table 1.1

Optimal Rates of Return for SLPEs as Suggested by Ipe to the Ninth Finance Commission

Parameter/Category	*Manufacturing*	*Trading & Manufacturing*	*Financial*	*Promotional*	*Welfare*
Debt-Equity Ratio	—	1:4	1:5	1:1	1:1
Rate of interest on debt	—	—	—	12%	10%
Rateof return on equity	—	—	—	4%	—
Spread of interest	—	—	3%	—	—
Turnover	—	2%	6%	1%	1%
Operational expenses	—	—	50%	—	—
Minimum rate of profit per turn over	—	1%	3%	—	—
PBIT	12%	10%	9%	8%	5%

point of view of practical implementation. The present work, after giving due regard to this criticism, divides the SLPEs into just three categories, namely, commercial, commercial-cum-promotional, and promotional. It suggests a rate of return of 7.5%, 5% and 2.5% per annum respectively for the commercial, commercial-cum-promotional, and promotional SLPEs.

Conceptual Framework for Rates of Returns

A 7.5% per annum rate of return has been suggested for the commercial enterprises which are mainly involved in undertaking manufacturing and allied operations. This composite rate of 7.5% per annum to be earned by the commercial enterprises on their capital employed is being suggested to provide enough leverage for sustenance, declaring dividends, and going in for expansion. 2.5% of the rate of return can be appropriated for sustenance, another 2.5% should be used for declaring dividends, and the remaining 2.5% should be used for expansion. This allocation of the rate of return into these three obligations would later on unfold the logic for suggesting lower rates of return for the commercial-cum-promotional and promotional enterprises.

The commercial enterprises in the private corporate sector earn a rate of return of 12% per annum. The Bureau of Industrial Costs & Prices has also suggested a rate of return of 12% for enterprises predominantly commercial in nature. However, a study of the rate of return earned by the central public enterprises, which are predominantly commercial in nature, as revealed in Table 1.2 during 1985-86 to 1994-95, shows that the return on their equity averaged to 7.5% per annum. The commercial SLPEs should be treated on par with the central public enterprises in this context and, therefore, earn a rate of return of a minimum of 7.5% per annum on their capital employed.

Table1.2
Return on Equity in Central Enterprises During 1985-86 to 1994-95

Year	*Indicator*	*Total*
1985-86	Paid up capital	20,507.00
	Net Profit	1,189.00
	Return on equity (in %)	5.80
1986-87	Paid up capital	24,678.00
	Net Profit	1,770.00
	Return on equity (in %)	7.17
1987-88	Paid up capital	28,665.00
	Net Profit	2,183.00
	Return on equity (in %)	7.62
1988-89	Paid up capital	31,082.00
	Net Profit	3,782.00
	Return on equity (in %)	10.75
1989-90	Paid up capital	42,360.00
	Net Profit	2,368.00
	Return on equity (in %)	5.59
1990-91	Paid up capital	44,841.00
	Net Profit	2,472.00
	Return on equity (in %)	5.52
1991-92	Paid up capital	45,802.00
	Net Profit	2,475.00
	Return on equity (in %)	5.37
1992-93	Paid up capital	51,868.00
	Net Profit	3,396.00
	Return on equity (in %)	7.74
1993-94	Paid up capital	55,683.00
	Net Profit	4,435.00
	Return on equity (in %)	7.84
Average	Return on equity (in %)	7.50

Source: Bureau of Public Enterprises, Ministry of Finance, Government of India", Annual Survey of Public Enterprises", Volume-I, 1985-86 to 1994-95, New Delhi.

The commercial-cum-promotional enterprises are categorised by two polar extremities. On the one hand, they are involved in executing commercial functions and, on the other, they are mandated to fulfil promotional obligations. We, therefore, suggest a rate of return of 5% per annum to be earned on their capital employed, of which 2.5% should be used for sustenance, and the rest for remunerating the owners by way of providing dividends. If the State Governments are interested in their expansion, they should extend the funding for the purpose.

The promotional enterprises discharge social obligations of the Government, earlier being undertaken by the departmental enterprises which were converted into Government companies for the purpose of institutional mobilisation of funds, and commercialisation and corporatisation of their businesses. As these enterprises do not undertake activities with profit-making as the final goal, it is suggested that they should earn a minimum of 2.5% per annum as the rate of return on their capital employed. This should allow them to sustain their operations in the long-term. It would, however, not provide for funds to declare dividends and go in for expansion. The State Governments would have to forego dividends and provide funds to them for the purposes of expansion.

The conceptual framework for the rates of return to be earned by the three groups of the SLPEs is innovative in many regards. Firstly, it takes into consideration the commercial and the social aspects of the functioning of the SLPEs; secondly, it encourages a classification of these enterprises along these lines; and, thirdly, it provides a basis for suggesting a realistic framework of rate of return to be earned by these enterprises.

Sectoral Dimensions

In this section we propose to discuss the state-wise distribution of the SLPEs forming a part of the study and their sector-wise distribution. Table 1.3 provides the sector-wise distribution of the SLPEs. Of the total 882 SLPEs in 25

Table 1.3

Total Capital Employed

Sector	1985-86	1986-87	1987-88	1988-89	1989-90	1990-91	1991-92	1992-93	1993-94
Commercial	3264.58	3645.58	3916.14	4434.88	4891.51	5503.34	6404.98	7197.86	8152.76
Comml-cum-prom	4153.51	4874.29	5653.13	7078.30	8305.64	9541.87	11100.00	12987.20	13215.32
Promotional	240.11	271.83	311.90	1077.61	1300.01	1745.76	2375.97	2411.31	2460.45
Total	7658.20	8791.70	9881.17	12590.79	14497.16	16790.97	19880.95	22596.37	23828.53

states, 436 were commercial enterprises, 314 were discharging commercial-cum-promotional functions, and 132 belonged to the promotional category. The responses of 471 SLPEs are covered in this report. This shows that the study has covered more than 50% of the SLPEs on an average. When related to the States, it is found that the coverage was more than 50% in the case of Andhra Pradesh, Arunachal Pradesh, Assam, Goa, Gujarat, Haryana, Himachal Pradesh, Jammu & Kashmir, Karnataka, Kerala, Maharashtra, Meghalaya, Punjab, and West Bengal. The States having a response rate of around 50% included Madhya Pradesh, Mizoram, Nagaland, Rajasthan, and Sikkim. The response rate was found to be less than 25% in the case of Bihar, Manipur, Orissa, Tamil Nadu, and Tripura. While the number of SLPEs was very large in the case of Uttar Pradesh, namely 74, only 25 enterprises sent responses for the study. Some State, such as Karnataka and Kerala, submit Public Enterprise Surveys to their respective Assemblies, together with the budget papers, in the budget session. Thus, the response rate appears to be very high and crossed the mark of 50% in such cases. On the other hand, in States like Bihar, Manipur, and Tripura, Annual Surveys on Public Enterprises are not prepared in time, and not submitted as a part of the budget papers in the budget session. The response rate in such cases naturally turned out to be very low. In some States either the annual accounts were not finalised, or the state administration was not performing its task for fulfilling public accountability to the State legislature. This resulted in a delay in the preparation and finalisation of accounts. In fact, in the case of a large number of SLPEs, the preparation and finalisation of accounts in time was a major problem. These remained in arrears for a period varying between one and fifteen years.

The response rate was about 50% in the case of the commercial enterprises. The states exceeding the average rate of response included Haryana, Himachal Pradesh, Jammu & Kashmir, Karnataka, Kerala, Maharashtra, Meghalaya, Punjab, and West Bengal. The States with a response rate of 25% or less were Goa, Manipur, Tamil Nadu, and Tripura. The States where there was a concentration of SLPEs in this category included Andhra Pradesh, Assam, Gujarat, Haryana, Karnataka, Kerala, Orissa, Rajasthan, Tamilnadu, Uttar Pradesh, and West Bengal.

193 of the 314 commercial-cum-promotional enterprises filled in the questionnaire. The response rate was about 60%. The States where this rate exceeded the average included Andhra Pradesh, Arunachal Pradesh, Assam, Goa, Gujarat, Haryana, Himachal Pradesh, Karnataka, Kerala, Maharashtra, Meghalaya, Punjab, Nagaland, Sikkim, and West Bengal. The response rate turned out to be less than 25% in the case of Bihar. The concentration of such SLPEs in terms of numbers was very high in the case of Andhra Pradesh, Bihar, Gujarat, Haryana and Himachal Pradesh.

Only 56 out of the 132 promotional enterprises responded. Thus, the response rate turned out to be a mere 40%. The States which exceeded this response rate comprised Assam, Goa, Haryana, Himachal Pradesh, Madhya Pradesh, Maharashtra, Orissa, Punjab and Rajasthan. The States which recorded a response of less than 25% comprised Andhra Pradesh, Bihar, and Tripura. Maharashtra and Uttar Pradesh had a higher concentration of SLPEs in this category.

Table 1.4 shows that the total capital employed in the SLPEs covered by this study increased from Rs. 7,658 crore in 1985-86 to Rs.23,829 crore in 1993-94. Thus, the capital employed multiplied by three times, and the investment grew at a compound average rate of growth (CARG) of 22% during the period under study, which was more than the CARG of the gross domestic product of all the States taken

Table 1.4

Profit After Tax Divided By Total Capital Employed

Sector Name	*1985-86*	*1986-87*	*1987-88*	*1988-89*	*1989-90*	*1990-91*	*1991-92*	*1992-93*	*1993-94*
Commercial	-1.29	-2.58	-1.38	-0.90	2.69	-1.32	-1.04	-2.35	-0.32
Comml-cum-prom	0.23	1.19	1.62	0.78	0.39	0.72	1.37	1.15	0.82
Promotional	-4.07	0.54	0.70	-0.35	0.36	0.18	0.09	0.00	-0.14
Total	0.48	-0.45	0.35	0.08	1.06	-0.10	0.42	- 0.10	0.20

together. The investment in commercial-cum promotional enterprises in terms of pace matched the growth of the overall investment in the SLPEs. The promotional enterprises had a ten-fold increase in the investment. However, due credit has to be given to the fact that the pace of investment in 1985-86, in the case of the promotional enterprises, was far less as compared to the investment in the other categories. The investment in commercial enterprises lagged behind and was to the tune of two and a half times of the base year investment in 1985-86. Possibly the disenchantment of the various States with the performance of the commercial SLPEs might have been the reason responsible. Added to this, their sub-optimal performance, and consequently lack of budgetary support, also emerged as a bottleneck in the growth of the investment in this sector. The dependence of the various State Governments on the promotional corporations to fulfil the socio-economic objectives increased substantially during the period of the study. These acted as extended arms of the State Governments. This justifies a ten-fold increase in the investments in these enterprises during the period of the study. The promotional element in the commercial-cum promotional enterprises turned out to be the mainstay for their continuation and increased budgetary support form the various State Governments. This resulted in a three-fold increase of the capital employed in these enterprises.

In the case of the commercial enterprises, the States which recorded a higher growth rate than the average for all the States taken together, turned out to be Andhra Pradesh, Goa, Gujarat, Haryana, Madhya Pradesh, Maharashtra, Punjab, Rajasthan and Sikkim. In the case of the other States, the growth was less than the average growth taken together for all the States. Interestingly for some States the investment turned out to be in minus. Nagaland, Uttar Pradesh and West Bengal were the cases in point. In the case of Manipur, the minus values became plus in the closing years of the study. The erosion of net worth might have resulted in the minus values in the case of these States. Though in the case of Karnataka the investment did not multiply at the rate of 2.5 times, substantial additions were made to investments in the SLPEs in this State.

In the case of the commercial-cum-promotional enterprises, capital employed grew faster than the average for all the 25 States taken together in the case of Andhra Pradesh. Goa, Haryana, Karnataka, Kerala, Maharashtra and Mizoram. These States emphasised a balanced development and portfolio in the realm of the SLPEs.

In the case of the promotional enterprises, investments grew faster than the national average in the case of Andhra Pradesh, Assam, Gujarat and Madhya Pradesh. These, and the other States where substantial additions took place in the investments, exhibit their concern for using these enterprises as an instrument of public policy. It is no secret that SLPEs in all the three categories did not perform well. Rather, their performance turned out to be highly dissatisfying.

Return on Capital Employed

The financial goals of the SLPEs range from keeping their net worth in tact to its maximisation. The commercial enterprises being competitive in nature should earn as much profits as possible. They should ensure in any case a rate of return of 7.5% per annum. But the commercial enterprises, as depicted in Table 1.5 had registered negative returns during the period of the study, excepting for 1989-90 in which year they earned a rate of 2.69% on their capital employed. The commercial-cum-promotional enterprises were also way behind. The prescribed rate of return on capital employed in their case was 5% per annum. During none of the years of the study they had earned that rate of

Table 1.5

Profit after Tax Divided by Total Capital Employed (Percentage)

Sector:Commercial

State Name	*1985-86*	*1986-87*	*1987-88*	*1988-89*	*1989-90*	*1990-91*	*1991-92*	*1992-93*	*1993-94*
Andhra Pradesh	11.82	-9.38	-3.06	0.97	-3.28	-16.91	-20.01	-20.84	-18.29
Arunachal Pradesh	*	*	*	*	*	*	-37.50	-23.60	-16.00
Assam	7.53	15.77	18.12	20.17	13.69	10.09	6.99	2.97	2.64
Bihar	-67.21	-217.5	-2189.00	*	*	*	*	*	*
Goa	2.73	-2.07	0.57	0.93	1.49	3.79	4.16	1.85	2.13
Gujarat	10.78	9.35	7.78	8.15	8.07	8.72	9.27	7.79	6.59
Haryana	-3.27	4.25	6.89	7.02	11.08	4.78	-0.61	12.02	14.73
Himachal Pradesh	2.02	2.04	2.03	2.04	2.05	2.05	2.04	2.12	1.99
Jammu & Kashmir	-2.17	2.62	4.97	2.49	8.73	20.25	21.85	34.25	186.80
Karnataka	1.96	0.13	0.68	-0.39	7.64	2.78	4.34	-1.35	0.63
Kerala	-2.03	-2.06	0.10	1.26	0.88	-2.12	-10.91	1.34	1.42
Madhya Pradesh	7.54	8.64	6.01	4.47	9.63	10.61	19.28	9.93	12.93
Maharashtra	7.36	12.89	17.07	6.20	-1.51	0.81	4.09	4.07	4.42
Manipur	33.33	—	*	*	*	*	33.33	16.22	7.27
Meghalaya	-11.26	-5.84	-6.09	-5.99	11.46	16.27	26.82	1.93	5.87
Mizoram	*	*	*	*	*	*	*	*	0.00

Nagaland	-63.62	-176.70	*	*	*	*	*	*	*
Orissa	7.78	4.90	7.39	5.40	18.65	-1.81	-0.83	0.75	1.99
Punjab	-15.60	-9.61	-9.02	-7.69	4.48	-2.38	5.25	10.51	26.21
Rajasthan	7.18	6.06	4.54	6.91	6.86	3.77	7.05	1.57	4.40
Sikkam	0.00	0.00	0.00	0.00	4.61	2.70	7.69	5.32	1.59
Tamil Nadu	-3.26	-6.68	-7.05	-5.63	6.53	8.87	8.23	8.65	6.44
Tripura	*	*	*	*	*	*	*	*	*
Uttar Pradesh	-0.55	-7.28	-15.21	-29.55	-29.30	-24.98	-23.17	-38.75	*
West Bengal	*	*	*	*	-734.10	-219.70	-298.60	-707.90	*
Country Ratio	-1.29	-2.58	-1.38	-0.90	2.69	-1.32	-1.04	-2.35	-0.32

*-Total Capital Employed Negative.

return. However, one positive feature of the profit-earning in the case of these enterprises was that all through the study they had earned positive rates of return. The promotional enterprises had to earn a rate of return of 2.5% per annum. Their record was no better than the commercial enterprises. As a result of the dismal performance of the enterprises in all the three groups, the overall rate of return of the SLPEs on their capital employed, for all the States taken together, was either in negative or very paltry, ranging between the lowest of 0.08% in 1988-89 to the highest of 1.06% recorded in 1989-90.

Overview of Financial Performance

In this section we study the overall financial performance of the SLPEs in three categories by comparing their actual performance with the targeted rate of return on the capital employed.

Commercial SLPEs

The commercial SLPEs in this category have to earn a 7.5% per annum rate of return on their capital employed which has been though of as optimal. This is much closer to the average overall rate of return earned by the central enterprises. Though the commercial enterprises in the private sector have been earning a rate of return of 12%, 7.5% rate of return has been suggested to put the enterprises in this category on the profit track. It has been found that even in the case of the central public enterprises there are some units which have been earning a 12% rate of return. This shows a need to create an environment conducive to competitive profit-earning, which can bring these enterprises on par with the private sector enterprises and central public enterprises earning high rates of return. A study of the profit-earning of these enterprises as depicted in Table 1.6, shows that excepting for the year 1989-90 when they earned a nominal rate of return of 2.69% on their

Table 1.6

Profit after Tax Divided by Total Capital Employed (Percentage)

Sector:Commercial-cum-Promotional

State Name	*1985-86*	*1986-87*	*1987-88*	*1988-89*	*1989-90*	*1990-91*	*1991-92*	*1992-93*	*1993-94*
Andhra Pradesh	-0.75	-0.92	-1.75	-1.25	-1.47	0.30	-0.86	-0.41	-0.24
Arunachal Pradesh	1.59	8.71	-0.94	2.34	-7.58	-0.31	0.71	0.32	2.53
Assam	-4.55	-3.70	-3.04	-2.39	-1.07	-2.71	-3.37	-5.86	-6.13
Bihar	2.36	2.00	1.09	0.33	0.05	0.04	1.28	0.88	0.96
Goa	-13.78	-1.20	-1.77	1.17	3.24	6.07	2.43	4.77	2.01
Gujarat	4.65	9.18	15.71	17.12	5.94	7.60	12.16	10.71	9.18
Haryana	1.88	1.59	2.34	2.51	4.13	4.74	4.11	4.52	2.63
Himachal Pradesh	0.86	-0.76	1.06	-0.10	-0.32	-0.51	1.48	0.62	0.72
Jammu & Kashmir	*	*	*	*	*	*	*	*	*
Karnataka	1.16	1.22	1.18	0.77	0.83	0.72	1.02	1.53	0.83
Kerala	-0.55	0.11	-9.12	-10.91	-5.86	-5.69	4.20	-18.55	-1.35
Madhya Pradesh	1.52	1.38	1.50	1.82	1.85	1.74	-1.42	1.76	-2.92
Maharashtra	0.50	0.89	0.77	0.34	0.26	0.35	0.83	1.00	0.65
Manipur	5.26	0.00	2.53	-0.63	-3.74	-4.95	-4.81	15.14	-3.33

(Contd.)

Table 1.6 (contd.)

State Name	*1985-86*	*1986-87*	*1987-88*	*1988-89*	*1989-90*	*1990-91*	*1991-92*	*1992-93*	*1993-94*
Meghalaya	0.00	0.00	0.00	0.00	2.07	0.30	-0.31	-0.31	-0.20
Mizoram	*	*	*	*	*	-0.59	-11.11	-12.57	-12.57
Nagaland	-1.99	-0.08	-0.43	-4.08	-3.63	-5.97	-6.49	-5.94	-5.62
Orissa	-1.47	0.30	0.28	0.46	-1.32	-1.84	-0.47	1.42	-12.66
Punjab	*	*	*	-263.00	-35.72	2.13	15.19	17.27	28.39
Rajasthan	-0.40	-0.16	0.58	-0.38	1.50	1.07	3.49	3.68	3.34
Sikkam	0.90	0.83	0.61	0.70	0.00	0.00	0.00	0.00	0.00
Tamil Nadu	7.56	8.52	5.41	2.33	0.91	1.11	3.80	7.88	3.19
Tripura	0.00	-2.79	0.30	1.83	-1.98	1.52	-0.14	0.00	0.12
Uttar Pradesh	0.45	0.54	-0.05	-0.52	0.40	-0.38	0.48	-0.47	1.07
West Bengal	1.49	0.23	0.17	-2.46	-1.33	-0.66	-1.33	-2.44	1.53
Country Ratio	0.23	1.19	1.62	0.78	0.39	0.72	1.37	1.15	0.82

*-Total Capital Employed Negative

capital employed, in all the other years they incurred losses. The enterprises in this regard in Andhra Pradesh, Arunachal Pradesh, Bihar, Mizoram, Nagaland, Uttar Pradesh and West Bengal were the loss leaders. Some States have recorded a mixed performance, wherein during some years these enterprises earned profits, and in others they incurred losses. Such States comprised Haryana, Jammu & Kashmir, Karnataka, Maharashtra, Meghalaya, Orissa, Punjab and Tamil Nadu. There were some States which had a clean record of having a positive rate of return and these included Assam, Gujarat, Himachal Pradesh, Madhya Pradesh and Rajasthan. These States could again be divided into two categories. In the first category were the States where the commercial enterprises consistently earned a high rate of return of about 7.5% per annum and above. Gujarat and Madhya Pradesh figure in this category. In the second category there were States in which the commercial enterprises earned profits, but far lower than the optimal rate of return of 7.5% per annum on the capital employed. The States comprised Assam, Himachal Pradesh and Rajasthan. These highest percentage of the profit earned on the basis of capital employed was 186.80% in 1993-94 by the commercial enterprises in Jammu & Kashmir. The maximum loss incurred was in the case of commercial SLPEs in Bihar in 1987-88 of 21.89%. This shows that the profit performance of these enterprises swung widely between positive profit performance and negative profit performance. It was not possible for these enterprises to follow the example of Jammu & Kashmir in which case the profit-earning percentage doubled between 1989-90 and 1990-91, and went up to as much as 187% in 1993-94.

Commercial-cum-Promotional Enterprises

The optimal rate of return that these enterprises should earn on their capital employed has been fixed at 5% per annum. The overall rate of return earned by these enterprises during the various years of the study as depicted

Table 1.7

Profit after Tax Divided by Total Capital Employed (Percentage)

Sector:Promotional

State Name	*1985-86*	*1986-87*	*1987-88*	*1988-89*	*1989-90*	*1990-91*	*1991-92*	*1992-93*	*1993-94*
Andhra Pradesh	27.87	19.53	15.15	10.10	7.95	6.04	5.81	5.22	6.46
Arunachal Pradesh	*	*	*	*	*	*	*	*	*
Assam	1.00	0.66	3.69	3.47	3.98	2.52	1.53	0.43	0.50
Bihar	0.00	0.00	0.00	0.00	0.00	0.00	0.00	*	0.00
Goa	0.19	0.66	1.04	0.00	0.90	0.73	0.69	1.07	1.20
Gujarat	-6.56	-3.82	-5.28	-0.91	-0.43	-0.36	-0.49	-0.60	-0.62
Haryana	-67.70	-0.21	-0.30	-7.03	-0.66	0.27	0.51	0.31	-1.64
Himachal Pradesh	-2.54	-1.51	-1.97	-3.92	-1.41	-0.64	-1.26	2.32	4.90
Jammu & Kashmir	*	*	*	*	*	*	*	*	*
Karnataka	*	*	*	*	4.76	1.14	4.34	6.55	4.15
Kerala	0.00	0.00	0.00	0.06	0.00	0.00	0.00	0.00	0.00
Madhya Pradesh	3.97	-0.98	1.94	0.00	1.33	0.73	-1.82	-1.65	-1.71
Maharashtra	1.91	4.94	4.78	3.96	2.85	2.99	5.84	0.46	-0.60
Manipur	*	*	*	*	*	*	*	*	*

Meghalaya	*	*	*	*	*	*	*	*	*
Mizoram	*	*	*	*	*	*	*	*	*
Nagaland	*	*	*	*	*	*	*	*	*
Orissa	-19.46	-14.96	-17.57	-4.16	-2.71	-2.59	-1.67	0.54	6.72
Punjab	3.60	11.02	12.06	11.09	10.89	17.47	*	187.06	161.84
Rajasthan	0.72	1.17	2.35	1.02	2.67	1.30	1.84	1.14	0.37
Sikkam	*	*	*	*	*	*	*	*	*
Tamil Nadu	*	*	*	*	*	*	*	*	0.00
Tripura	*	*	*	*	*	*	*	*	*
Uttar Pradesh	2.30	3.11	2.90	1.06	3.31	2.83	4.73	4.91	0.39
West Bengal	*	*	*	*	*	*	*	*	*
Country Ratio	-4.07	0.54	0.70	-0.35	0.36	0.18	0.09	0.00	-0.14

*-Total Capital Employed Negative.

in Table 1.7, shows that 1.62% was the maximum that these enterprises earned in 1987-88. Another interesting feature to be noted that it is only in this category of enterprises that the profits earned for all the States taken together, during all the years of the study, were in positive. The commercial-cum-promotional enterprises in Assam, Jammu & Kashmir, Mizoram and Nagaland recorded a negative rate of return throughout the period of the study. These enterprises in the States of Bihar, Gujarat, Haryana, Karnataka, Maharashtra and Tamil Nadu recorded positive rates of return on their capital employed. The remaining States fell in the mixed category, wherein these enterprises earned profits in certain years and incurred losses during the remaining years. The highest percentage of the losses recorded on capital employed was 263 in Punjab in 1988-89. The highest percentage of profit earned was also recorded in the case of Punjab, i.e 28.39% in 1993-94. This shows two things: (1) There was a high degree of variation in profit-earning in the commercial-cum-promotional enterprises in the same State. (2) There was a great scope for improving the profit-earning capacity in the case of all the States, which could have gone even beyond the 5% prescribed as the optimal rate of return.

Promotional Enterprises

The promotional enterprises should earn a rate of return of 2.5% per annum. However, as indicated in Table 1.8, these enterprises incurred losses for the country as a whole in 1985-86, 1988-89, and 1993-94, whereas during the remaining years of the study their profit-earning record was far below the mark. Andhra Pradesh and Punjab presented a better picture. The profit earning was negative throughout the period of the study in the case of Arunachal Pradesh, Jammu & Kashmir, Manipur, Meghalaya, Mizoram, Nagaland, Sikkim, Tamil Nadu, Tripura and West Bengal. The highest percentage of profits earned was 187.06 in

Table 1.8

Total Capital Employed

Sector: Commercial

(Rs. in Crore)

State Name	*1985-86*	*1986-87*	*1987-88*	*1988-89*	*1989-90*	*1990-91*	*1991-92*	*1992-93*	*1993-94*	*CARG*
Andhra Pradesh	358.40	507.58	619.36	756.16	820.30	939.87	1010.71	1034.68	1021.73	13.99
Arunachal Pradesh	0.00	0.00	0.00	0.00	0.00	0.00	0.08	0.38	0.75	206.19
Assam	56.95	51.49	55.81	60.54	59.31	57.89	58.63	69.46	69.23	2.47
Bihar	14.64	10.35	1.40	-6.40	-12.91	-29.69	-7.99	-78.94	-80.49	*
Goa	4.40	4.82	5.25	7.54	9.42	9.23	8.65	13.09	13.59	15.14
Gujarat	249.81	324.60	418.23	634.53	760.59	1038.97	1300.61	1591.01	1839.12	28.34
Haryana	49.22	55.57	63.26	79.01	110.85	135.66	174.23	200.43	240.64	21.94
Himachal Pradesh	206.96	205.17	206.24	204.48	203.48	203.79	205.04	258.53	286.13	4.13
Jammu & Kashmir	60.69	55.28	50.75	48.94	40.66	31.81	27.55	19.71	6.44	-24.45
Karnataka	1364.30	1466.40	1568.49	1667.00	1852.40	2012.82	2398.10	2715.43	3100.54	10.81
Kerala	320.30	335.33	345.50	356.13	378.64	392.00	376.68	413.43	410.24	3.14
Madhya Pradesh	19.64	23.95	29.13	30.67	51.51	76.63	63.80	55.68	62.59	15.59
Maharashtra	55.03	72.60	77.11	113.32	129.53	153.50	156.79	179.33	211.41	18.32

(Contd.)

Table 1.8 (contd.)

State Name	*1985-86*	*1986-87*	*1987-88*	*1988-89*	*1989-90*	*1990-91*	*1991-92*	*1992-93*	*1993-94*	*CARG*
Manipur	0.03	-0.02	-0.10	-0.19	-0.03	-0.13	0.03	0.37	0.55	43.85
Meghalaya	17.05	16.94	20.19	12.35	9.86	9.65	12.12	18.61	18.24	0.85
Mizoram	0.00	0.00	0.00	0.00	0.00	0.00	0.00	0.00	0.12	0.00
Nagaland	33.40	16.67	-1.40	-17.50	-43.63	-60.13	-84.41	-115.67	-131.02	*
Orissa	11.05	14.09	16.67	17.42	16.73	13.80	14.41	14.73	15.60	1.46
Punjab	44.11	57.04	69.20	71.04	90.20	81.48	118.63	132.73	157.06	17.20
Rajasthan	38.60	43.24	42.95	57.72	86.42	120.82	156.39	206.46	230.92	25.06
Sikkam	0.55	0.45	0.41	0.39	1.52	3.70	4.03	4.32	4.39	29.65
Tamil Nadu	238.28	241.01	228.74	219.73	225.68	224.82	319.23	409.92	692.98	14.28
Tripura	0.00	0.00	0.00	0.00	0.00	0.00	0.00	0.00	0.00	0.00
Uttar Pradesh	147.74	147.85	100.63	122.04	98.81	81.13	85.43	51.37	-2.52	*
West Bengal	-26.85	-4.83	-1.68	-0.04	2.17	5.75	6.24	2.80	-15.48	-6.63
Total	3264.58	3645.58	3916.14	4434.88	4891.51	5503.34	6404.98	7197.86	8152.76	12.12

1992-932 and 161.84 in 1993-94 in the case of Punjab, whereas the highest percentage of losses incurred was 67.70 in 1985-86 in the case of the promotional SLPEs of Haryana. The profit-earning record in these enterprises points to a potential for enhancing their profit-earning in the various States, if regard has to be given to profit performance of these enterprises during 1992-93 and 1993-94 in the case of Punjab.

Issues and Problems

Despite severe budgetary problems, the various State Governments invested heavily in their SLPEs to achieve their socio-economic and political objectives. The instrumentality of the SLPEs was used to set up commercial, commerical-cum-promotional, and promotional enterprises. Though it is difficult to specify a financial goal for the diverse kinds of the SLPEs, it could be stated that these enterprises should at the minimum keep their net worth in tact and, if possible, should try to maximise their profit-earning on the other hand. A study of the financial performance of these enterprises shows, on the contrary, that they have incurred heavy losses. They were also found to be lax with regard to various financial parameters. Their capital employed was growing in the face of an erosion in their net worth. Their performance with regard to value added was disheartening. They faced operational problems. Their interface with the State Governments was not conducive to their commercial functioning. Though they were organised as commercial entities, they severely lacked corporate and commercial traits.

CHAPTER 2

FINANCIAL PERFORMANCE OF COMMERCIAL STATE LEVEL PUBLIC ENTERPRISES

The purpose of this chapter is to discuss the scope of the commercial SLPEs in India, their genesis and growth, objectives, financial and economic dimensions of their functioning, and problems and issues confronting their working.

Scope

The commercial enterprises form an important component of the SLPE system in India. In terms of numbers, they account for nearly 50% strength of these enterprises. In terms of coverage, the same percentage of these enterprises responded. These include engineering, electronics, textiles, mining, drugs and chemicals, sugar and cement sector enterprises. The telecommunication enterprises also find a place in this category. Most of these enterprises are in competitive sectors. A study of the working of these enterprises has gained importance in the present context, as most of the State Governments are thinking about their public enterprise portfolio. The general consensus is in favour of giving up such enterprises which have consistently been making profits. On the other hand, there is a great deal of unanimity on the issue of winding up or privatising such enterprises which have been consistently incurring cash losses, and whose net worth has undergone a considerable erosion due to accumulation of losses.

Objectives

Though the objectives of these enterprises vary very widely, some of the common objectives in the setting up of these enterprises were:

- Filling up the entrepreneurial gap caused by the private sector in the various States.
- Undertaking capital-intensive and risk-prone industrial activity.
- Supplementing and supplanting the efforts of the private sector in the industrial development of the States.
- Exploiting technological advantage in favour of States in areas of high-tech base.
- Operating monopoly business in the State sector.
- Generating surplus for the planned development of the States and for their own growth.

Financial and Economic Dimensions

The various financial and economic dimensions of the commercial SLPEs are discussed below:

Capital Employed

Table 2.1 shows that the capital employed in these enterprises increased from Rs. 3,265 crore in 1985-86 to Rs. 8,153 crore in 1993-94. The CARG turned out to be 12% for the period under study. The average rate of growth was 28%. The base year percentage growth was about 250% during the same period. The States in which a phenomenal growth was recorded in investment comprised Andhra Prades, Arunachal Pradesh, Goa, Gujarat, Haryana, Madhya Pradesh, Maharashtra, Manipur, Punjab,

Table 2.1

Debt Equity Ratio
[(Total Long Term Loans) divided by Equity]

Sector: Commercial

State Name	*1985-86*	*1986-87*	*1987-88*	*1988-89*	*1989-90*	*1990-91*	*1991-92*	*1992-93*	*1993-94*
Andhra Pradesh	2.06	1.77	2.07	2.22	2.63	2.61	2.74	2.81	2.66
Arunachal Pradesh	***	***	***	***	***	***	0.09	0.02	0.01
Assam	1.57	1.54	1.63	1.72	1.42	1.40	1.23	0.76	0.69
Bihar	4.40	4.22	4.39	4.67	5.06	6.20	6.67	8.34	7.53
Goa	2.76	2.25	2.16	1.60	1.78	1.84	1.88	2.06	2.62
Gujarat	0.29	0.61	0.90	1.20	0.73	0.95	1.11	1.26	1.06
Haryana	0.78	0.77	0.77	0.97	1.15	1.14	1.23	1.23	1.07
Himachal Pradesh	8.44	8.51	8.28	8.21	8.00	7.63	7.33	6.90	6.68
Jammu & Kashmir	0.61	0.67	0.67	0.40	0.43	0.75	0.95	1.17	1.71
Karnataka	4.70	5.06	5.01	5.33	3.63	1.91	1.86	1.90	1.40
Kerala	1.45	1.40	1.47	1.34	1.27	1.42	1.26	1.35	1.47
Madhya Pradesh	0.40	0.34	0.30	0.47	0.72	0.71	0.60	0.08	0.06
Maharashtra	0.86	0.99	1.16	1.45	1.72	1.71	1.73	1.98	2.03
Manipur	0.58	0.61	0.59	0.59	0.35	0.38	0.30	0.23	0.21
Meghalaya	1.22	1.13	1.04	1.46	0.89	0.83	0.70	0.93	0.45

Mizoram	***	***	***	***	***	***	***	***	0.00
Nagaland	1.21	1.34	1.40	1.20	1.20	1.47	1.47	1.46	1.46
Orissa	2.51	2.16	2.21	2.40	2.51	2.51	2.44	1.55	2.32
Punjab	0.46	0.50	0.52	0.55	0.58	0.44	0.50	0.52	0.43
Rajasthan	0.59	0.60	0.39	0.35	0.26	0.25	0.40	0.69	0.69
Sikkam	1.72	1.93	2.23	1.23	1.54	0.37	0.35	0.33	0.33
Tamil Nadu	1.61	1.60	1.60	1.58	1.47	1.25	1.91	1.58	2.41
Tripura	***	***	***	***	***	***	***	***	***
Uttar Pradesh	0.59	0.50	0.54	0.49	0.49	0.48	0.64	0.61	0.60
West Bengal	9.52	11.93	14.88	12.35	14.51	13.29	12.92	13.06	13.72
Total	2.12	2.11	2.23	2.22	1.97	1.74	1.77	1.80	1.63

Rajasthan, Sikkim, and Tamil Nadu. In some States the growth suffered a setback as the investment figures in these enterprises recorded a negative status. Bihar, Jammu & Kashmir, Nagaland, Uttar Pradesh, and West Bengal were the States in this category. A higher than the average growth suggests the preference the respective Governments accorded to the importance of these enterprises and vice versa.

Debt-Equity Ratio

The investments in these enterprises were financed mostly through equity and debt coming from the respective State Governments. A very small fraction of such investments was financed by the Central Government/ financial institutions. The internal resources also turned out to be insignificant.

Normally, the central public enterprises follow the principle of 1:1 debt-equity ratio for capital structuring. Table 2.2 shows that the debt-equity ratio in the case of enterprises under discussion was 2.12 in 1985-86. It declined to 1.63 in 1993-94. In fact, in the case of commercial enterprises, the debt-equity ratio should be much higher than 1:1, provided they are earning profits. Contrary to this, a decline in the debt-equity ratio in the case of these enterprises shows that they were not fulfilling this condition, and the losses incurred in these enterprises had been made good by the infusion of new equity. The States where the debt-equity ratios were higher than the average included Andhra Pradesh, Bihar, Goa, Himachal Pradesh, Jammu & Kashmir, Maharashtra, Orissa, Tamil Nadu, and West Bengal. In most of the States, these enterprises did not earn profits as a whole, and as the State Governments declined to extend equity support to sustain the losses incurred, their debts swelled. In some cases the cash losses are made good by way of debt and social obligations in respect of which losses incurred were made good by the debt component.

Table 2.2

Total Revenue

Sector:
Commercial

State Name	*1985-86*	*1986-87*	*1987-88*	*1988-89*	*1989-90*	*1990-91*	*1991-92*	*1992-93*	*1993-94*	*CARG*
Andhra Pradesh	468.39	509.06	587.06	813.97	925.74	1032.71	1340.89	1162.29	1084.72	11.07
Arunachal Pradesh	0.00	0.00	0.00	0.00	0.00	0.00	0.00	0.04	0.06	50.00
Assam	53.52	58.02	60.78	70.80	79.61	81.03	82.92	85.16	86.19	6.14
Bihar	21.47	50.94	60.28	56.95	75.67	72.30	71.39	87.25	88.87	19.43
Goa	2.87	3.76	4.22	5.91	7.12	9.95	13.15	12.42	9.53	16.19
Gujarat	442.26	508.41	540.24	890.38	980.27	1043.61	1342.89	1496.53	1614.07	17.57
Haryana	215.81	251.90	272.92	182.33	330.45	431.58	602.47	637.58	875.63	19.13
Himachal Pradesh	38.33	44.50	47.79	53.01	91.10	53.92	52.14	65.68	78.60	9.39
Jammu & Kashmir	41.30	44.36	53.77	72.16	61.56	38.76	64.50	71.93	58.84	4.52
Karnataka	386.67	467.23	628.21	696.24	808.30	864.11	928.25	962.10	1215.28	15.39
Kerala	409.82	447.63	504.12	553.54	601.19	684.26	767.77	916.61	959.34	11.22
Madhya Pradesh	32.50	28.16	32.90	33.91	57.21	87.65	127.57	54.12	52.54	6.19
Maharashtra	145.00	161.54	184.55	196.86	232.59	240.16	263.82	272.88	259.17	7.53

(Contd.)

Table 2.2 (contd.)

State Name	*1985-86*	*1986-87*	*1987-88*	*1988-89*	*1989-90*	*1990-91*	*1991-92*	*1992-93*	*1993-94*	*CARG*
Manipur	0.32	-0.09	0.05	0.22	0.07	0.09	0.18	0.36	0.53	6.51
Meghalaya	9.69	10.65	9.60	10.68	18.66	22.83	26.48	22.13	24.28	12.17
Mizoram	0.00	0.00	0.00	0.00	0.00	0.00	0.00	0.00	0.12	0.00
Nagaland	6.24	5.42	6.85	2.85	1.58	4.45	5.01	1.26	2.00	-13.26
Orissa	59.43	59.17	75.57	78.63	81.31	80.52	92.11	82.23	98.20	6.48
Punjab	72.12	952.54	132.85	143.33	181.49	215.55	242.14	308.27	350.23	21.84
Rajasthan	56.27	63.03	69.97	88.36	127.19	136.44	158.44	202.70	249.87	20.48
Sikkam	0.46	0.42	0.26	0.48	0.96	1.62	2.42	2.90	2.14	23.00
Tamil Nadu	343.36	340.55	363.91	392.20	408.88	459.09	526.43	569.70	599.12	7.21
Tripura	0.00	0.00	0.00	0.00	0.00	0.00	0.00	0.00	0.00	0.00
Uttar Pradesh	124.99	118.73	144.63	172.68	169.36	171.06	154.49	193.26	247.94	8.94
West Bengal	23.94	30.19	40.48	41.69	53.10	50.98	62.98	68.63	75.13	15.37
Total	2954.76	3299.12	3821.01	4557.18	5297.41	5782.67	6928.44	7296.03	8032.71	13.32

Total Revenue

Table 2.3 reveals that the total revenue of these enterprises increased from Rs. 2,955 crore in 1985-86 to Rs.8,033 crore in 1993-94, at a CARG of 13.32%, which was higher than the CARG of capital employed, but lower than the CARG of net worth. In this connection, it may be noted that the ratio of total revenue to capital employed was about 1:1 in 1993-94, the final year of the study. In 1985-86 this ratio was less than 1:1, indicating the fact that one rupee of capital employed produced less than one rupee of revenue. In the case of the private corporate sector and central public enterprises, this ratio was on the higher side, suggesting to us the scope for higher utilisaiton of capacities in these enterprises and a review of their product lines and also their capacities. Some of the States where the growth of total revenue was less than the national average included Andhra Pradesh, Assam, Himachal Pradesh, Jammu & Kashmir, Kerala, Madhya Pradesh, Maharashtra, Manipur, Meghalaya, Nagaland, Orissa, Tamil Nadu, and Uttar Pradesh. It appears that these were also the States where the capital employed to total revenue ratio eluded optimality.

Net Worth

Table 2.4 points out that the net worth of these enterprises increased from Rs.604 crore in 1985-86 to Rs. 2,044 crore in 1993-94. The CARG of net worth was 16.47%, which was higher than the CARG of capital employed, indicating the fact that there were heavy equity infusions in these enterprises. In some States the net worth figure was in minus. In States such as Bihar, Jammu & Kashmir, Nagaland, Uttar Pradesh, and West Bengal, it is seen that heavy cash losses impaired the equity and reserve balances, so much so that the net worth figure turned into negative. In some other States, such as Assam and Kerala, the net worth balances were lower in 1993-94 as compared

Table 2.3

Net Worth

(Rs. in Crore)

Sector: Commercial

State Name	*1985-86*	*1986-87*	*1987-88*	*1988-89*	*1989-90*	*1990-91*	*1991-92*	*1992-93*	*1993-94*	*CARG*
Andhra Pradesh	30.57	72.39	54.32	101.20	46.17	52.69	57.27	49.63	57.87	8.30
Arunachal Pradesh	0.00	0.00	0.00	0.00	0.00	0.00	0.07	0.37	0.74	225.14
Assam	27.67	35.75	37.33	41.66	34.98	34.11	31.00	20.89	18.72	-4.77
Bihar	-68.99	-85.50	-112.78	-132.52	-163.25	208.84	-250.34	-308.07	-304.94	*
Goa	0.63	0.82	0.80	2.17	2.23	2.59	2.61	2.65	2.61	19.44
Gujarat	167.18	179.66	186.31	232.52	377.10	521.80	563.93	635.71	818.38	21.97
Haryana	16.39	16.41	24.00	31.80	48.97	6.70	81.87	107.28	150.63	31.95
Himachal Pradesh	25.32	33.11	33.69	36.18	36.35	37.82	38.15	47.13	36.63	4.72
Jammu & Kashmir	26.51	21.99	22.49	24.91	19.96	11.40	6.62	-3.87	-27.08	*
Karnataka	210.24	201.95	209.67	187.92	320.63	619.79	745.34	821.60	1167.57	23.90
Kerala	67.75	51.24	47.90	55.27	58.46	49.91	5.21	-10.39	30.41	-9.53
Madhya Pradesh	14.47	18.68	23.93	31.36	34.43	44.64	40.42	68.74	78.12	23.46
Maharashtra	27.00	34.83	51.22	59.50	61.27	58.75	63.59	60.21	69.75	12.60
Manipur	0.03	-0.02	-0.10	-0.13	-0.04	-0.12	0.03	0.37	0.70	48.25

Meghalaya	9.68	10.62	11.41	12.46	18.33	16.85	18.03	20.13	19.16	8.91
Mizoram	0.00	0.00	0.00	0.00	0.00	0.00	0.00	0.00	0.12	0.00
Nagaland	-23.14	-46.26	-66.76	-88.87	-112.09	-132.23	-155.76	-179.42	-201.53	*
Orissa	32.89	37.54	44.72	51.73	54.67	55.61	60.56	67.17	70.49	10.00
Punjab	3.53	10.81	51.24	26.14	39.93	51.60	69.31	85.09	125.65	56.29
Rajasthan	19.35	22.23	26.47	39.69	65.28	92.49	105.34	118.74	131.51	27.07
Sikkam	0.57	0.57	0.57	0.95	2.16	4.18	4.71	5.32	5.41	32.48
Tamil Nadu	16.51	12.05	5.28	1.75	46.96	33.81	29.08	85.24	113.39	27.23
Tripura	0.00	0.00	0.00	0.00	0.00	0.00	0.00	0.00	0.00	0.00
Uttar Pradesh	99.52	99.02	39.49	43.04	22.24	7.03	-5.25	-33.29	-85.20	*
West Bengal	-99.95	-125.29	-145.70	-155.73	-164.11	-176.89	-193.27	-216.14	-235.17	*
Total	603.65	602.54	495.49	602.98	850.63	1865.83	1318.49	1445.08	2043.94	16.47

Table 2.4

Profit After Tax

(Rs. in Crore)

Sector: Commercial

State Name	*1985-86*	*1986-87*	*1987-88*	*1988-89*	*1989-90*	*1990-91*	*1991-92*	*1992-93*	*1993-94*	*CARG*
Andhra Pradesh	42.36	-47.65	-18.96	7.32	-26.91	-158.96	-202.24	-215.59	-186.86	*
Arunachal Pradesh	0.00	0.00	0.00	0.00	0.00	0.00	-0.03	-0.09	-0.12	*
Assam	4.04	8.66	10.49	11.56	7.69	5.90	4.12	2.05	1.94	-8.76
Bihar	-8.81	-21.89	-29.04	-23.25	-34.82	-44.26	-47.62	-54.21	-51.20	*
Goa	0.12	-0.10	0.03	0.07	0.14	0.35	0.36	0.24	0.25	9.61
Gujarat	26.92	30.34	33.04	51.72	61.39	90.65	120.55	123.94	121.27	20.70
Haryana	-2.06	1.87	3.98	5.11	11.88	6.05	-1.53	23.63	34.90	*
Himachal Pradesh	4.18	4.18	4.18	4.39	4.41	4.18	4.18	5.49	5.70	3.95
Jammu & Kashmir	-1.32	1.45	2.52	1.22	3.55	6.44	6.02	6.75	12.03	*
Karnataka	26.69	1.90	11.22	-7.19	142.75	59.68	106.37	-35.88	21.41	-2.72
Kerala	-6.12	-7.32	-0.19	3.78	4.76	-9.51	-44.00	6.22	6.74	*
Madhya Pradesh	1.48	2.07	1.75	1.37	4.96	8.13	12.30	5.53	8.09	23.75
Maharashtra	4.05	9.38	13.16	7.05	1.33	1.25	6.41	7.32	9.34	11.01
Manipur	0.01	0.00	-0.03	0.03	-0.11	-0.02	0.01	0.06	0.04	18.92

State										
Meghalaya	-1.92	-0.99	-1.23	-0.74	1.13	1.57	3.25	0.36	1.07	*
Mizoram	0.00	0.00	0.00	0.00	0.00	0.00	0.00	0.00	0.00	0.00
Nagaland	-21.25	-29.45	-27.70	-29.55	-30.25	-33.11	-26.58	-24.56	-24.86	*
Orissa	-0.21	-1.65	-3.83	-6.02	-0.74	-1.34	-5.16	-4.83	-1.78	*
Punjab	-6.88	-5.34	-6.14	-5.39	4.16	-1.83	6.38	14.09	41.39	*
Rajasthan	2.77	2.62	1.95	3.99	5.93	4.56	11.02	3.25	10.17	17.65
Sikkam	0.00	0.00	0.00	0.00	0.07	0.10	0.31	0.23	0.07	0.00
Tamil Nadu	-7.76	-16.10	-16.12	-12.38	15.70	21.27	28.65	36.80	49.13	*
Tripura	0.00	0.00	0.00	0.00	0.00	0.00	0.00	0.00	0.00	0.00
Uttar Pradesh	0.18	-9.77	-14.32	-35.07	-27.96	-18.97	-24.73	-43.62	-57.63	*
West Bengal	-14.51	-16.30	-18.82	-17.90	-17.61	-14.65	-24.35	-26.00	-27.50	*
Total	41.96	-94.09	-54.06	-39.88	131.45	-72.52	-66.31	-168.82	-26.41	*

*-CARG ignored in case of negative values

to 1985-86, indicating the fact that all these States also accumulated losses impairing their net worth balances.

Profit After Tax

Profit after tax represents the bottom line of all operational and non-operational revenues earned by an enterprise. A study of Table 2.5 shows that out of the nine-year study period these enterprises, for all the States taken together, earned net losses, excepting, for the years 1986-87 and 1989-90. The CARG was "Nil" for all the States taken together for the various years of the study. It was positive individually in the case of Goa, Gujarat, Himachal Pradesh, Madhya Pradesh, Maharashtra, Manipur, and Rajasthan. In the case of the other States, the trends in profit-earning were erratic, but it required no complexity to understand the behaviour of the overall profit-earning by the various States which was negative for the study as a whole.

Accumulated Losses

Table 2.6 discloses that the accumulated losses of these enterprises increased by three and a half times over the nine-year period of the study, from Rs. 984 crore in 1985-86 to Rs. 3,228 crore in 1993-94. In terms of volume, Andhra Pradesh, Bihar, Kerala, Uttar Pradesh, and West Bengal topped the table by recording accumulated losses several times more than their net worth. The accumulated losses were about 67% of the net worth in 1985-86 for all the 25 States taken together. The accumulated losses overtook the net worth balance in 1993-94, in which year these amounted to Rs. 3,228 crore compared to Rs. 2,044 crore of net worth.

Current Ratio

As depicted in Table 2.7, the current ratio in these enterprises fluctuated between 1.38 in 1985-86 and 1.29 in

Table 2.5

Accumulated Loss

Sector: Commercial (Rs. in Crore)

State Name	*1985-86*	*1986-87*	*1987-88*	*1988-89*	*1989-90*	*1990-91*	*1991-92*	*1992-93*	*1993-94*
Andhra Pradesh	159.84	122.09	155.52	172.56	282.75	452.39	668.76	680.89	676.16
Arunachal Pradesh	0.00	0.00	0.00	0.00	0.00	0.00	0.03	0.12	0.24
Assam	24.10	30.12	37.14	43.83	43.00	44.77	48.81	50.86	52.83
Bihar	87.86	110.37	141.03	163.98	199.61	244.41	292.69	347.50	345.8
Goa	3.10	3.26	3.28	3.27	3.22	2.86	2.86	3.01	3.2
Gujarat	27.39	32.53	39.91	46.76	50.65	56.04	45.48	41.36	30.43
Haryana	30.06	31.78	32.50	31.30	26.78	28.28	41.37	53.21	64.93
Himachal Pradesh	13.12	16.40	18.49	21.46	22.06	25.04	27.27	28.27	29.49
Jammu & Kashmir	15.57	18.93	21.99	24.53	30.47	39.95	46.65	56.51	71.76
Karnataka	44.55	59.78	72.72	99.87	112.27	119.38	152.60	184.81	199.63
Kerala	127.76	154.42	187.81	207.49	243.13	285.61	370.54	398.36	369.59
Madhya Pradesh	0.11	0.51	0.84	1.46	5.14	0.00	0.00	0.00	0.00
Maharashtra	32.79	42.04	55.91	62.04	64.53	73.56	84.99	109.35	110.36

(Contd.)

Table 2.5 (contd.)

State Name	*1985-86*	*1986-87*	*1987-88*	*1988-89*	*1989-90*	*1990-91*	*1991-92*	*1992-93*	*1993-94*
Manipur	0.28	0.33	0.42	0.45	0.61	0.70	0.86	0.80	0.82
Meghalaya	15.72	18.03	20.68	21.39	23.46	23.13	20.52	21.00	19.95
Mizoram	0.00	0.00	0.00	0.00	0.00	0.00	0.00	0.00	0.00
Nagaland	69.31	92.50	113.08	148.09	171.42	180.60	204.34	228.10	250.40
Orissa	27.38	29.87	35.00	43.44	46.67	49.87	55.82	63.52	66.01
Punjab	26.09	31.17	39.33	43.88	40.54	47.79	64.03	82.61	85.92
Rajasthan	13.75	13.43	13.31	11.31	11.39	12.05	12.14	12.04	9.09
Sikkam	0.65	0.72	0.90	0.90	0.92	1.01	1.03	1.23	1.23
Tamil Nadu	94.18	103.84	110.95	116.61	84.37	103.41	116.92	117.73	124.79
Tripura	0.00	0.00	0.00	0.00	0.00	0.00	0.00	0.00	0.00
Uttar Pradesh	51.47	73.66	108.80	155.48	189.48	219.58	257.97	314.68	375.78
West Bengal	118.79	159.67	182.55	201.80	219.98	241.74	270.51	309.16	339.27
Total	983.87	1145.54	1392.16	1621.90	1872.45	2252.17	2786.19	3105.12	3227.91

Table 2.6

Current Assets Divided by Current Liabilities

Sector: Commercial

State Name	*1985-86*	*1986-87*	*1987-88*	*1988-89*	*1989-90*	*1990-91*	*1991-92*	*1992-93*	*1993-94*
Andhra Pradesh	1.52	1.70	1.56	1.58	1.25	1.09	0.96	0.96	0.92
Arunachal Pradesh	*	*	*	*	*	*	1.00	30.00	16.50
Assam	1.17	1.04	1.03	1.03	1.03	1.19	1.18	1.46	1.40
Bihar	1.05	1.02	0.93	0.89	0.75	0.68	0.82	0.74	0.75
Goa	0.87	1.01	1.15	1.43	1.50	1.47	1.33	1.70	2.50
Gujarat	1.44	1.42	1.48	1.70	1.72	1.46	1.16	1.32	1.39
Haryana	1.05	1.11	1.40	1.77	2.07	1.47	1.53	1.66	1.56
Himachal Pradesh	1.49	1.46	1.47	1.48	1.43	1.44	1.31	1.39	1.54
Jammu & Kashmir	1.46	1.18	1.10	1.04	0.97	0.89	0.82	0.77	0.71
Karnataka	1.59	1.62	1.60	1.51	1.90	1.41	1.86	1.56	1.60
Kerala	1.27	1.19	1.24	1.25	1.26	1.29	1.19	1.21	1.24
Madhya Pradesh	1.09	0.45	1.40	0.57	1.30	1.28	1.49	2.01	2.35
Maharashtra	1.23	1.31	1.31	1.64	2.03	1.98	1.91	2.00	2.35

(Contd.)

Table 2.6 (contd.)

State Name	*1985-86*	*1986-87*	*1987-88*	*1988-89*	*1989-90*	*1990-91*	*1991-92*	*1992-93*	*1993-94*
Manipur	0.84	0.76	0.65	0.58	0.79	0.65	0.83	1.60	2.00
Meghalaya	0.78	0.80	0.81	0.96	1.02	1.07	1.06	1.02	0.99
Mizoram	*	*	*	*	*	*	*	*	1.38
Nagaland	0.34	0.23	0.20	0.13	0.07	0.15	0.08	0.05	0.03
Orissa	0.78	0.80	0.80	0.73	0.79	0.78	0.70	0.66	0.67
Punjab	1.17	1.19	1.28	1.31	1.45	1.35	1.41	1.38	1.69
Rajasthan	1.26	1.25	1.19	1.26	1.44	1.36	1.21	1.33	1.34
Sikkam	1.79	1.00	0.92	0.95	1.71	1.29	1.44	1.42	1.66
Tamil Nadu	1.38	1.31	1.24	1.19	1.20	1.20	1.64	2.07	2.47
Tripura	*	*	*	*	*	*	*	*	*
Uttar Pradesh	1.43	1.27	1.05	0.91	0.80	0.75	0.75	0.65	0.5
West Bengal	0.56	0.60	0.67	0.79	0.85	0.85	0.82	0.74	0.93
Country Ratio	1.38	1.36	1.36	1.39	1.40	1.26	1.23	1.26	1.29

Table 2.7
(Value Added (Wages+Net Profit+Interest))

Sector: Commercial (Rs. in.Crore)

State Name	*1985-86*	*1986-87*	*1987-88*	*1988-89*	*1989-90*	*1990-91*	*1991-92*	*1992-93*	*1993-94*	*CARG*
Andhra Pradesh	266.80	191.50	279.54	365.45	376.55	325.59	409.18	397.55	420.70	5.06
Arunachal Pradesh	0.00	0.00	0.00	0.00	0.00	0.00	-0.02	-0.03	-0.30	*
Assam	14.08	21.02	24.51	27.21	21.91	20.93	20.15	19.62	19.30	4.07
Bihar	8.53	1.64	-0.60	-0.57	-1.37	-3.34	-2.60	-1.78	-0.52	*
Goa	2.91	2.82	2.99	3.09	3.41	4.06	2.50	4.97	5.73	8.84
Gujarat	77.84	94.08	123.64	185.24	179.81	236.40	317.85	386.87	482.44	25.61
Haryana	5.08	10.33	14.58	15.62	29.89	27.33	32.42	59.05	118.00	48.29
Himachal Pradesh	9.04	9.31	10.38	12.21	12.62	12.04	13.01	14.39	16.07	7.46
Jammu & Kashmir	9.02	13.07	16.61	21.04	21.18	22.42	28.35	35.00	41.71	21.10
Karnataka	134.46	167.49	211.90	211.46	397.70	307.57	393.23	292.36	364.32	13.27
Kerala	86.64	95.21	107.70	110.86	130.33	134.48	126.83	193.27	195.36	10.70
Madhya Pradesh	5.03	6.44	7.43	7.03	13.70	21.32	24.10	16.88	22.60	20.66
Maharashtra	41.93	51.62	61.25	56.34	57.71	64.35	74.69	81.09	81.49	8.66

(Contd.)

Table 2.7 (contd.)

State Name	*1985-86*	*1986-87*	*1987-88*	*1988-89*	*1989-90*	*1990-91*	*1991-92*	*1992-93*	*1993-94*	*CARG*
Manipur	0.06	0.06	0.01	0.08	0.00	0.07	0.12	0.16	0.14	11.17
Meghalaya	1.57	2.55	1.89	3.31	6.21	6.89	8.93	6.46	4.39	13.72
Mizoram	0.00	0.00	0.00	0.00	0.00	0.00	0.00	0.00	0.02	0.00
Nagaland	-9.19	-14.85	-14.40	-14.47	-14.47	-15.15	-7.18	-3.59	-4.34	*
Orissa	11.14	11.35	9.93	9.19	17.09	18.08	19.48	19.29	23.16	9.58
Punjab	7.32	12.34	16.64	17.45	33.69	32.03	45.37	67.94	98.05	38.31
Rajasthan	17.62	19.86	20.32	22.80	29.32	30.71	43.59	47.14	67.38	18.25
Sikkam	0.21	0.22	0.28	0.36	0.55	0.79	1.09	1.11	0.92	20.28
Tamil Nadu	102.08	102.78	114.34	132.88	164.62	194.60	231.24	252.53	286.29	13.76
Tripura	0.00	0.00	0.00	0.00	0.00	0.00	0.00	0.00	0.00	0.00
Uttar Pradesh	30.72	23.91	26.10	11.40	22.74	35.71	35.03	32.79	24.92	-2.58
West Bengal	3.85	8.23	9.75	9.41	14.17	19.68	17.01	16.72	20.89	23.54
Total	826.74	830.98	1044.79	1207.39	1517.36	1496.56	1034.87	1939.79	2289.95	13.58

1993-94. A current ratio of more than 1:1 means an excessive deployment of funds in current assets. The low use of capital employed in relation to total revenue, as pointed out earlier, also indicates that a higher than desirable level of current ratio in these enterprises meant only excessive acquisition of capital assets, such as inventory, receivables, and cash. The States exceeding the national average for the entire period, or during a large period of time, included Arunachal Pradesh, Assam, Goa, Gujarat, Haryana, Himachal Pradesh, Karnataka, Madhya Pradesh, Maharashtra, Manipur, Mizoram, Punjab, Rajasthan, Sikkim and Tamil Nadu. A more than requisite deployment of funds in current assets in several States points to the net worth status of capital management in the States.

Value Added

According to Table 2.8, the value added in the case of the commercial SLPEs increased from Rs. 827 crore in 1985-86 to Rs.2,290 crore in 1993-94, with a CARG of 13.58%, which was slightly higher than the growth in the total revenue and capital employed of these enterprises. Some of the States where the CARG of the value added was lower than the national average included Andhra Pradesh, Assam, Goa, Himachal Pradesh, Kerala, Maharashtra, Manipur, Nagaland, Orissa, and Uttar Pradesh. That the CARG of value added was higher than the CARG of total revenue in certain States in indicative of the fact that these States very effectively managed their shop floor operations but erred on capital gearing and planning of administrative and selling costs.

Issues and Problems

The major problem of these enterprises pertain to site selection, purchase of plant and machinery, effective project implementation, high costs, over-manning, and excessive

Table 2.8
Total Capital Employed

Sector: Commercial-Cum-Promotional (Rs. in.Crore)

State Name	*1985-86*	*1986-87*	*1987-88*	*1988-89*	*1989-90*	*1990-91*	*1991-92*	*1992-93*	*1993-94*	*CARG*
Andhra Pradesh	564.30	717.61	928.08	1081.05	1268.73	1616.74	1712.17	1990.53	2223.07	18.69
Arunachal Pradesh	3.14	5.05	5.33	5.98	5.54	6.51	5.67	6.25	8.69	13.57
Assam	116.32	143.42	169.07	216.35	217.60	244.85	279.91	368.54	253.47	10.23
Bihar	58.52	94.18	117.36	116.50	130.52	159.36	187.21	195.43	179.95	15.07
Goa	9.00	13.29	13.01	14.51	23.75	29.83	35.83	32.08	69.76	29.17
Gujarat	363.78	456.67	486.83	491.75	545.56	586.37	694.22	783.30	905.58	12.08
Haryana	206.40	168.35	232.10	265.93	276.19	336.37	405.73	507.24	701.24	16.52
Himachal Pradesh	48.85	60.35	76.34	87.23	100.14	105.44	122.87	119.95	131.30	13.16
Jammu & Kashmir	0.00	0.00	0.00	0.00	0.00	0.00	0.00	0.00	0.00	0.00
Karnataka	309.53	372.02	437.34	524.70	602.16	725.23	912.73	1122.92	1228.20	18.80
Kerala	67.28	122.08	99.70	133.09	135.11	129.46	146.98	197.92	208.12	15.16
Madhya Pradesh	165.06	213.80	259.55	309.38	372.40	92.16	419.53	427.19	430.85	12.74
Maharashtra	1294.17	1536.47	1672.26	2408.56	2997.59	3627.98	4040.45	4941.76	4699.95	17.49
Manipur	0.38	1.05	8.29	11.19	17.10	20.19	21.81	9.18	18.01	61.98
Meghalaya	6.99	8.42	8.65	12.65	14.50	16.50	19.48	22.86	25.10	17.33
Mizoram	0.00	0.00	0.00	0.00	0.00	1.98	2.61	3.66	3.66	22.73

Nagaland	9.06	13.28	9.25	14.22	12.93	15.07	14.79	14.65	13.16	4.78
Orissa	427.16	432.12	489.73	542.56	615.03	677.97	746.39	806.66	568.32	3.63
Punjab	-14.52	-90.49	-79.34	8.91	6.83	34.70	56.60	48.76	58.58	*
Rajasthan	121.92	137.18	152.78	159.96	180.39	207.14	258.81	308.09	333.08	3.39
Sikkam	4.44	6.06	9.84	11.47	13.69	15.22	16.81	18.42	17.03	18.30
Tamil Nadu	36.62	39.66	47.90	51.86	52.55	55.87	58.97	57.97	72.12	8.84
Tripura	1.74	2.51	3.36	4.93	5.04	6.57	7.14	7.63	8.56	22.04
Uttar Pradesh	179.62	209.86	257.98	312.23	369.75	421.79	476.91	505.52	553.74	15.11
West Bengal	173.73	211.42	247.73	293.35	342.54	408.57	456.38	490.69	503.78	14.23
Total	4153.51	4874.29	5653.13	7078.30	8305.64	9541.87	11100.00	12987.20	13215.32	15.57

interest burden. They had a very poor marketing image. Marketing departments did not exist in these enterprises and sales personnel lacked the requisite drive and initiative. They lacked commercialisation as they did not develop appropriate pricing and costing systems. They were also weak on corporatisation as they lacked adequate management information systems, internal audit and budgeting. The Government-SLPE relationship was such as not to permit adequate operational freedom to these enteprises. Except in a few cases, such as the New Government Electric Factory and Hyderabad Allwyn Limited, the other enterprises had not obtained ISO 9000 accreditation. No joint ventures existed in the case of these enterprises. The R & D departments were either non-existent or non-performing. The work force, including executives at the different levels, did not have opportunities to develop themselves through educational and training programmes. Though many of these States had Bureaus of Public Enterprises, they did not provide training facilities. The accounting systems were not in order, which led to the preparation of inadequate accounts. Long delays were a common feature of the accounting system was maintenance accounting. The valuation of the assets was not done from time to time.

The working capital imbalances did not allow these enterprises to maximise their output. Another common feature of these enterprises was that they did not projectise new ideas and solely depended on the financial support from their respective State Governments. Though many States could have benefited by drawing upon the experience of other States in running similar enterprises, hardly any attempt was made in this direction.

CHAPTER 3

FINANCIAL PERFORMANCE OF COMMERCIAL-CUM-PROMOTIONAL STATE LEVEL PUBLIC ENTERPRISES

The purpose of this chapter is to discuss the scope of the term commercial-cum-promotional enterprises and analyse their genesis and growth, objectives, financial and economic dimensions of their functioning, and problems and issues confronting their working.

Scope

These enterprises are characterised by twin elements of business, i.e., they blend a mix of commercial and promotional goals directing their functioning. Their commercial goals force them to go in for profit-earning and their promotional goals lead them to execute economic activities at the behest of the Government on profit or no profit basis. These enterprises include the SLPEs dealing with dairy development, fisheries, development, industrial finance, industrial development, infrastructure development, development of leather industry, civil supplies, essential commodities, housing etc. They are different from commercial SLPEs in terms of restrictions placed on their latitude to fix prices for their services and products.

Genesis and Growth

Most of these enterprises were set up between the 1950s and 1970s. The State Financial Corporations Act was passed in the 1950s, paving the way for setting up such

Corporations by the various States in different parts of the country. Twenty-two such Corporations have been set up in the country. They have become an important component of the development banking system in the country. Leading States such as Andhra Pradesh, Gujarat, Karnataka, Maharashtra, and Uttar Pradesh have seen their State Financial Corporations exceeding the sanction and disbursement targets of Rs. 1,000 crore long back. As the State Financial Corporations concern themselves with the financing of small units, the Industrial Development Corporations in the country, set up between the 1950s and 1970s, promote the establishment of medium and large industrial units. The Infrastructure Corporations have been set up to develop and promote infrastructure for industrial development in the various States. These are now expected to play a very important role in the development of infrastructure. The Housing Corporations have been set up under different names in the various States with the objective of removing housing shortages in the country. There are States where mass housing programmes are underway being handled by Housing Boards, Housing Corporations, Police Housing Corporations, Housing Corporations for Weaker Sections, etc. Food security is a major problem for any developing economy. One of the aspects of the food security is an efficient and effective distribution. The Civil Supplies Corporations and the Essential Commodities Corporations have been set up in the various States to help the Food Corporation of India in the procurement of foodgrains and they operate as a lifeline for the distributional network of foodgrains under the control of the various State Governments. The Leather Industries Development Corporations were set up to help small cobblers by making adequate provisions for extending financial support to them, as well as helping them in marketing their products. The commercial-cum-promotional enterprises constitute 33-1/3% of the total number of SLPEs in terms of both their number and those which have been covered by the present study. In terms of responses, a heavy concentraiton of such enterprises has been found in relation ot Andhra Pradesh, Assam, Goa, Gujarat, Haryana, Himachal Pradesh, Karnataka, Kerala, Maharashtra, and Punjab. These States used the instrument of SLPEs as a public policy to achieve both the commercial and non-commercial goals.

Objective

The commercial-cum-promotional enterprises have been set up with the following as their objectives:

- Marketing of goods produced by some producers undertaking production of perishable and durable consumable items;
- Removing poverty, unemployment, and strengthening the economic base of producers by providing financial assistance, modernising their production, organisation and marketing of their products;
- Achieving economy in execution of construction works;
- Accelerating the rate of industrialisation in the various States;
- Removing regional imbalances in the industrial development of the States;
- Promoting the growth of tiny, small, and medium industries; and
- Formulating programmes for proper utilisation of resources.

Financial and Economic Dimensions

The various financial and economic dimensions of the commercial-cum-promotional enterprises are placed below:

Capital Employed

Table 3.1 shows that the capital employed of these enterprises increased three times from Rs. 4,154 crore to Rs. 13,215 crore between 1985-86 and 1993-94, with a CARG of 15.57%. It was natural that the growth of investment in these enterprises should have been lower as compared to the rate of growth of investment in commercial enterprises. The States which recorded a higher than average rate of growth of investment in capital employed included Andhra Pradesh, Goa, Haryana, Karnataka, Maharashtra, Manipur, Meghalaya, Mizoram, Sikkim, and Tripura. Though in some of these States initially the commercial content of the SLPEs had received better attention, there is a gradual shift in this importance from the commercial to the promotional sector. A high rate of growth of investment in the commercial-cum-promotional sector of enterprises also points to the fact that these States initially thought of cropping up entrepreneurial activities, having the ultimate objective of passing it on to the entrepreneurs in the private sector.

Debt-Equity Ratio

The debt-equity ratio of these enterprises, as depicted in Table 3.2, fluctuated between 3.75 in 1985-86 and 3.49 in 1993-94. Keeping in mind the profit-earning record of these enterprises, it could be surmised that the debt-equity ratio was not geared to maximise their profitability. The States which exceeded the average for all the 25 States in this regard comprised Andhra Pradesh where the debt-equity ratio was as high as 6.49 in 1993-94 and could be termed excessive by terms of any canon of financial structuring. Karnataka was also a part of this story. In the case of Punjab, the debt-equity ratio cam down from 13.41 in 1985-86 to 2.78 in 1993-94. The State which was under central rule for a long period might have had an access to easy finance. There were some States such as Arunachal

Table 3.1

Total Long Term Loans Divided by Equity

Sector: Commercial-Cum-Promotional

State Name	*1985-86*	*1986-87*	*1987-88*	*1988-89*	*1989-90*	*1990-91*	*1991-92*	*1992-93*	*1993-94*
Andhra Pradesh	3.49	3.52	3.72	3.89	4.18	5.05	5.13	5.65	6.49
Arunachal Pradesh	0.62	0.60	0.63	0.86	0.80	1.00	1.14	1.38	1.86
Assam	3.16	3.53	2.91	2.90	1.60	1.42	1.29	1.40	1.54
Bihar	2.37	2.60	2.72	2.91	2.94	3.01	4.68	1.93	1.62
Goa	1.85	1.84	1.85	1.88	2.20	2.21	2.09	2.21	2.13
Gujarat	4.81	5.18	4.86	4.86	5.47	5.45	6.10	6.57	6.43
Haryana	5.56	5.59	5.50	5.79	5.68	4.70	4.81	5.50	6.81
Himachal Pradesh	0.94	1.22	1.28	1.26	1.40	1.45	1.51	1.51	1.61
Jammu & Kashmir	*	*	*	*	*	*	*	*	*
Karnataka	.35	5.69	4.06	4.16	4.35	4.72	5.16	6.00	5.96
Kerala	2.79	2.72	2.74	2.91	2.67	2.05	1.58	2.29	2.59
Madhya Pradesh	3.65	3.46	3.37	2.92	2.88	2.83	2.80	2.78	2.85
Maharashtra	3.27	3.09	3.01	2.98	3.00	2.78	2.56	2.66	2.73

(Contd.)

Table 3.1 (contd.)

State Name	*1985-86*	*1986-87*	*1987-88*	*1988-89*	*1989-90*	*1990-91*	*1991-92*	*1992-93*	*1993-94*
Manipur	0.03	2.92	1.78	1.66	1.10	0.82	0.76	0.89	0.89
Meghalaya	0.44	0.48	0.50	0.36	0.41	0.41	0.39	0.22	0.19
Mizoram	*	*	*	*	*	*	*	*	*
Nagaland	0.57	0.54	0.62	0.65	0.67	0.57	0.59	0.55	0.5
Orissa	2.27	3.36	2.65	2.28	2.40	2.26	2.10	1.95	1.98
Punjab	13.41	11.24	0.61	0.95	1.19	2.04	0.90	0.51	2.78
Rajasthan	1.11	1.18	1.25	1.28	1.35	1.60	1.77	1.76	1.60
Sikkam	0.83	1.01	1.31	1.17	1.13	1.24	1.08	1.23	1.16
Tamil Nadu	0.58	0.47	0.54	0.61	0.62	0.57	0.47	0.35	0.69
Tripura	0.02	0.06	0.05	0.05	0.12	0.20	0.20	0.19	0.16
Uttar Pradesh	1.92	2.13	2.41	2.38	2.49	2.57	2.63	2.81	3.13
West Bengal	2.69	2.95	3.02	2.82	2.74	2.82	2.90	3.09	2.46
Country Ratio	3.75	3.80	3.38	3.34	3.35	3.35	3.22	3.29	3.49

Table 3.2

Total Revenue

Sector: Commercial-Cum-Promotional (Rs. in Crore)

State Name	*1985-86*	*1986-87*	*1987-88*	*1988-89*	*1989-90*	*1990-91*	*1991-92*	*1992-93*	*1993-94*	*CARG*
Andhra Pradesh	189.42	260.00	278.46	234.63	254.42	343.91	364.96	360.79	374.84	8.91
Arunachal Pradesh	7.83	10.54	17.58	18.12	14.43	17.73	18.03	18.21	18.66	11.47
Assam	139.95	140.94	146.08	144.02	147.81	144.99	146.74	139.23	172.39	2.64
Bihar	24.84	30.92	32.68	34.56	34.15	34.35	43.25	36.40	39.60	6.00
Goa	24.25	24.04	33.94	39.31	43.52	48.01	52.53	69.75	80.52	16.18
Gujarat	570.73	731.49	1208.08	1223.32	785.27	1009.44	1071.30	980.14	962.42	6.75
Haryana	128.82	129.03	153.88	134.48	241.27	292.58	395.29	390.31	389.40	14.83
Himachal Pradesh	104.46	128.57	147.29	135.42	149.68	160.05	203.75	237.37	266.93	12.44
Jammu & Kashmir	0.00	0.00	0.00	0.00	0.00	0.00	0.00	0.00	0.00	0.00
Karnataka	302.30	327.33	400.65	279.72	365.49	450.31	493.61	593.46	623.79	9.48
Kerala	293.60	311.08	323.30	361.55	382.85	397.92	382.38	484.89	355.99	2.44
Madhya Pradesh	83.43	52.46	52.39	74.79	105.83	138.32	145.19	121.04	113.83	3.96
Maharashtra	405.77	447.14	533.71	637.94	723.98	830.15	901.96	1208.85	1274.26	15.38

(Contd.)

Table 3.2 (contd.)

State Name	*1985-86*	*1986-87*	*1987-88*	*1988-89*	*1989-90*	*1990-91*	*1991-92*	*1992-93*	*1993-94*	*CARG*
Manipur	0.22	0.92	1.82	2.30	2.60	2.95	3.25	3.67	4.13	44.27
Meghalaya	0.72	0.84	1.27	1.67	2.13	1.97	1.96	2.17	2.42	16.36
Mizoram	0.00	0.00	0.00	0.00	0.00	0.12	0.24	0.54	0.54	65.10
Nagaland	0.45	0.65	0.83	0.56	0.76	0.56	0.52	0.65	0.65	4.70
Orissa	253.30	258.13	367.24	403.18	428.88	429.08	466.35	493.44	419.26	6.50
Punjab	376.50	588.62	656.15	554.02	526.29	237.94	1096.44	1015.00	1332.12	17.11
Rajasthan	55.89	52.95	65.84	76.77	88.34	101.42	159.23	187.18	177.47	15.54
Sikkam	0.37	0.59	0.83	1.13	0.63	0.33	0.67	0.55	0.73	8.87
Tamil Nadu	52.43	48.67	49.96	59.81	82.80	109.02	124.01	114.30	154.35	14.45
Tripura	0.06	0.15	0.48	1.17	1.46	1.66	2.05	2.17	2.17	56.60
Uttar Pradesh	128.60	117.87	145.68	138.67	196.52	241.99	348.90	464.70	482.75	17.98
West Bengal	35.54	35.04	40.32	51.63	60.41	74.00	83.28	85.94	94.91	13.06
Total	3179.48	3698.85	4658.46	4608.77	4639.52	5068.90	6305.89	7010.75	7344.13	11.03

Pradesh, Rajasthan, and Tamil Nadu, where this ratio fluctuated between 1.0/1.5:1. This shows the concern for balancing the debt and equity in right proportions, which was in line with business propriety, as these enterprises were involved in both the promotional and commercial activities.

Total Revenue

Table 3.3 shows that the total revenue of these enterprises grew from Rs.3,179 crore in 1985-86 to Rs. 7,344 crore in 1993-94 having a CARG of 11.03% which was lower as compared to the CARG of capital employed and net worth, signifying the fact that the utilisation of the capital employed was not encouraging, leaving much less scope to reward the investments made by the equity holders, namely, the various State Governments. The States which did not fare well on the score of earning such revenues comprised Andhra Pradesh, Assam, Bihar, Gujarat, Karnataka, Kerala, Madhya Pradesh, Nagaland, Orissa, and Sikkim.

Net Worth

Table 3.4 shows that the net worth of these enterprises grew from Rs. 727 crore in 11985-86 to Rs. 2,320 crore in 1993-94, signifying an increase of 300%. What is interesting in this figure is to observe that the net worth at any point of time varied between 15% and 20% of the capital employed in these enterprises, which shows that these enterprises very tactfully raised debts on a small capital base. However, a peep into the finances of these enterprises reveals that most of such debt came from the State Governments which were not serviced regularly. The growth of net worth was very low in the case of Andhra Pradesh, Arunachal Pradesh, Himachal Pradesh, Jammu & Kashmir, Kerala, Nagaland, Orissa, Uttar Pradesh, and West Bengal, which shows that these enterprises were not proving financially viable.

Table 3.4

Profit After Tax

Sector: Commercial-Cum-Promotional (Rs. in Crore)

State Name	*1985-86*	*1986-87*	*1987-88*	*1988-89*	*1989-90*	*1990-91*	*1991-92*	*1992-93*	*1993-94*	*CARG*
Andhra Pradesh	-4.24	-6.61	-16.23	-13.49	-18.68	4.87	-14.24	-9.59	-7.15	***
Arunachal Pradesh	0.05	0.44	-0.05	0.14	-0.42	-0.02	0.04	0.02	0.22	20.35
Assam	-5.29	-5.16	-5.02	-4.99	-2.33	-6.64	-9.44	-21.60	-15.54	***
Bihar	1.38	1.88	1.28	0.39	0.06	0.06	2.40	1.72	1.72	2.79
Goa	-1.23	-0.14	-0.21	0.21	0.81	1.85	0.90	1.55	1.45	***
Gujarat	17.36	41.51	75.74	85.05	35.66	46.57	87.11	85.77	85.21	22.00
Haryana	4.45	2.90	5.90	7.70	12.71	17.86	18.60	22.92	19.69	20.43
Himachal Pradesh	0.56	-0.31	0.85	-0.05	-0.47	-0.74	1.82	0.75	0.95	6.83
Jammu & Kashmir	0.00	0.00	0.00	0.00	0.00	0.00	0.00	0.00	0.00	0.00
Karnataka	3.66	4.60	5.24	4.14	5.64	5.63	9.81	17.24	10.26	13.75
Kerala	-0.35	0.22	-9.39	-14.92	-8.28	-7.20	6.29	-36.58	-2.71	***
Madhya Pradesh	2.51	2.96	3.89	5.62	6.89	-2.20	-5.95	7.51	-12.56	***
Maharashtra	8.11	13.64	12.96	8.23	7.85	12.54	33.41	49.56	37.93	21.27
Manipur	0.02	0.00	0.21	-0.07	-0.64	-1.00	-1.05	1.39	-0.60	***
Meghalaya	0.00	0.00	0.00	0.00	0.30	0.05	-0.06	-0.07	-0.05	***

Mizoram	0.00	0.00	0.00	0.00	0.00	-0.17	-0.29	-0.46	-0.46	***
Nagaland	-0.18	-0.01	-0.04	-0.58	-0.47	-0.90	-0.96	-0.87	-0.74	***
Orissa	-5.92	1.31	2.24	2.69	-8.11	-12.30	-3.32	11.62	-71.77	***
Punjab	-16.34	-4.88	7.21	-21.51	-1.34	6.92	14.37	13.99	26.98	***
Rajasthan	-0.82	0.54	3.31	3.81	6.33	6.58	14.80	18.92	18.71	***
Sikkam	0.04	0.05	0.06	0.08	0.00	0.00	0.00	0.00	0.00	25.99
Tamil Nadu	2.59	3.69	2.60	1.29	0.49	0.62	2.24	4.58	2.30	-1.47
Tripura	0.00	-0.07	0.01	0.09	-0.10	0.10	-0.01	0.00	0.01	***
Uttar Pradesh	0.59	1.39	0.47	-1.70	1.29	-1.27	2.17	-7.63	6.24	34.29
West Bengal	2.58	0.49	0.43	-7.21	-4.56	-2.71	-6.07	-11.95	7.73	14.70
Total										35.43

***- CARG ignored in case of negative values

Table 3.5

Accumulated Loss

Sector: Commercial-Cum-Promotional (Rs. in Crore)

State Name	*1985-86*	*1986-87*	*1987-88*	*1988-89*	*1989-90*	*1990-91*	*1991-92*	*1992-93*	*1993-94*
Andhra Pradesh	43.09	50.43	65.09	78.66	101.90	115.10	130.24	150.45	170.99
Arunachal Pradesh	0.00	0.00	0.16	0.09	0.39	0.98	1.62	2.16	2.60
Assam	47.83	50.06	52.33	55.28	56.72	58.98	72.20	82.26	96.04
Bihar	0.00	0.00	0.00	0.00	3.65	24.63	5.14	101.82	172.52
Goa	2.17	1.70	2.43	2.43	2.89	2.90	2.90	2.98	3.03
Gujarat	28.36	56.92	117.33	152.10	190.19	217.19	258.55	373.49	412.73
Haryana	30.88	36.23	36.25	37.76	39.96	36.36	33.44	32.92	32.73
Himachal Pradesh	2.60	3.76	4.12	4.95	10.35	9.22	7.50	6.83	5.98
Jammu & Kashmir	0.00	0.00	0.00	0.00	0.00	0.00	0.00	0.00	0.00
Karnataka	5.04	4.78	5.54	7.27	9.18	9.54	8.46	8.72	8.44
Kerala	95.72	59.97	113.53	132.41	144.81	156.62	156.95	228.32	256.87
Madhya Pradesh	1.33	1.38	1.51	1.49	1.84	6.20	13.10	19.62	31.42
Maharashtra	16.61	19.29	23.23	24.06	27.26	31.28	34.67	38.01	42.11
Manipur	0.34	0.32	0.11	0.18	0.82	1.82	2.87	1.48	2.08
Meghalaya	0.55	0.91	1.07	1.53	1.45	1.47	1.53	1.63	1.73

Mizoram	0.00	0.00	0.00	0.00	0.00	0.17	0.46	0.92	0.92
Nagaland	0.60	0.52	0.57	2.93	3.40	4.30	5.26	6.13	6.35
Orissa	31.70	5.97	6.18	7.10	18.71	33.62	39.58	40.14	106.50
Punjab	104.32	113.09	108.84	144.37	146.35	147.46	142.64	139.82	124.82
Rajasthan	17.34	16.85	19.95	22.51	22.56	24.67	29.90	41.03	39.57
Sikkam	0.00	0.00	0.00	0.00	0.00	0.15	0.60	1.31	3.29
Tamil Nadu	4.39	4.00	3.84	3.73	2.61	2.48	1.42	0.71	0.14
Tripura	0.05	0.13	0.18	0.08	0.24	0.22	0.34	0.26	0.96
Uttar Pradesh	2.44	2.9 1	4.48	7.19	9.77	12.80	12.68	26.07	27.21
West Bengal	2.21	3.38	4.32	16.07	24.43	31.55	39.59	68.05	64.75
Tot al	437.57	432.60	571.06	702.19	819.48	929.71	1001.64	1375.13	1613.78

Profit After Tax

Profit after tax shows the net profitability of all operations, namely, commercial and non-commercial. Table 3.5 shows that the commercial-cum-promotional enterprises had earned net profits all through the study, ranging from Rs. 10 crore in 1985-86 to Rs. 108crore in 1993-94. Interestingly, the CARG for profit after tax turned out to be 33.43% for the entire period for all the States as a whole. The States which had done very well included Arunachal Pradesh, Gujarat, Haryana, Karnataka, Maharashtra, and Sikkim. States like Uttar Pradesh and West Bengal had a high CARG not due to a consistent trend of profit-making but because of a high profit-earning in 1993-94 which was the final year of the study. In the preceding years these States had recorded losses.

Accumulated Losses

As depicted in Table 3.6, these shot up from Rs. 438 crore in 1985-86 to Rs. 1,614 crore in 1993-94. The maximum losses being incurred by Andhra Pradesh, Bihar, Gujarat, Kerala, Orissa and Punjab.

Current Ratios

Table 3.7 shows that the current ratio of the commercial-cum-promotional enterprises rose from 1.91 in 1985-86 to 2.15 in 1993-94, against the time-honoured level of 1:1 prescribed by financial analysts. The States exceeding the national average included Andhra Pradesh, Bihar, Kerala, Madhya Pradesh, Maharashtra, Manipur, Meghalaya, Mizoram, Nagaland, Rajasthan, Sikkim, Tripura and Uttar Pradesh.

This abnormality in the current ratios of the States very clearly points to the inefficient management of working capital. It also points to the lack of effort the managers of

Table 3.6

Current Assets Divided by Current Liabilities

Sector: Commercial-Cum-Promotional (Rs. in Crore)

State Name	*1985-86*	*1986-87*	*1987-88*	*1988-89*	*1989-90*	*1990-91*	*1991-92*	*1992-93*	*1993-94*
Andhra Pradesh	2.24	2.40	3.09	2.87	3.21	3.44	3.04	3.86	4.43
Arunachal Pradesh	0.95	1.07	1.02	1.16	0.96	0.99	0.99	0.97	1.06
Assam	1.38	1.39	1.47	1.46	1.31	1.30	0.80	1.26	1.16
Bihar	4.24	4.51	5.45	4.25	3.89	3.56	2.64	2.20	2.26
Goa	1.15	1.25	1.26	1.17	1.25	1.25	1.25	1.22	0.94
Gujarat	2.05	1.96	1.94	1.87	1.85	1.85	1.98	2.11	2.04
Haryana	1.27	1.03	0.93	0.79	0.64	0.70	0.79	0.80	0.90
Himachal Pradesh	1.49	1.46	1.47	1.48	1.43	1.44	1.31	1.39	1.54
Jammu & Kashmir	***	***	***	***	***	0.00	***	***	***
Karnataka	2.02	1.95	1.88	1.94	1.75	1.70	1.49	2.00	1.65
Kerala	1.37	1.46	1.42	1.70	2.13	1.96	1.95	2.27	2.62
Madhya Pradesh	1.80	2.27	2.33	2.10	1.89	2.16	2.04	2.22	2.18
Maharashtra	2.71	2.13	2.12	2.56	3.16	3.03	3.04	1.52	2.84

(Contd.)

Table 3.6 (contd.)

State Name	*1985-86*	*1986-87*	*1987-88*	*1988-89*	*1989-90*	*1990-91*	*1991-92*	*1992-93*	*1993-94*
Manipur	5.22	1.27	1.35	1.37	1.69	2.01	2.06	1.53	2.57
Meghalaya	10.59	5.93	3.35	4,36	3.40	3.39	5.49	6.11	6.27
Mizoram	***	***	***	***	***	36.33	21.00	4.81	4.81
Nagaland	21.85	24.88	8.61	13.52	10.72	10.68	8.23	5.88	5.47
Orissa	2.19	1.87	2.60	1.85	1.73	1.66	1.45	1.67	1.34
Punjab	0.99	0.84	0.78	1.06	1.00	1.14	1.30	1.17	1.16
Rajasthan	3.51	3.28	3.00	2.90	2.75	2.42	2.20	2.34	2.64
Sikkam	15.83	22.89	10.51	24.52	97.29	89.18	66.64	17.32	13.33
Tamil Nadu	1.75	1.77	1.81	1.72	1.68	1.54	1.48	1.36	1.42
Tripura	50.75	81.73	38.83	19.40	27.12	45.29	9.88	8.30	10.37
Uttar Pradesh	5.24	6.12	6.57	6.80	6.16	5.48	4.97	4.35	4.07
West Bengal	2.20	2.14	2.10	2.03	1.95	1.97	2.09	1.68	1.50
Tot al	1.91	1.78	1.94	2.13	2.25	2.23	2.14	1.80	2.15

Table 3.7

(Value Added (Wages + Net Profit + Interest))

Sector: Commercial-Cum-Promotional (Rs. in Crore)

State Name	*1985-86*	*1986-87*	*1987-88*	*1988-89*	*1989-90*	*1990-91*	*1991-92*	*1992-93*	*1993-94*	*CARG*
Andhra Pradesh	23.54	40.36	39.37	30.13	35.18	59.50	53.05	68.78	93.57	18.83
Arunachal Pradesh	4.39	5.18	7.79	7.98	7.41	8.43	8.65	8.83	9.34	9.90
Assam	16.74	18.25	20.21	21.75	24.77	20.18	19.02	8.16	11.00	-5.11
Bihar	14.37	19.06	20.61	23.67	28.43	35.21	36.01	48.98	46.40	15.78
Goa	6.25	9.04	12.24	13.51	14.52	18.43	16.96	28.18	34.20	23.67
Gujarat	64.30	120.85	179.09	196.12	150.64	173.16	235.90	250.40	245.90	18.25
Haryana	57.07	57.52	69.23	72.36	96.90	114.48	117.39	159.65	195.51	16.64
Himachal Pradesh	12.70	18.80	24.38	16.74	102.57	23.10	30.06	30.04	31.34	11.95
Jammu & Kashmir	0.00	0.00	0.00	0.00	0.00	0.83	0.00	0.00	0.00	0.00
Karnataka	40.94	45.33	53.10	55.76	67.88	80.80	101.94	137.04	160.70	18.64
Kerala	36.58	39.54	34.76	41.95	48.53	53.35	63.63	48.01	49.32	3.81
Madhya Pradesh	17.98	22.17	24.51	28.21	34.92	21.55	28.57	45.61	30.00	6.61
Maharashtra	158.50	204.08	222.89	248.82	280.32	325.71	348.97	550.46	509.29	15.71

(Contd.)

Table 3.7 (contd.)

State Name	*1985-86*	*1986-87*	*1987-88*	*1988-89*	*1989-90*	*1990-91*	*1991-92*	*1992-93*	*1993-94*	*CARG*
Manipur	0.06	0.14	0.62	0.74	0.26	0.05	0.23	2.48	0.56	32.21
Meghalaya	0.47	0.67	0.87	1.34	1.61	1.54	1.58	1.66	1.74	17.78
Mizoram	0.00	0.00	0.00	0.00	0.00	-0.10	-0.16	-0.15	-0.15	***
Nagaland	0.25	0.40	0.62	0.31	0.52	0.28	0.19	0.34	0.38	5.37
Orissa	35.53	47.10	58.52	59.50	63.38	61.36	80.89	110.11	16.65	-9.04
Punjab	52.48	76.97	84.80	44.42	74.56	109.67	140.91	135.38	193.35	17.70
Rajasthan	13.74	16.35	21.35	25.01	30.22	34.20	44.40	51.87	55.70	19.12
Sikkam	0.15	0.18	0.24	0.29	0.25	0.27	0.32	0.36	0.36	11.56
Tamil Nadu	7.91	9.72	9.22	9.45	9.23	10.65	13.15	17.46	18.49	11.20
Tripura	0.03	0.03	0.25	0.69	0.56	0.96	0.83	0.75	0.79	50.51
Uttar Pradesh	14.67	17.25	22.04	27.61	35.34	38.75	48.32	49.90	71.93	21.99
West Bengal	12.01	12.03	15.11	5.69	15.65	21.41	21.82	28.66	60.42	22.38
Tot al	590.66	781.02	921.82	932.05	1123.65	1213.77	1417.63	1782.96	1836.79	15.24

these enterprises might have made to raise current liabilities which could have given them opportunities for acquiring fresh finance and reducing thereby their cost of operations.

Value Added

The value added to total revenue could be taken as a proxy for the ratio of value added to sales as most of the total revenue was composed of values arising out of sales. Table 3.8 shows that the value added increased from Rs. 591 crore in 1985-86 to Rs.1,837 crore in 1993-94, with a CARG of 15.24%, which was much lower than the CARG of capital employed, total revenue, and net worth. The value added as a percentage of total revenue was 43% in the case of commercial-cum-promotional enterprises. An increase in value added was possible only through the reduction in the wage component and interest payments. The consumption of materials was also on the high side, besides the expenses incurred on maintenance of administration and marketing and promotional efforts.

Issues and Problems

Some of the important problems of these enterprises across the country were as follows:

Lack of vision: As these enterprises were involved in diverse activities, they failed to develop a vision governing their business operations. This brought complacency and resulted in wastages.

Absence of business systems: These enterprises had not installed certain basic business systems. They did not have a comprehensive personnel policy which was pivotal to the success of their efficient functioning as they required personnel having attributes to appreciate the business purpose of these enterprises on the one hand and their social goals on the other. Their Marketing Departments in

Table 3.8

Total Capital Employed

Sector: Promotional

(Rs. in Crore)

State Name	*1985-86*	*1986-87*	*1987-88*	*1988-89*	*1989-90*	*1990-91*	*1991-92*	*1992-93*	*1993-94*	*CARG*
Andhra Pradesh	0.61	1.28	1.98	2.97	3.90	4.80	6.02	7.09	7.59	37.05
Arunachal Pradesh	0.00	0.00	0.00	0.00	0.00	0.00	0.00	0.00	0.00	0.00
Assam	3.99	4.57	5.15	5.48	11.32	21.80	27.46	34.97	34.33	30.87
Bihar	2.45	3.66	5.42	4.83	6.58	6.43	7.86	0.00	7.95	15.85
Goa	26.63	34.71	46.33	59.05	72.52	87.80	100.87	112.00	123.82	21.18
Gujarat	84.82	86.30	85.66	797.18	986.73	1384.02	1986.33	1988.55	1981.28	48.27
Haryana	6.75	9.43	16.69	13.65	15.24	18.74	19.73	25.60	27.43	19.16
Himachal Pradesh	12.21	13.26	15.26	18.63	22.01	25.17	27.70	28.89	32.62	13.07
Jammu & Kashmir	0.00	0.00	0.00	0.00	0.00	0.00	0.00	0.00	0.00	0.00
Karnataka	0.00	0.00	0.00	0.00	0.63	3.50	3.92	6.56	9.40	96.54
Kerala	11.13	12.13	12.35	15.93	16.85	18.36	19.97	19.19	17.61	5.90
Madhya Pradesh	1.51	2.04	4.13	6.53	9.81	12.35	13.77	14.51	16.33	34.66

(Contd.)

Table 3.8 (contd.)

State Name	*1985-86*	*1986-87*	*1987-88*	*1988-89*	*1989-90*	*1990-91*	*1991-92*	*1992-93*	*1993-94*	*CARG*
Maharashtra	7.32	8.91	10.46	11.87	15.46	19.37	18.31	15.36	30.25	19.41
Manipur	0.00	0.00	0.00	0.00	0.00	0.00	0.00	0.00	0.00	0.00
Meghalaya	0.00	0.00	0.00	0.00	0.00	0.00	0.00	0.00	0.00	0.00
Mizoram	0.00	0.00	0.00	0.00	0.00	0.00	0.00	0.00	0.00	0.00
Nagaland	0.00	0.00	0.00	0.00	0.00	0.00	0.00	0.00	0.00	0.00
Orissa	1.85	2.34	2.39	3.04	3.32	3.48	3.60	3.70	4.76	12.54
Punjab	6.67	7.71	9.37	9.02	8.63	6.64	-2.31	1.70	2.28	-12.56
Rajasthan	37 .63	45.36	48.85	53.35	55.50	59.15	63.07	67.40	69.58	7.99
Sikkam	0.00	0.00	0.00	0.00	0.00	0.00	0.00	0.00	0.00	0.00
Tamil Nadu	0.00	0.00	0.00	0.00	0.00	0.00	0.00	0.00	3.17	0.00
Tripura	0.00	0.00	0.00	0.00	0.00	0.00	0.00	0.00	0.00	0.00
Uttar Pradesh	36.54	40.19	47.86	76.08	71.55	74.15	80.72	86.88	92.05	12.24
West Bengal	0.00	0.00	0.00	0.00	0.00	0.00	0.00	0.00	0.00	0.00
Tot al	240.11	271.83	311.90	1077.61	1300.02	1745.76	2375.97	2411.31	2460.45	33.76

particular were not staffed with proper personnel having a sensitisation of social marketing. Their internal audit systems, budgetary control and account-keeping was in a very poor shape.

Low utilisation of resources: Capacities installed were utilised very inadequately. The turnover of capital employed ratio was less than 1:1. In fact, in enterprises such as the Dairy Development Corporation or Leather Industries Development Corporation, there was no reason that this ratio should have been that low.

Duplication of activities: In many States more than one SLPE was engaged in the same activity. The study reveals that in housing there were as many as four to five Corporations engaged in the various States. In some States, in the field of forestry there was more than one enterprise. There is a need to remove this duplication.

Over-dependence on the State Governments and poor Government-enterprise interface: These enterprises depend heavily on the State support which is against the spirit of the purpose for which these enterprises were set up. It was expected that they would subsides the costs of their social obligations by effective management of their commercial activities. However, in practice they lost on both. As they had a mixed bag of objectives, the Government-enterprise relationship in these SLPEs was not smooth. No effort was made to develop parameters in terms of which the efficiency of these enterprises could have been measured.

CHAPTER 4

FINANCIAL PERFORMANCE OF PROMOTIONAL STATE LEVEL ENTERPRISES

The purpose of this chapter is to discuss the scope of the promotional SLPEs, their genesis and growth, objectives, financial and economic dimensions of their functioning, and problems and issues confronting their working.

Scope

These enterprises are public units operating at the State-level to undertake promotional activities of the various State Governments on a commercial and corporate basis. In the case of these enterprises, promotion is the primary objective and profit-earning becomes a secondary consideration. In the process of fulfilling their primary objective, these enterprises should not incur losses. In other words, these enterprises must discharge their obligations on the basis of the principle of breakeven and not incur any financial loss. These enterprises include in their ambit the Women Development Corporations, Scheduled Castes Finance Corporations, Scheduled Tribes Finance Corporation, Backward Classes Corporations, Corporations for Handicapped, Area Development Boards and Authorities, and Minorities Development Corporations. As promotion is the primary objective of these enterprises, and in view of the imperative of their working on the principle of breakeven it is suggested that these enterprises must earn a rate of return of 2.5% per annum. This is essential for their continued operations. The growth and development of these enterprises should be funded by the respective State Governments. A 2.5% rate of return would help them in keeping their net worth in tact and ensuring continual support from the financial institutions, and also give them the advantage of a helpful considerations for obtaining funds from the financial institutions in India and abroad.

Genesis and Growth

There are in all 132 promotional SLPEs in India. Of these, 56 responded to our study. Thus, the response rate was about 40%. The States which have used promotional enterprises as an instrumentality of development and implementation of the public policy are Andhra Pradesh, Bihar, Maharashtra, Tripura, and Uttar Pradesh. The States where the response rate has exceeded the national average are Goa, Himachal Pradesh, Jammu & Kashmir, Maharashtra, and Punjab. In the case of Uttar Pradesh, though the response rate was less than 40%, the national average, the number of enterprises responding was next only to Maharashtra, in which case 10 out of 14 enterprises responded to the study.

The various State Governments between the 1950s and the early 1970s had initiated a number of welfare activities for discharging their obligations in this regard. These State Governments had set up special departments. It was found that departmentalisation of such activities deprived the various State Governments of the advantage of obtaining long-term and short-term finances from the development banks, commercial banks, and global sources. It was also observed that the bureaucratic style of the functioning of the Government prevailing in the various departments of the central secretariat affected the smooth functioning of such departments in charge of carrying out these important welfare programmes and activities of the Government. Among the major problems faced by the departmental operations to execute their activities, were lack of cost-consciousness and non-adherence to time schedules. Buck passing emerged to be another major handicap. All these reasons culminated into the setting up of a special breed of SLPEs to handle the promotional activities of the various SLPEs. In the latter part of the 1970s and 1980s, most of the States used the company form of organisation to carry out their promotional activities. However, in the case of some States, the cooperative form of organisation has been adopted. The Government of Gujarat led this movement.

Objectives

The major objectives of these enterprises are as follows:

- Promotion of economic activities through encouraging private entrepreneurs by their direct involvement.

- Acting as nodal agencies in their area of operations charged with the responsibility of preparing and implementing the plans for the development of respective activities assigned to them; and

- Carrying out commercial activities as and when assigned to them but only on a perfunctory basis, as profit-earning is applied as a secondary criterion to evaluate their performance.

Capital Employed

As could be seen from Table 4.1 the total capital employed in these enterprises had the highest rate of growth. The volume of capital employed increased from Rs. 240 crore in 1985-86 to Rs. 2,460 crore in 1993-94. The CARG was 33.76% for the period under study, against a CARG of 15.57% and 12.12% in the case of commercial-cum-promotional and commercial enterprises respectively for the period under reference. The States where the CARG exceeded the nationala verage included Andhra Pradesh,

Table 4.1

Total Long Term Loans Divided By Equity

Sector: Promotional (Rs.in Crores)

State Name	*1985-86*	*1986-87*	*1987-88*	*1988-89*	*1989-90*	*1990-91*	*1991-92*	*1992-93*	*1993-94*
Andhra Pradesh	0.02	0.00	0.00	0.00	0.00	0.00	0.05	0.06	0.03
Arunachal Pradesh	***	***	***	***	***	***	***	***	***
Assam	1.34	1.87	0.43	0.66	2.34	4.53	6.69	9.50	9.14
Bihar	0.12	0.10	0.06	0.06	***		0.05	***	0.04
Goa	1.67	1.47	1.51	1.42	1.54	1.44	1.44	1.45	1.59
Gujarat	1.31	1.29	1.17	0.96	0.77	1.03	1.01	1.02	0.95
Haryana	0.09	0.08	0.07	0.07	0.06	0.05	0.08	0.08	0.10
Himachal Pradesh	15.67	11.89	10.97	12.04	8.84	12.00	11.69	9.94	9.66
Jammu & Kashmir	***	***	***	***	***	***	***	***	***
Karnataka	***	***	***	***	0.00	0.00	0.00	0.00	0.00
Kerala	0.00	0.00	0.00	0.00	0.00	0.00	0.00	0.00	0.00
Madhya Pradesh	0.00	0.09	0.13	0.00	0.06	0.20	0.26	0.25	0.25
Maharashtra	0.55	0.60	0.64	0.61	0.63	0.70	0.77	0.77	0.77
Manipur	***	***	***	***	***	***	***	***	***
Meghalaya	***	***	***	***	***	***	***	***	***

Mizoram	***	***	***	***	***	***	***	***	***
Nagaland	***	***	***	***	***	***	***	***	***
Orissa	0.42	0.30	0.19	0.19	0.16	0.15	0.05	0.05	0.05
Punjab	0.00	0.00	0.00	0.00	0.00	0.00	0.18	0.11	0.11
Rajasthan	0.15	0.11	0.16	0.11	0.13	0.25	0.26	0.21	0.08
Sikkam	***	***	***	***	***	***	***	***	***
Tamil Nadu	3.74	.37	2.86	2.69	2.29	2.42	2.33	2.67	2.04
Tripura	***	***	***	***	***	***	***	***	***
Uttar Pradesh	0.79	0.64	0.42	0.79	0.74	0.58	0.53	0.53	0.52
West Bengal	***	***	***	***	***	***	***	***	***
Tot al	1.08	1.09	1.02	1.04	0.96	1.07	1.18	1.23	1.16

Gujarat, Karnataka, and Madhya Pradesh. In the case of Punjab, the CARG turned out to be negative.

Debt-Equity Ratio

The debt-equity ratio of these enterprises should be 1:1 as suggested by the Institute of Public Enterprise in its report to the Ninth Finance Commission (See: Institute of Public Enterprise, Rate of Return on State Level Public Enterprieses, Report submitted to the Ninth Finance Commission, February, 1989). Table 4.2 shows that the debt-equity ratio for all the enterprises taken together during the period of the study was veering around this region. Some of the States where the debt element turned out to be very high included Assam and Himachal Pradesh. One of the reasons for poor profitability of promotional enterprises in these States was unoptimality in their debt-equity ratio.

Total Revenue

As depicted in Table 4.3, the total revenue in these enterprises increased from Rs. 132 crore in 1985-86 to Rs. 414 crore in 1993-94, with a CARG of 15.34%. The growth of CARG to total revenue was just 50% of the growth of the CARG of net worth and capital employed, indicating the fact that there was a lot of scope to improve the utilisation of assets and funds for turnover in these enterprises. The States where the CARG of total revenue was higher than the national average included Asssam, Goa, Himachal Pradesh, Karnataka, Madhya Pradesh, Orissa, Punjab, Rajasthan, and Tamil Nadu. Some States had not done well at all and these included Andhra Pradesh, Haryana, and Kerala, where the CARG of total revenue was less than one digit. The investment in capital employed when related to total revenue indicates that the total revenue was about 15% of capital employed for all the States taken together in the last year of the study, i.e., 1993-94.

Table 4.2

Net Worth

Sector: Promotional (Rs. in Crore)

State Name	*1985-86*	*1986-87*	*1987-88*	*1988-89*	*1989-90*	*1990-91*	*1991-92*	*1992-93*	*1993-94*	*CARG*
Andhra Pradesh	0.59	1.28	1.98	2.97	3.90	4.80	5.65	6.55	7.26	39.72
Arunachal Pradesh	0.00	0.00	0.00	0.00	0.00	0.00	0.00	0.00	0.00	0.00
Assam	0.64	0.62	0.59	0.75	1.61	2.24	2.78	2.93	2.93	20.94
Bihar	0.00	0.00	0.00	0.00	0.00	0.00	0.00	0.00	0.00	0.00
Goa	11.30	15.91	21.24	26.72	31.65	38.82	43.44	48.05	50.33	20.53
Gujarat	44.84	47.15	50.94	708.49	931.05	1281.86	1806.50	1802.27	1796.85	58.62
Haryana	6.08	8.85	16.07	13.63	15.30	17.52	22.90	23.10	24.07	18.77
Himachal Pradesh	10.71	11.65	13.39	16.07	19.22	22.32	24.65	26.64	32.02	14.67
Jammu & Kashmir	0.00	0.00	0.00	0.00	0.00	0.00	0.00	0.00	0.00	0.00
Karnataka	0.00	0.00	0.00	0.00	0.64	3.51	3.93	6.56	9.41	95.82
Kerala	0.40	0.40	0.40	0.95	1.24	1.73	1.70	1.72	0.40	0.00
Madhya Pradesh	1.69	2.15	3.70	6.46	8.97	9.10	10.03	10.05	9.83	24.70
Maharashtra	3.46	4.68	6.46	6.90	9.90	12.17	12.53	15.48	18.11	22.99

(Contd.)

Table 4.2 (contd.)

State Name	*1985-86*	*1986-87*	*1987-88*	*1988-89*	*1989-90*	*1990-91*	*1991-92*	*1992-93*	*1993-94*	*CARG*
Manipur	0.00	0.00	0.00	0.00	0.00	0.00	0.00	0.00	0.00	0.00
Meghalaya	0.00	0.00	0.00	0.00	0.00	0.00	0.00	0.00	0.00	0.00
Mizoram	0.00	0.00	0.00	0.00	0.00	0.00	0.00	0.00	0.00	0.00
Nagaland	0.00	0.00	0.00	0.00	0.00	0.00	0.00	0.00	0.00	0.00
Orissa	0.84	1.30	1.42	1.85	2.16	2.31	2.25	2.22	2.98	17.15
Punjab	4.24	5.31	7.89	9.47	10.79	13.91	14.27	17.12	163.79	18.77
Rajasthan	6.82	7.65	9.32	10.58	12.73	14.37	14.44	14.41	15.32	10.65
Sikkam	0.00	0.00	0.00	0.00	0.00	0.00	0.00	0.00	0.00	0.00
Tamil Nadu	0.00	0.00	0.00	0.00	0.00	0.00	0.00	0.00	0.00	0.00
Tripura	0.00	0.00	0.00	0.00	0.00	0.00	0.00	0.00	0.00	0.00
Uttar Pradesh	20.47	23.10	33.61	38.70	43.85	52.31	62.79	67.50	77.54	18.11
West Bengal	0.00	0.00	0.00	0.00	0.00	0.00	0.00	0.00	0.00	0.00
Tot al	111.99	130.05	167.01	843.54	1093.01	1476.97	2027.86	2044.60	2063.84	43.94

Table 4.3

Profit Aftertax

Sector: Promotional (Rs. in Crore)

State Name	*1985-86*	*1986-87*	*1987-88*	*1988-89*	*1989-90*	*1990-91*	*1991-92*	*1992-93*	*1993-94*	*CARG*
Andhra Pradesh	0.17	0.25	0.30	0.30	0.31	0.29	0.35	0.37	0.49	14.15
Arunachal Pradesh	0.00	0.00	0.00	0.00	0.00	0.00	0.00	0.00	0.00	0.00
Assam	0.04	0.03	0.19	0.20	0.45	0.55	0.42	0.15	0.17	19.83
Bihar	0.00	0.00	0.00	0.00	0.00	0.00	0.00	0.00	0.00	0.00
Goa	0.05	0.23	0.48	0.00	0.65	0.64	0.70	1.20	1.49	52.85
Gujarat	-5.56	-3.30	-4.52	-7.24	-4.26	-4.93	-9.79	-12.02	-12.26	***
Haryana	-4.57	-0.02	-0.05	-0.96	-0.10	0.05	0.10	0.08	-0.45	***
Himachal Pradesh	-0.31	-0.20	-0.30	-0.73	-0.31	-0.16	-0.35	0.67	1.60	***
Jammu & Kashmir	0.00	0.00	0.00	0.00	0.00	0.00	0.00	0.00	0.00	0.00
Karnataka	-0.05	-0.09	-0.10	-0.93	-0.22	-0.22	-0.19	0.07	0.03	***
Kerala	0.00	0.00	0.00	0.00	0.00	0.00	0.00	0.00	0.00	0.00
Madhya Pradesh	0.06	-0.02	0.08	0.00	0.13	0.09	-0.25	-0.24	-0.28	***
Maharashtra	-0.59	2.32	2.86	3.13	3.34	2.93	3.51	1.46	1.21	***

(Contd.)

Table 4.3 (contd.)

State Name	*1985-86*	*1986-87*	*1987-88*	*1988-89*	*1989-90*	*1990-91*	*1991-92*	*1992-93*	*1993-94*	*CARG*
Manipur	0.00	0.00	0.00	0.00	0.00	0.00	0.00	0.00	0.00	0.00
Meghalaya	0.00	0.00	0.00	0.00	0.00	0.00	0.00	0.00	0.00	0.00
Mizoram	0.00	0.00	0.00	0.00	0.00	0.00	0.00	0.00	0.00	0.00
Nagaland	0.00	0.00	0.00	0.00	0.00	0.00	0.00	0.00	0.00	0.00
Orissa	-0.36	-0.35	-0.42	-0.14	-0.09	-0.09	-0.06	0.02	0.32	***
Punjab	0.24	0.85	1.13	1.00	0.94	1.16	2.65	3.18	3.69	40.72
Rajasthan	0.27	0.53	1.15	0.76	1.48	0.77	1.16	0.77	0.26	-0.47
Sikkam	0.00	0.00	0.00	0.00	0.00	0.00	0.00	0.00	0.00	0.00
Tamil Nadu	0.00	0.00	0.00	0.00	0.00	0.00	0.00	0.00	0.00	0.00
Tripura	0.00	0.00	0.00	0.00	0.00	0.00	0.00	0.00	0.00	0.00
Uttar Pradesh	0.84	1.25	1.39	0.81	2.37	2.10	3.82	4.27	0.36	-10.05
West Bengal	0.00	0.00	0.00	0.00	0.00	0.00	0.00	0.00	0.00	0.00
Tot al	-9.77	1.48	2.19	-3.79	4.69	3.10	2.07	-0.02	-3.37	-12.46

***-CARG ignored in case of negative values.

Almost all the States, irrespective of the level of their economic development, suffered from this handicap.

Networth

Table 4.4 reveals that the net worth of these enterprises increased from Rs. 112 crore in 1985-86 to Rs. 2,064 crore in 1993-94, having a CARG of 43.94% for the entire period, which was higher as compared to 16.47% in the case of commercial SLPEs and 15.60% in the case of commercial-cum-promotional enterprises. The States where the CARG exceeded the national average included Gujarat and Karnataka. As the promotional enterprises dealt with very sensitive sections of society, the various State Governments injected fresh equity into their capital stock. Maharashtra also followed the same approach. One of the reasons for the high rate of growth of the CARG in some States was the efficient commercial functioning of these enterprises. For instance, in the case of Karnataka, Haryana, and Punjab, most of these corporations added new shcemes to their protfolio. They gave serious thought to their business plans and worked for backward and forward linkages. They went in for unconventional schemes which resulted in significant value additions. For instance, in the case of Karnataka, its SC/BC Corporation had a tie up with HMT Ltd., which farmed out certain ancillary activities to the Corporation. The Corporation also set up Engineering and Medical Colleges for the SCs and BCs. In the case of Punjab and Haryana, the average size of lending was more as compared to the other States and this put the SC/BC Corporations in Haryana and Punjab in an advantageous position. In States like Arunachal Pradesh, Mizoram, and Nagaland, the net worth of such Corporations appears as "Nil". This was because in these States SC/BC Corporations do not exist. In the case of Uttar Pradesh, SC/BC Corporations did not matter much in respect of the hilly areas of the State.

Table 4.4

Accumulated Loss

Sector: Promotional (Rs. in Crore)

State Name	*1985-86*	*1986-87*	*1987-88*	*1988-89*	*1989-90*	*1990-91*	*1991-92*	*1992-93*	*1993-94*
Andhra Pradesh	0.24	0.49	0.79	1.10	1.40	1.69	2.03	2.34	2.83
Arunachal Pradesh	0.00	0.00	0.00	0.00	0.00	0.00	0.00	0.00	0.00
Assam	0.49	0.78	0.78	0.79	1.00	1.12	1.13	1.13	1.13
Bihar	0.00	0.00	0.00	0.00	0.00	0.00	0.00	0.00	0.00
Goa	0.00	0.00	0.00	0.00	0.00	0.03	0.04	0.03	0.03
Gujarat	18.43	22.01	27.11	38.98	44.45	29.26	40.34	53.87	68.51
Haryana	5.49	6.02	1.91	2.75	3.08	3.25	3.48	3.61	4.46
Himachal Pradesh	1.60	1.80	2.11	2.82	3.14	3.33	3.69	3.03	1.44
Jammu & Kashmir	0.00	0.00	0.00	0.00	0.00	0.00	0.00	0.00	0.00
Karnataka	0.30	0.38	0.48	1.41	1.66	1.92	2.28	2.28	2.28
Kerala	0.06	0.06	0.06	0.35	0.09	0.09	0.09	0.07	0.06
Madhya Pradesh	0.24	0.22	0.20	0.15	0.15	0.27	0.78	0.78	1.09
Maharashtra	4.16	3.65	4.30	4.87	5.76	6.50	7.38	7.78	8.16
Manipur	0.00	0.00	0.00	0.00	0.00	0.00	0.00	0.00	0.00
Meghalaya	0.00	0.00	0.00	0.00	0.00	0.00	0.00	0.00	0.00

Mizoram	0.00	0.00	0.00	0.00	0.00	0.00	0.00	0.00	0.00
Nagaland	0.00	0.00	0.00	0.00	0.00	0.00	0.00	0.00	0.00
Orissa	0.78	1.13	1.55	1.69	1.78	1.86	1.92	1.96	1.64
Punjab	0.93	1.17	1.41	1.75	2.13	2.51	3.15	3.93	4.79
Rajasthan	0.10	0.00	0.00	0.00	0.26	0.61	0.57	0.92	1.79
Sikkim	0.00	0.00	0.00	0.00	0.00	0.00	0.00	0.00	0.00
Tamilnadu	12.31	14.90	9.76	0.83	0.00	0.00	0.00	4.27	0.00
Tripura	0.00	0.00	0.00	0.00	0.00	0.00	0.00	0.00	0.00
Uttar Pradesh	1.79	1.47	1.84	2.51	2.20	2.05	1.52	1.22	2.60
West Bengal	0.00	0.00	0.00	0.00	0.00	0.00	0.00	0.00	0.00
Total	46.92	54.00	52.30	60.00	67.10	54.99	68.40	87.22	100.81

Profit after Tax

The profit after tax shows the overall financial viability of the total operations of an enterprise. The promotional enterprises by virtue of the non-profit-earning mandate given to them are not expected to earn high profits. It is interesting to note from Table 4.5 that these enterprises had earned overall profits for all the States taken together during the years 1986-87, 1987-88, 1989-90, 1990-91 and 1991-92. For the rest of the years of the study they incurred losses. The profit after tax was Rs. 10 crore in 1985-86 and Rs. 3 crore in 1993-94. The CARG of these enterprises for the country as a whole for the entire period of the study was –12.46%, which pointed to the need for urgently making their operations commercially viable. Some of the States having a positive CARG continuously with regard to profit after tax included Andhra Pradesh, Assam, Goa, and Punjab. The other States either had a negative CARG throughout the study, or during one or more years of the study for the period under reference.

Accumulated Losses

As profit-earning did not find favour with these enterprises, the accumulated losses of these enterprises rose from Rs. 47 crore in 1985-86 to Rs. 101 crore in 1993-94, as could be seen from Table 4.6. Despite this, these enterprises had a positive net worth only because of continuous injections of equity support by the various State Governments. Andhra Pradesh, Gujarat, Karnataka, Maharashtra, Punjab, and Uttar Pradesh presented a very uncomfortable picture of rampant accumulated losses incurred by these enterprises.

Current Ratio

Table 4.7 shows that the current ratio for all the promotional enterprises taken together for all the States was less than 2:1, excepting in 1986-87 and 1993-94. The less

Table 4.5
Current Assets Divided by Current Liabilities

Sector: Promotional (Rs. In crore)

State Name	1985-86	1986-87	1987-88	1988-89	1989-90	1990-91	1991-92	1992-93	1993-94
Andhra Pradesh	1.07	1.17	1.28	1.52	1.47	1.66	1.89	1.92	2.21
Arunachal Pradesh	***	***	***	***	***	***	***	***	***
Assam	4.57	3.57	3.37	3.20	5.70	4.44	4.84	9.57	4.00
Bihar	3.26	2.88	3.79	2.98	2.80	2.59	2.70	.***	3.04
Goa	13.90	10.17	6.87	5.95	5.73	6.16	6.07	6.45	5.61
Gujarat	2.97	2.65	2.38	1.70	1.94	2.59	4.55	4.53	4.41
Haryana	8.58	10.43	5.76	5.17	6.15	5.13	4.19	4.95	3.76
Himachal Pradesh	0.91	0.92	0.92	0.91	0.98	0.93	0.94	0.98	1.05
Jammu & Kashmir	***	***	***	***	***	***	***	***	***
Karnataka	49.50	37.80	51.25	16.25	10.33	38.58	24.30	13.68	14.07
Kerala	41.00	41.00	41.00	41.00	66.00	41.00	87.50	48.50	41.00
Madhya Pradesh	1.47	1.39	2.23	2.58	2.20	3.65	3.86	3.38	3.80
Maharashtra	1.43	2.24	1.56	1.40	1.49	1.40	1.41	1.42	1.46
Manipur	***	***	***	***	***	***	***	***	***

(Contd.)

Table 4.5 (contd.)

State Name	1985-86	1986-87	1987-88	1988-89	1989-90	1990-91	1991-92	1992-93	1993-94
Meghalaya	***	***	***	***	***	***	***	***	***
Mizoram	***	***	***	***	***	***	***	***	***
Nagaland	***	***	***	***	***	***	***	***	***
Orissa	2.33	2.17	2.12	3.55	3.15	2.09	2.23	2.31	4.78
Punjab	1.36	1.41	1.44	1.38	1.31	1.18	0.95	1.02	1.03
Rajasthan	1.21	1.19	1.08	1.23	1.28	1.67	1.31	1.27	1.36
Sikkim	***	***	***	***	***	***	***	***	***
Tamilnadu	1.24	1.33	1.38	1.43	1.54	1.68	1.78	1.87	2.49
Tripura	***	***	***	***	***	***	***	***	***
Uttar Pradesh	1.30	1.22	1.23	1.32	1.32	1.26	1.29	1.29	1.34
West Bengal	***	***	***	***	***	***	***	***	***
Total	1.43	2.05	1.51	1.51	1.61	1.77	1.85	1.92	2.00

Table 4.6

Value Added (Wages+Net Profit+Interest)

Sector: Promotional (Rs. in Crore)

State Name	*1985-86*	*1986-87*	*1987-88*	*1988-89*	*1989-90*	*1990-91*	*1991-92*	*1992-93*	*1993-94*	*CARG*
Andhra Pradesh	0.69	0.98	1.21	1.08	1.33	1.38	1.55	1.75	2.15	15.27
Arunachal Pradesh	0.00	0.00	0.00	0.00	0.00	0.00	0.00	0.00	0.00	0.00
Assam	0.35	0.39	0.75	0.83	1.09	1.59	1.55	1.68	1.68	21.66
Bihar	0.12	0.14	0.19	0.22	0.23	0.31	0.28	0.00	0.32	13.04
Goa	0.33	0.53	0.80	0.30	1.24	1.21	1.40	1.97	2.37	27.95
Gujarat	-0.38	3.06	4.21	1.69	4.11	4.98	2.18	2.20	3.15	***
Haryana	-3.93	0.77	0.87	0.11	1.09	1.41	1.58	1.61	1.25	***
Himachal Pradesh	0.22	0.39	0.52	0.19	0.87	1.22	1.05	2.22	3.45	41.07
Jammu & Kashmir	0.00	0.00	0.00	0.00	0.00	0.00	0.00	0.00	0.00	0.00
Karnataka	0.00	-0.02	-0.01	-0.87	-0.09	-0.08	0.01	0.27	0.23	***
Kerala	0.21	0.28	0.32	0.35	0.42	0.53	0.53	0.52	0.49	11.17
Madhya Pradesh	0.44	0.49	0.93	0.87	1.30	1.57	1.46	1.60	1.65	17.97
Maharashtra	5.20	15.62	20.00	19.64	22.24	24.00	31.88	12.24	45.36	31.09

(Contd.)

Table 4.6 (contd.)

State Name	*1985-86*	*1986-87*	*1987-88*	*1988-89*	*1989-90*	*1990-91*	*1991-92*	*1992-93*	*1993-94*	*CARG*
Manipur	0.00	0.00	0.00	0.00	0.00	0.00	0.00	0.00	0.00	0.00
Meghalaya	0.00	0.00	0.00	0.00	0.00	0.00	0.00	0.00	0.00	0.00
Mizoram	0.00	0.00	0.00	0.00	0.00	0.00	0.00	0.00	0.00	0.00
Nagaland	0.00	0.00	0.00	0.00	0.00	0.00	0.00	0.00	0.00	0.00
Orissa	-0.11	-0.09	-0.17	0.08	0.11	0.24	0.25	0.31	0.76	***
Punjab	0.89	1.55	2.15	2.25	2.46	2.76	4.37	5.44	6.14	27.31
Rajasthan	0.36	0.64	1.28	0.85	1.84	1.16	1.55	1.16	0.65	7.67
Sikkim	0.00	0.00	0.00	0.00	0.00	0.00	0.00	0.00	0.00	0.00
Tamilnadu	16.13	18.06	21.66	26.51	33.86	40.66	41.99	51.65	60.56	17.98
Tripura	0.00	0.00	0.00	0.00	0.00	0.00	0.00	0.00	0.00	0.00
Uttar Pradesh	6.51	7.65	7.02	7.49	10.33	12.17	17.19	19.24	18.08	16.62
West Bengal	0.00	0.00	0.00	0.00	0.00	0.00	0.00	0.00	0.00	0.00
Total	27.03	50.44	61.73	61.59	82.43	95.11	108.82	103.86	148.29	23.71

Table 4.7

Gross Margin

Sector: Commercial (Rs.in crore)

State Name	*1985-86*	*1986-87*	*1987-88*	*1988-89*	*1989-90*	*1990-91*	*1991-92*	*1992-93*	*1993-94*
Andhra Pradesh	112.08	114.44	61.67	112.37	100.62	34.31	58.91	47.64	30.17
Arunachal Pradesh	0.00	0.00	0.00	0.00	0.00	0.00	-0.01	-0.09	-0.12
Assam	14.58	15.28	15.35	18.52	16.82	16.56	16.37	14.03	12.94
Bihar	-0.99	13.05	12.78	9.78	-0.33	8.15	13.08	27.46	27.91
Goa	0.46	0.28	0.51	0.69	0.77	1.10	1.52	1.13	0.59
Gujarat	95.52	86.45	116.95	167.49	169.71	237.12	303.14	334.27	357.84
Haryana	5.77	9.21	10.74	10.20	17.57	13.53	20.86	51.25	107.77
Himachal Pradesh	1.12	2.25	2.21	2.12	6.96	2.86	3.53	2.53	3.26
Jammu & Kashmir	5.77	1.59	5.04	6.63	2.52	-1.07	2.58	0.59	-3.72
Karnataka	131.42	156.88	204.50	209.97	244.33	251.48	265.82	219.85	346.05
Kerala	52.72	51.69	72.57	91.56	84.97	92.74	76.30	132.35	149.93
Madhya Pradesh	5.61	6.41	7.34	6.05	8.66	22.35	31.85	14.41	18.00
Maharashtra	11.76	14.23	25.76	25.86	22.06	20.19	31.44	31.37	40.99

(Contd.)

Table 4.7 (contd.)

State Name	*1985-86*	*1986-87*	*1987-88*	*1988-89*	*1989-90*	*1990-91*	*1991-92*	*1992-93*	*1993-94*
Manipur	0.03	0.02	-0.02	0.04	-0.08	0.00	0.04	0.02	0.06
Meghalaya	1.02	1.69	1.06	1.81	4.30	4.65	6.39	3.63	3.80
Mizoram	0.00	0.00	0.00	0.00	0.00	0.00	0.00	0.00	0.01
Nagaland	-5.81	-4.62	-5.74	-5.82	-5.74	-7.43	-6.20	-6.82	-5.39
Orissa	4.94	4.52	3.22	1.24	6.76	6.20	4.17	6.31	12.56
Punjab	3.47	7.14	15.19	16.27	32.13	33.65	29.77	55.85	87.85
Rajasthan	9.15	13.33	16.40	12.60	19.79	25.24	35.21	44.67	51.04
Sikkim	0.09	0.06	-0.11	-0.12	-0.04	-.11	0.18	0.05	0.05
Tamilnadu	79.64	73.28	81.16	80.42	88.30	93.20	99.49	111.14	125.95
Tripura	0.00	0.00	0.00	0.00	0.00	0.00	0.00	0.00	0.00
Uttar Pradesh	17.90	7.69	0.22	-14.25	-0.99	4.41	-4.7	-16.20	-24.27
West Bengai	-9.21	-10.44	-8.32	-11.56	-9.65	-10.66	-14.23	-14.82	-14.57
Total	537.04	564.43	638.48	741.85	809.44	848.47	975.43	1060.62	1328.70

than 2:1 current ratio during most of the years of the study points to their illiquidity and lack of control of working capital. However, there were States, such as Assam, Goa, Gujarat, Karnataka, Kerala, and Orissa where the current ratio in respect of their promotional enterprises turned out to be much higher than 2:1. This represented another extreme. In these States the enterprises were allowed to play with the public money. They seemed to have no idea of the cost of working capital and appeared to indulge in over-stocking, generous credit granting and large cash holdings.

Value Added

Table 4.8 reveals that the value added for all the SLPEs taken together went from Rs. 27 crore in 1985-86 to Rs. 148 crore in 1993-94. The CARG of value added in the promotional SLPEs was 23.71%.

Issues and Problems

These enterprises had a very weak middle management. The Chairman-cum-Managing Director/Vice-Chairman-cum-Managing Director were supported by junior functionaries as managers or deputy managers, since the senior management posts were lying vacant for long periods and it proved to be difficult for these enterprises to attract managers to man such posts. The top management in these enterprises suffered from severe handicaps. The chief executives came on short tenures and the members of the board of directors did not have continuity. This resulted in the absence of an enterprise-specific culture. Most of the managers came on deputation from the Government and so were the chief executive officers. This hampers the process of business development and lack of will to learn the rules of the market. Though these enterprises were created as autonomous entities, they continued to function as departmental enterprises on account of the presence of

Table 4.8

Gross Margin

Sector: Commercial-Cum-Promotional (Rs.in Crore)

State Name	*1985-86*	*1986-87*	*1987-88*	*1988-89*	*1989-90*	*1990-91*	*1991-92*	*1992-93*	*1993-94*
Andhra Pradesh									
Andhra Pradesh	13.60	22.16	19.45	16.52	17.40	42.61	29.14	34.28	55.64
Arunachal Pradesh	3.72	4.86	6.86	7.02	6.25	7.73	7.92	7.99	8.45
Assam	9.71	9.58	10.04	10.66	11.89	9.40	11.08	1.47	6.31
Bihar	13.42	17.82	17.50	18.43	21.05	18.73	27.26	16.65	18.82
Goa	2.67	4.29	5.50	6.42	7.12	9.35	9.53	13.94	24.89
Gujarat	32.42	40.99	53.83	59.21	26.48	31.09	45.41	39.54	37.50
Haryana	26.13	29.15	34.94	34.46	40.52	49.78	55.21	69.94	199.71
Himachal Pradesh	5.80	9.95	13.83	6.09	5.58	6.97	11.59	8.91	10.03
Jammu & Kashmir	0.00	0.00	0.00	0.00	0.00	0.00	0.00	0.00	0.00
Karnataka	34.91	34.09	42.20	45.05	52.07	53.84	78.16	122.21	145.99
Kerala	-8.12	-6.49	-11.42	-9.25	-2.51	-2.48	6.94	-12.33	-8.34
Madhya Pradesh	13.80	17.93	22.71	27.27	33.11	15.84	23.08	27.49	22.93
Maharashtra	142.40	167.30	192.49	214.83	244.06	280.68	310.05	495.84	524.92
Manipur	0.02	0.09	0.11	0.88	1.26	1.91	2.13	2.52	2.79

Meghalaya	0.03	0.05	0.09	0.20	0.20	0.20	0.22	0.22	0.25
Mizoram	0.00	0.00	0.00	0.00	0.00	-0.12	-0.18	-0.38	-0.38
Nagaland	0.18	0.27	0.45	0.15	0.34	-0.02	-0.06	0.03	0.02
Orissa	35.05	33.11	40.37	40.88	41.96	43.71	59.33	83.10	2.58
Punjab	-0.54	0.42	1.74	4.11	3.97	3.15	9.94	2.22	3.49
Rajasthan	0.26	-0.02	-0.07	0.74	0.11	0.26	1.70	4.09	4.06
Sikkim	0.05	0.17	0.07	0.09	0.01	0.63	0.43	0.70	1.96
Tamilnadu	6.06	6.70	8.04	6.95	8.30	10.87	12.47	13.70	14.17
Tripura	0.01	-0.06	0.02	0.16	-.02	0.16	0.04	0.05	0.07
Uttar Pradesh	29.56	44.16	42.48	43.03	68.75	76.70	104.15	157.20	83.94
West Bengal	8.58	7.65	9.90	8.45	7.75	11.62	12.18	15.42	24.85
Total	356.12	422.01	491.68	525.83	578.25	630.00	788.58	1070.52	1129.01

Government functionaries, as both the debt and equity came from the Government coffers. The innovations in business were at a discount in these enterprises, most of which continued to function with the same schemes. These enterprises also suffered from duplication of activities and lack of coordination. For instance, in each district of a State, the SC/BC, Women's Development, and Tribal Corporations function sometimes competing for the same end. They do not coordinate their activities with one another. This added to the cost of their transactions. In the case of some enterprises, instead of earning profits through disbursal and recovery of funds, the money was put in the bank in fixed deposits and high rates of interest were earned to show profit-earning.

CHAPTER 5

AN OVERVIEW OF SLPEs IN INDIA

Andhra Pradesh

Introduction

The Industrial Policy Resolution of 1956 which continues to be the cornerstone of our nations industrial policy and the planning process envisages an important role for the States in certain sectors of Industries. There is a widespread feeling that the SLPEs in A.P. have been created in a haphazard manner without giving due regard to the public purpose they are to serve and that they were set up mostly on account of the pressure for providing sound placement opportunities to public men and bureaucrats.

Profile

There are 59 SLPEs in Andhra Pradesh comprising 21 Commercial, 27 Commercial-cum-promotional and 11 Promotional SLPEs. Of these 10 Commercial, 17 Commercial-cum-Promotional and 2 Promotional (total 29) form a part of this study as the filled in data sheets were not received from the remaining SLPEs. The response from the SLPEs of Andhra Pradesh was quite satisfactory since 50% of them responded.

Total Investment

The total investment in 29 SLPEs went up from Rs. 923 crore in 1985-86 to Rs. 3,252 crore in 1993-94, registering a CARG 17%. Table 5.1 gives data on sector-wise total investment in the SLPEs. The growth in total investment

Table 5.1

Sector	*1985-86*	*1986-87*	*1987-88*	*1988-89*	*1989-90*	*1990-91*	*1991-92*	*1992-93*	*1993-94*
Comm	358.40	507.58	619.36	756.16	820.30	939.87	1010.71	1034.68	1021.7
C-P	564.30	717.61	928.00	1081.05	1268.73	1616.74	1712.17	1990.53	2223.02
Prom	0.61	1.28	1.98	2.97	3.90	4.80	6.02	7.09	7.59
Total	1923.31	1226.47	1549.42	1840.18	2092.93	2561.41	2728.90	3032.30	3252.39

Comm: Commercial, C-P:Commercial-cum-Promotional, Prom:Promotional.

of Commercial-cum-Promotional SLPEs as a whole was faster as compared to the other two sectors.

Net Worth

The aggregate net worth of the SLPEs of Andhra Pradesh under study went up from Rs.141.80 crore to Rs.230.65 crore during the period under referrence, thus showing 6.26% CARG. Among all the SLPEs, the A.P. State Financial Corporation Limited remained at the top in terms of net worth throughout the period from 1985-86 to 1993-94. Its net worth went up from Rs.56.98 crore to Rs.126.89 crore during this period. This was possible due to the infusion of more equity to the organisation in the same period. The A.P. Heavy Machinery & Engineering Limited and The Federation of Sericulture and Silk Weavers Cooperative Society have already eroded their net worth. Similarly the following SLPEs had zero or negligible net worth at the end of 1993-94:

Andhra Pradesh Scooters Limited
The Singareni Collieries Company Limited
A.P. Technology Services Limited
A.P. Dairy Development Cooperative Federation
A.P. State Housing Corporation.

Andhra Pradesh Cooperative Oilseeds Growers Federation after showing a negative net worth in 1992-93, turned around and showed a positive net worth in the following year.

Sales

The Singareni Collieries Limited maintained its top position among all the SLPEs in terms of sales in all the years under study. Its sales went up from Rs. 369.75 crore in 1985-86 to Rs. 662.43 crore in 1994-95. The Godavari Fertilizers and Chemicals Limited followed with a sales of

Rs.224.23 crore in 1994-95. The aggregate sales of the SLPEs under the study went up at a CARG of 10.14% from Rs. 576.44 crore in 1985-86 to Rs. 1,248.19 crore in 1993-94. However, in 1991-92 the aggregate sales was Rs. 1,539.63 crore. In 1993-94, the commercial SLPEs contributed more than 80% of the total sales of all the SLPEs.

The AP Foods Limited was found to be showing highest growth rate (21.94% CARG) in the turnover. Its sales went up from Rs. 3.88 crore in 1985-86 to Rs. 18.97 crore in 1993-94. A number of SLPEs like Godavari Fertilizers Limited, A.P.Small Industries Development Corporation Limited, A.P. Cooperative Oil Seeds Growers Federation recorded a decline in the later half of the study in their turnover after showing upward trend in the first half.

Gross Profit

In 1993-94, out of 29 SLPEs, 15 SLPEs earned gross profit on their sales, while the rest incurred gross loss. The aggregate gross profit of the SLP ed gross profit till 1989-90 and then losses up to the last year of the study. 7 SLPEs earned gross profit throughout the period of the study. The prominent among them are Godavari Fertilizers and Chemicals Limited and A.P.Housing Board in commercial group are the A.P. State Irrigation Corporation in the promotional category. 6 SLPEs showed zero gross profit or gross loss in all the years during the study period.

Profit after Tax (PAT)

During 1985-86 to 1993-94, the SLPEs as a whole earned profits only in two years, i.e. 1985-86 and 1988-89. While in 1985-86, the aggregate profit was Rs. 38.89 crore. However the net loss corresponding to 1992-93 was Rs. 211.93 crore. Unlike 15 SLPEs earning gross proft, only 10 SLPEs showed net profits and the rest showed no profit or net loss. The Singareni Collieries Limited earned profits in

1985-86 and in 1988-89. In rest of the period, this company was the highest contributor to the loss of the SLPEs as a whole. The top 2 profit making SLPEs under study in A.P. in 1993-94 included:

1. A.P. State Financial Corporation (Rs. 16.20 crore)

2. Godavari Fertilizers & Chemicals Limited (Rs. 14.91 crore)

The above mentioned SLPEs also earned net profits through out the period under reference. Besides, the A.P. State Seeds Development Corporation Limited showed net profits in all the years.

Accumulated Losses

The aggregate accumulated losses went up by more than four times from Rs. 203.17 crore in 1985-86 to Rs. 849.98 crore in 1993-94. In all the years, the Singareni Collieries Limited had a share of more than 60% of the aggregate Accumulated Losses. Among the Commercial-cum-Promotional SLPEs, A.P. State Housing Corporation was the major contributor to the accumulated losses in all the years.

Return On Investment (ROI)

Among 29 SLPEs of A.P. under reference, 19 SLPEs earned positive ROI in 1993-94, while others showed zero or negative ROI. The A.P. State Film Development Corporation Ltd showed very high ROI of 186.67% in 1993-94, although it incurred net losses in the same year. The unusually high ROI of A.P. State Film Development Corporation was possible due to its low equity capital. 12 SLPEs earned ROI in all years under reference. Besides A.P.State Film Development Corporation Ltd., the prominent among them are:

1. A.P. Technology Services Limited
2. A.P. State Financial Corporation Limited
3. A.P. State Seeds Development Corporation

The average ROI for all the SLPEs came down drastically from 18.90% in 1985-86 to 3.44% in 1993-94.

Return on Paid-Up Capital (ROPUC)

In 1993-94, 10 SLPEs showed positive ROPUC, and the rest showed zero, neglible or negative ROPUC. A.P. State Housing Corporation Limited (APSHC) showed a very low ROPUC i.e.,-10720% on its meager equity capital or Rs. 0.25 crore. In that year, A.P. Mineral Development Corporation Limited and Godavari Fertilizers & Chemical Limited earned 65.87% and 46.38% ROPUC, respectively. Other prominent SLPEs earning negative ROPUC were the A.P. Heavy Machinery & Engineering Limited and The Singareni Collieries Co. Ltd. The average ROPUC of the 29 SLPEs came down from 12.49% in 1985-86 to 18.04% in 1993-94.

Return On Net Worth (RONW)

Only 10 SLPEs earned RONW in 1993-94. In that year A.P. Mineral Development Corporation Limited showed the highest RONW of 627.54%. A.P. State Cooperative Oil Seeds Growers' Federation showed 216.4% RONW. This was possible since its net worth was very low compared to PAT. SLPEs like Godavari Fertilizers and Chemicals Limited and The Nizam Sugars Limited showed more than 12% RONW in 1993-94. The average RONW of the SLPEs went up from 3.38% to 16.29%.

Gross Margin to Sales (GMS)

On an average 15-17 SLPEs were able to earn gross margin on their sales in the whole period under reference.

However, the average GMS came down from 19.66% in 1985-86 to 4.48% in 1993-94. The A.P. Irrigation Development Corporation showed 100% GMS, due to the nature of the organisation. The SLPEs like A.P. Technology Services Limited and the A.P. Mineral Development Corporation and A.P. Forest Development Corporation earned more than 20% GMS in 1993-94.

The A.P. Scooters Limited showed –707.3% GMS in 1991-92. This figure was repeated in the following years due to non availability of data. The next SLPE to follow in showing negative GMS in 1993-94 was Leather Industries Development Corporation Limited with –33.80%.

Debt-Equity Ratio (D/E Ratio)

The overall D/E ratio of A.P. SLPEs varied from 2.56 to 4.21 during the period under study. The Commercial SLPEs had a low level of long-term debt as compared to the Commercial-cum-Promotional SLPEs. In the former category, The Godavari Fertilizers and Chemicals Limited and the Singareni Collieries Company Limited had high debt-equity ratio of 3.17 and 2.98, respectively, in 1993-94. The A.P. State Housing Corporation and an unusually high D/E ratio of 4886.7 in 1993-94. This was caused due to nominal equity capital or Rs. 0.25 crore in that SLPE. Among all the SLPEs, 5 had D/E Ratio exceeding 3:1 in 1993-94. Among Commercial-cum-Promotional SLPEs, A.P. State Financial showed higher D/E ratio in all the years.

Current Ratios

The liquidity position of the SLPEs in A.P. was more than normal since the current ratio turned around to be 1.9 to 2.3 in various years. The Commercial SLPEs, as a whole had a low current ratio compared to the size of this ratio to the other categories. A.P. Foods and A.P. State Housing had higher level of current assets compared to the other SLPEs.

Value Added

The value added by the AP SLPEs increased from Rs. 292 crore to Rs. 516 crore during the period from 1985-86 to 1993-94. However during 1990-91 there was slight decrease in the total value added is it was Rs. 387 crore. Although each category was showing a continuous increase in value added during the period under reference, commercial category's contribution to total value added was more compared to the other two categories. Among commercial enterprises. The maximum value addition was done by the Singareni Collieries company Limited.

Arunachal Pradesh

Introduction

This State has only 5 SLPEs, the oldest being the Arunachal Pradesh Forest Development Corporation set up in March, 1997. This State is endowed with tremendous forest resources. The State Government's favourable attitude has been the major factor which contributed to the growth of the SLPEs in the State. However, by effecting improvement in technology and developing human resources, these SLPEs could substantially improve their performance.

Profile

There are 5 SLPEs in Arunachal Pradesh comprising 2 Commercial and 3 Commercial-cum-Promotional SLPEs. Only 3 SLPEs come under this study since filled-in data sheets were not received from the rest. The names of these 3 SLPEs are:

1. Arunachal Pradesh Mineral Development & Trading Corporation Limited.

2. Arunachal Pradesh Forest Corporation Limited.

3. Arunachal Pradesh Industrial Development and Finance Corporation Limited.

Total Investment

The total investment in these 3 SLPEs went up from Rs. 3.14 crore in 1985-86 to Rs. 9.44 crore thus registering 14.75% CARG. Among them highest investment was made in Arunachal Pradesh Forest Corporation. However the growth rate of investment in Arunachal Pradesh Industrial Development of Financial Corporation was faster than that in Arunachal Pradesh Forest Corporation. The investment in the Arunachal Pradesh Mineral Development & Trading Corporation Ltd went up from Rs. 0.08 crore in 1993-94 to Rs. 0.75 crore in 1993-94 as shown in Table 5.2.

Net Worth

The three SLPEs of Arunachal Pradesh showed an aggregate net worth of Rs. 4. 39 crore in 1985-86 which went up marginally to 4.62 crore in 1993-94. The Arunachal Pradesh Industrial Development of Financial Corporation had already eroded its net worth by Rs. 1.17 crore as at the end of 1993-94.

Sales

The sales of the SLPEs in Arunachal Pradesh showed a good growth, since it grew at 11% CARG from Rs. 6.54 crore in 1985-86 to Rs. 15.64 crore in 1993-94. The sales of Arunachal Pradesh Mineral Development & Trading Corporation which commenced its operation in 1991-92, was negligible. Arunachal Pradesh Forest Corporation contributed to more than 95% of the total sales of 3 SLPEs.

Gross Profit (GP)

The gross profit of the SLPEs under study went up from Rs. 3.46 crore in 19985-86 to Rs. 7.82 crore in 1993-94. It

Table 5.2

Sector	1985-86	1986-87	1987-88	1988-89	1989-90	1990-91	1991-92	1992-93	1993-94
Comm	0.00	0.00	0.00	0.00	0.00	0.00	0.00	0.38	0.75
C-P	3.14	5.05	5.33	5.98	5.54	6.51	5.67	6.25	8.69
Prom	0.00	0.00	0.00	0.00	0.00	0.00	0.00	0.00	0.00
Total	3.14	5.05	5.33	5.98	5.54	6.51	5.75	6.63	9.44

Comm: Commercial, C-P: Commercial-cum-Promotional, Prom: Promotional.

was commensurated with the sales growth. As usual, The Arunachal Pradesh Forest Corporation Ltd. contributed to more than 90% of the total loss profit of the SLPEs. However, The Arunachal Pradesh Mineral Development & Trading Corporation registered gross loss in all the 3 years of its operation.

Profit After Tax (PAT)

Compared to growth in sales and gross profit, profit after tax of all the SLPEs as a whole did not grow much. It went up from Rs. 0.05 crore to Rs. 0.10 crore during the study period. Only The Arunachal Pradesh Forest Corporation was able to earn net profit in all but 2 years of the study period.

Accumulated Losses

The accumulated losses of Arunachal Pradesh SLPEs were contributed in main by The Arunachal Pradesh Mineral Development & Trading Corporation and The Arunachal Pradesh Industrial Development of Financial Corporation. The accumulated losses went up from Rs. 0.06 crore in 1985-86 to Rs. 2.84 crore in 1993-94.

Return On Investment

The SLPEs of Arunachal Pradesh under study earned very high rate of Return on Investment compared to the other states although the Return on Investment came down from 118.47% in 1985-86 to 88.34% in 1993-94. Except in the Arunachal Pradesh Mineral Development Mineral Development & Trading Corporation, all the other SLPEs showed a positive Return on Investment. Arunachal Pradesh Forest Corporation showed a very high return on investment of 157.78% in 1993-94 compared to 20.21% in case of Arunachal Pradesh Industrial Development of Financial Corporation.

Return On Paid-Up Capital (ROPUC)

The ROPUC of Arunachal Pradesh SLPEs was more or less fluctuating in the period under reference. The average ROPUC came down from 1.41% in 1985-86 to –8.32% in 1989-90 to go up to 1.69% in 1993-94. The Arunachal Pradesh Financial Corporation earned the ROPUC of 11.09% in 1993-94. The other two SLPEs showed a negative ROPUC.

Return On Net Worth (RONW)

The RONW of Arunachal Pradesh SLPEs went up from 1.14% in 1988-89 to 2.16% in 1993-94. The Arunachal Pradesh Forest Corporation was showing higher RONW of 11.09% compared to other SLPEs. The Arunachal Pradesh Mineral Development & Trading Corporation showed negative RONW in all the years of its operations.

Gross Margin to Sales (GMS)

In terms of GMS, Arunachal Pradesh Forest Corporation and Arunachal Pradesh Industrial Development of Financial Corporation showed good results in all the years under reference. In 1993-94, the Arunachal Pradesh Industrial Development of Financial Corporation showed 12.03% GMS, which was possible due to the fact that, it earned more other incomes than sales in the particular year. Over all, the average GMS of these two SLPEs remained between 45 and 56 %.

Debt-Equity Ratio (D/E Ratio)

The Debt-Equity ratio of the Arunachal Pradesh SLPEs as a whole is represented by the D/E ratio of the Arunachal Pradesh Industrial Development of Financial Corporation, alone, since the Arunachal Pradesh Forest Corporation and the Arunachal Pradesh Mineral Development & Trading Corporation had neglligible long-term loans to be repaid.

The D/E ratio of the Arunachal Pradesh Industrial Development of Financial Corporation went up from 3.22 to 13.03 during 1985-86 to 1993-94.

Current Ratio

The overall liquidity position of Arunachal Pradesh SLPEs was more or less unsatisfactory, since the current ratio covered around 1:1 in all the years of study. Comparatively Arunachal Pradesh Mineral Development & Trading Corporation had very high liquidity since it had a current ratio of 16.50:1 in 1993-94. Arunachal Pradesh Industrial Development of Financial Corporation had a better current ratio of 1.20:1 in 1993-94. It was as high as 4.63:1 in 1988-89.

Value Added

The value added of Arunachal Pradesh SLPEs increased from Rs. 4 crore to Rs. 10 crore during the period under study. Among the commercial-cum-promotional enterprises the maximum value added was created by the Arunachal Pradesh Forest Corporation Limited. In this case during 1985-86, the value added was Rs. 4 crore which went up to Rs. 9 crore in 1993-94.

Assam

Introduction

Assam including the present day Meghalaya, Mizoram and Nagaland had no SLPEs during the pre-independence period. The total dependence of the inhabitants of the state on agriculture and lack of education on the benefits of industrialisation was responsible for this sad state of affaiRs. The enterprises in Assam were established to exploit the natural resources and provide employment, fulfill the public interest and take up welfare oriented activities. A major objective of SLPEs in Assam is to open avenues of employment for the growing work force and increase the per capita income of the state.

Profile

The State of Assam at present has 46 SLPEs comprising 23 commercial, 11 commercial-cum-promotional and 12 promotional units. Out of 46 SLPEs, 23 had responded by filling the required data. The response came from 10 commercial, 10 commercial-cum-promotional and 3 promotional units. A total of 23 SLPEs form a part of this study.

Total Investment

The total investment in the 23 SLPEs stood at Rs. 357.03 crore in 1993-94 as against Rs. 177.26 crore in 1985-86. During the period of reference the state registered a CARG of 9.15%. Table 3.1 gives data relating to the sector-wise total investment in the SLPEs.

Net Worth

The SLPEs in Assam under study had a net worth of Rs. 80.30 crore in 1993-94 as against Rs. 45.66 crore in 1985-86. During this period the net worth grew at a rate of 7.3%. in absolute terms it has been less than double. Out of the 23 SLPEs, the following 3 SLPEs eroded their net worth by 1987-88 itself and the 4th SLPE by 1990-91.

1. Assam Conductors and Tubes Ltd.
2. Assam Spun Silk Mills Ltd.
3. Assam State Fertilizers and Chemicals Ltd.
4. Assam Government Construction Corporation Ltd.

Though the Assam State Development Corporation for Scheduled Caste, had a negative net worth up to 1988-89

Table 5.3

Sector	*1985-86*	*1986-87*	*1987-88*	*1988-89*	*1989-90*	*1990-91*	*1991-92*	*1992-93*	*1993-94*
Comm	56.95	51.49	55.81	60.54	59.31	57.89	58.63	69.46	69.23
C-P	116.32	143.42	169.07	216.35	217.60	244.85	279.91	368.54	253.47
Prom	3.99	4.57	5.15	5.48	11.32	21.80	27.46	34.97	34.33
Total	177.26	199.48	230.03	282.37	288.23	324.54	366.00	472.97	357.03

Comm: Commercial, C-P: Commerical-cum-Promotional, Prom:Promotional.

it has registered a positive net worth during the period thereafter.

Sales

The sales of Assam SLPEs increased slowly and steadily. The Assam commercial-cum-promotional SLPEs registered higher sales than the commercial SLPEs as such. The maximum sales were that of Assam State Co-operative Marketing and Consumers Federation in 1993-94. The total sales of the 23 SLPEs amounted to Rs. 186.83 crore in 1985-86 which increased to Rs. 263.66 crore in 1993-94. During the above mentioned period the SLPEs registered a CARG of 8% in sales.

Gross Profit

Out of the 23 SLPEs in Assam, only 11 have shown gross profit throughout the 8 years (though many had marginal profits). Out of the remaining 12 enterprises seven SLPEs e registered negative gross profit almost throughout the period under study and the remaining 5 have had negative gross profits at least for 4 years. The 23 SLPEs on the aggregate have registered a decline in gross profit from Rs. 20.44 crore in 1985-86 to Rs. 9.53 crore in 1993-94.

Profit After Tax

In Assam out of the 23 SLPEs only 5 registered profit through out 1985-86 to 1993-94. These SLPEs are as follows:

1. Assam Petrochemicals Ltd.
2. Assam State Warehousing Corporation
3. The Assam Text Book Production and Publication Corporation

4. Assam State Financial Corporation

5. Assam Apex Weavers and Artisans Co-operative Federation

The rest of the SLPEs either had zero profits or negative profits. Some SLPEs such as the Assam Spim Silk Mills Ltd., Assam State Fertilizers and Chemicals Ltd., Assam Hills Small Industries Development Corporation, Assam State Co-operative Marketing and Consumers Federation incurred losses through out the period under study.

On the whole, only the commercial SLPEs could maintain a positive profit after tax though it declined from Rs. 4.04 crore to Rs. 1.94 crore during 1985-86 to 1993-94. Both the commercial-cum-promotional and promotional SLPEs registered negative profit after tax.

In aggregate the SLPEs recorded losses of Rs. 1.21 crore in 1985-86 which increased to Rs. 13.43 crore in 1993-94 though 1986-87, 1987-88, 1988-89 and 1989-90 registered marginal profits.

Accumulated Losses

Out of the 23 SLPEs, only 6 of them did not have accumulated losses throughout the period under study i.e 1985-86 to 1993-94. The highest losses through out the eight year period were registered by the Assam State Co-operative Marketing and Consumers Federation i.e. Rs. 40.05 crore in 1993-94 while the next place was occupied by the Assam State Industrial Development Corporation with accumulated losses of Rs. 38.51 crore. On the whole, the accumulated losses of 23 SLPEs which were Rs. 72.42 crore in 1985-86 increased to Rs. 150 crore in 1993-94.

Return On Investment (ROI)

The Return on Investment of the 23 Assam SLPEs was 23.28% in 1985-86 which declined to 13.09% in 1993-94.

Though the Commercial SLPEs registered the highest ROI in 1993-94 i.e 16.51%., there has been a reduction in the ROI as compared to that in 1985-86 which was 32.57%. The commercial-cum-promotional SLPEs also registered a reduction in ROI from 17.2% in 1985-86 to 10.03% in 1993-94. There have been no SLPEs which have been earning negative ROI through out the 8 year period in Assam. It is only the Assam State Minor Irrigation Department which had a negative ROI for 6 years continuously.

Current Ratio

The overall liquidity of the Assam SLPEs varied between 1.38 and 1.27 during the period of study. The Current ratio was the maximum for the Promotional units in Assam. The Assam Urban Water Supply and Sewerage Board recorded 195:1 in 1993-94 though itwas started in the year 1989-90.

Value Added

In the case of Bihar, the total value added of the SLPEs fluctuated from year to year. During 1985-86, the value added was Rs. 31 crore, which decreased to Rs. 29 crore in 1992-93. Again in 1993-94 it went up to Rs. 33 crore. Among all the SLPEs, the Assam Petrochemicals Limited has contributed the largest value added in all the years.

Bihar

Introduction

Bihar is one of relatively backward states of the country. The state is faced with the challenge of raising the living standards of the masses through an accelerated rate of economic development. However the state suffers from a serious resource crunch. The SLPEs in Bihar are expected to achieve certain specific socio-economic ends and generate commercial surpluses for the growth of the economy.

Profile

In Bihar there are in overall 50 enterprises comprising 15 commercial, 23 Commercial-cum-Promotional and 12 promotional enterprises. The data for the purpose of analysis is available for only 9 enterprises 50, comprising of 4 commercial, 4 Commercial-cum-Promotional and 1 promotional enterprise. The response received from the state of Bihar happens to be very poor.

Total Investment

The Total Investment in the SLPEs reported for the study at the end of fiscal 1993-94 stands at Rs. 104.7 crore. When compared to the figure at the end of 1985-86 it grew with a CARG of 4.15%. In case of Bihar Sugar Corporation Ltd. the total investment was totally eroded and had become negative to the extent of Rs. 102.89 crore.

Net Worth

For all the years of the study, the net worth was in negative terms. It was –28.53 in 1985-86 and –137.30 in the year 1993-94. More than Rs. 100 crore was lost in the enterprises reported. But if we observe the data closely, it is seen that the commercial were showing negative net worth, whereas the Commercial-cum-Promotional were keeping the head above water in case of the Bihar State Credit and Investment Corporation Ltd. which was showing positive net worth till 1992-93 had started showing negative net worth.

Sales

In terms of sales, the enterprises in Bihar nearly doubled their sales in the period of study showing an average sales of 60.64 crore showing a CARG of 8.61 per cent. In the case of the commercial enterprises, the increase was marginally less as the sales increased from 18.65 crore in 1985-86 to Rs. 34.39 crore over a period of 9 years.

Table 5. 4

Sector	*1985-86*	*1986-87*	*1987-88*	*1988-89*	*1989-90*	*1990-91*	*1991-92*	*1992-93*	*1993-94*
Comm	14.64	10.35	1.40	-6.40	-12.91	-29.69	-7.99	-78.94	-80.49
C-P	58.52	94.19	117.36	116.50	130.52	159.36	187.21	195.43	179.95
Prom	2.45	3.66	5.42	4.83	6.58	6.43	7.86	0.00	7.95
Total	75.61	108.19	124.18	114.93	124.19	136.10	187.08	116.49	107.41

Comm: Commercial, C-P: Commercial-cum-Promotional, Prom: Promotional

Gross Profit

In terms of gross profit all the enterprises reported were showing a positive Gross Profit. The Gross Profit increased from Rs. 12.80 crore in 1985-86 to Rs. 45.81 crore in the year 1993-94 representing a CARG of 17.28 per cent. The Gross Profit in the Bihar State Mineral Development Corporation Ltd. and the Bihar State Co-operative Milk Producers Federation Ltd. had been negative till 1991-92 Gross Profit for Commercial enterprises was showing a negative trend of –0.67% in 1985-86 but it turned a positive 27.32% in 1993-94.

Profit After Tax

In terms of PAT, the SLPEs of Bihar were showing negative profit during the period under study. In terms of losses the Bihar State Sugar Corporation Ltd. was continuously making losses and in case of the Bihar State Co-operative Milk Producers Federation Ltd., there was negative PAT till the year 1992-93 which improved to a positive figure of Rs. 1.69 crore in 1993-94. In case of the Bihar State Financial Corporation which has a positive PAT till 1988-89, the receding trend set in during the period thereafter.

Accumulated Losses

The SLPEs of the State had accumulated losses to the tune of Rs. 530.98 crore at the end of fiscal 1993-94. The figures stood at Rs. 88.59 crore at the end of 1985-86. The losses had increased almost 6 times in the SLPEs reproted. During the period of the study the Bihar Sugar Corporation Ltd. was leading the table with Rs. 326.85 crore and the Bihar State Financial Corporation followed with an accumulated losses of Rs. 156.16 crore at the end of fiscal 1993-94.

Return On Investment (ROI)

In terms of ROI, the SLPEs of Bihar have shown a five fold decline from 16.81 % at the end of 1985-86 to 73.28% at the end of 1993-94. In terms of ROI the Bihar State Financial Corporation came at the top of the list with an ROI of 117.22%. It was followed by the Bihar State Textbook Publishing Corporation Limited with 66.28%. The ROI was negative (-30.89%) in case of commercial category as a whole. Whereas in case commercial-cum-promotional category it was 12.88%, the promotional SLPEs as a whole earned a nil ROI.

Return On Paid-Up Capital

In terms of ROPUC, the overall Return on PUC on all enterprises together was negative, i.e., Rs. 2.87 crore. At the end of fiscal 1993-94 it stood at Rs. –16.68 crore negative to Rs. –37.81 crore in the year 1990-91. Bihar State Co-operative Milk Producers Federation Ltd. topped the list of negative ROPUC with Rs. –444.7 crore and on the other The Bihar State Text Book Publishing Corporation Ltd. topped the list with a positive ROI of Rs. 31.62 crore. Out of the enterprises reproted, only two enterprises showed a positive ROPUC and all other were either showing negative or zero PUC.

Return On Net Worth (RONW)

It is interesting to note that the net worth was negative in all the enterprises.

Gross Margin to Sales (GMS)

Gross Margin to sales in the SLPEs of Bihar was ranging between 24.20 and 37.84 at the end of fiscal 1993-94 the Gross Margin to Sales was 31.87%. The Bihar State Financial Corporation topped the list with a Gross Margin of 137.87% to sales followed by Bihar State Textbook Publishing Corporation Ltd. with 18.68%. On an average the Gross Margin to Sales in the SLPEs during the period of study was around 28 per cent.

Debt-Equity Ratio (D/E Ratio)

The Debt-Equity ratio for the SLPEs of Bihar ranged between 2.17 and 4.97. It was very high at 10.10 and 5.35 in the case of the Bihar State Sugar Corporation Ltd. and the Bihar State Credit and Investment Corporation Ltd. respectively. Overall, for all the SLPEs taken together the ratio stood at 1:4.95 in the year 1991-92.

Current Ratio

In the case of Bihar SLPEs, the overall current ratio ranged from 1.04 to 1.57 during the period under reference. At the end of the year 1993-94 , the ratio for all that enterprises taken together turned out to be 1.04. In terms of current ratio, the Bihar State Hydro Electric Power Corporation Limited led the table with 5.11:1 followed by the Ranchi Industrial Area Development Authority with 3.04:1.

Value Added

During 1985-86, the value added was Rs. 23 crore. The Value added had increased by two fold during the period under review. In the case of each enterprise, the value added has been increasing constantly over the period. Under the category of the commercial SLPEs the Bihar State Sugar Corporation Limited's contribution to total value added was of Rs. 6.68 crore in 1985-86 which turned out to be a negative of Rs. 623 crore in 1993-94. In the Commercial-cum-Promotional SLPEs the value added increased from Rs. 14.37 crore in 1985-86 to Rs. 46.40 crore in 1993-94.

Goa

Introduction

Goa, which became a part of the Indian Union in 1961 was granted statehood in 1987. The SLPEs in Goa are engaged in the task of modernising the state as well as strengthening the economy in its traditional sectors.

Profile

The Goa State is having 23 SLPEs, comprising 14 Commercial, 8 Commercial-cum-Promotional and 1 Promotional. Of these only 3 Commercila, 10 Commercial-cum-Promotional and 3 Promotional (total 16) SLPEs form a part of this study as the filled-in data sheets were not received from the other SLPEs.

Total Investment

The Total Investment in the 16 SLPEs of Goa stood at Rs. 214.42 crore at the end of 1993.94 compared to Rs. 40.03 crore at the end of 1985-86. During the period under reference, it had a CARG of 23.34%. Table 5.1 gives data relating to the sector-wise total investment in the SLPEs.

Net Worth

The SLPEs in Goa under study had a net worth of Rs. 27.81 crore in 1985-86 and the figure increased to Rs. 99.38 crore in 1993-94. During this period the net worth grew at a CARG of 17.25. Out of 16 SLPEs , 8 enterprises have already eroded their net worth.

The Goa Financial Leasing Services Limited successfully turned around in 1989-90 and Goa State Schedule Caste & other Backward Cast Finance & Development Corporation Ltd. have been adding positively to their net worth.

Table 5.5

Sector	*1985-86*	*1986-87*	*1987-88*	*1988-89*	*1989-90*	*1990-91*	*1991-92*	*1992-93*	*1993-94*
Comm	4.40	4.82	5.25	7.54	9.42	9.23	8.65	13.09	13.59
C-P	9.00	13.29	13.01	14.51	23.75	29.83	35.83	32.08	69.76
Prom	26.63	34.71	46.33	59.05	72.52	87.00	100.87	112.00	123.82
Total	40.03	52.82	64.59	81.10	105.69	126.86	145.35	157.17	207.17

Comm: Commercial, C-P: Commercial-cum-Promotional, Prom: Promotional.

Sales

During the study period the total sales of 16 SLPEs went up from Rs. 12.41 crore to Rs. 48.40 crore during the period 1985-86 to 1993-94. The Goa State Co-operative Bank Ltd. toped the SLPEs in terms of sales in1993-94 with a turnover of Rs. 24.26 crore, followed by Goa Handicrafts Rural & Small Scale Industries Development Corporation with a turnover of Rs. 11.02 crore. Throughout the period of study Promotional SLPEs showed better turnover in aggregate compared to the commercial SLPEs.

Gross Profit

Out of 16 SLPEs in 1993-94, 9 showed gross profit and the rest had either zero or negative gross profit. The Goa State Co-operative Bank Ltd. had been maintaining the top position in gross profit throughout the period. Its gross profit went up from Rs. 1.87 crore to Rs. 19.23 crore during the period 1985-86 to 1993-94. Economic Development Corporation of Goa, Daman & Diu Ltd. showed increasing trend in gross profit from Rs. 0.14 crore to Rs. 3.96 crore during the same period. Besides these two, Goa Auto Accessories Ltd., Goa Handicrafts, Rural & Small Scale Industries Development, Goa Tourism Development Corporation Limited and Goa Urban Co-operative Bank Ltd. earned gross profit in all the years of the study. The aggregate gross profit of 16 SLPEs went up from Rs. 2.54 crore in 1985-86 to Rs. 27.25 crore in 1993-94 at a CARG of 34.52%.

Profit After Tax

In 1993-94, 9 SLPEs had shown profit and the rest of the enterprises recorded loss. Among the profit making SLPEs, the following SLPEs earned profits throughout the period 1985-86 to 1993-94:

1. The Goa State Co-operative Housing Finance & Federation
2. Goa Handicrafts, Rural & Small Scale Industries Development Corporation
3. Goa Tourism Development Corporation
4. Goa Urban Co-operative Bank Ltd.
5. Economic Development Corporation of Goa, Daman, & Diu, Ltd.

The Kadamba Transport Corporation had incurred losses throughout the study period excepting 1990-91.The aggregate profit of 16 SLPEs had increased from Rs. -1.06 crore to Rs. 3.19 crore during the study period.

Accumulated Losses

Among 16 SLPEs in Goa 3 had accumulated losses in 1993-94, whereas in 1985-86 4 SLPEs figured in this category. The Goa Meat Complex Limited, the Kadamba Transport Corporation Ltd. had incurred losses throughout the study period Total accumulated losses of the SLPEs shot up from Rs. 5.27 crore to Rs. 6.45 crore during the period 1985-86 to 1993-94.

Return On Investment (ROI)

The SLPEs of Goa could generate 21.16% ROI in 1993-94 as compared to the ROI of 16.91% in 1985-86. The promotional SLPEs were in a better position to generate the ROI as compared with the SLPEs in the other sectors.

Return On Paid-Up Capital

The equity share holders of the SLPEs as a whole earned 3.18% ROPUC in 1993-94 and in 1985-86 it was –1.19%. In 1993-94, the Goa Auto Accessories Limited had a negative ROPUC. Six out of the 16 SLPEs had zero ROPUC and the top position in earning ROPUC was occupied by the Citizen Co-operative Bank Ltd. with 13.51%.

Return On Net Worth (RONW)

In aggregate the SLPEs earned 1.78% RONW in 1993-94. In 1985-86 this figure was –5.29%. The Goa Financial and Leasing Services Limited was toped the list earning 11.11% RONW in 1993-94. 2 SLPEs had negative RONW and 9 SLPEs had zero RONW in 1993-94. 4 SLPEs had RONW more than the state average in 1993-94.

Gross Margin to Sales (GMS)

The GMS of the SLPEs as a whole increased from 21.43% to 46.28% during the period 1985-86 to 1993-94. The Commercial SLPEs showed a lower GMS compared to Commercial-cum-Promotional. The Goa, Daman & Diu Industrial Development Corporation had highest GMS in 1992-93 compared to other SLPEs with 413.33% and it followed by the Goa Land Army Corporation Ltd. which had a negative GMS in 1992-93 and1993-94. 9 SLPEs had zero GMS in 1993-94.

Debt-Equity Ratio

The overall D/E ratio of the Goa SLPEs increased from 1.85 to 1.91 during the period 195-86 to 1993-94. The Citizen Co-operative Bank Ltd. had highest D/E ratio throughout the study period.

Current Ratio

The overall liquidity seemed to be satisfactory with the current ratio varying from 1.74 to 1.55 during the study period. Promotional SLPEs had a high current ratio compared to other secrors. The Goa State Co-operative Housing Finance & Federation had a current ratio of 13:1 in 1993-94, and it was followed by the Citizen Co-operative Bank Ltd. with 11:1 current ratio.

Value Added

The total value added by the SLPEs multiplied by five folds as it increased from Rs. 9 crore to Rs. 42 crore between the years 1985-86 and 1993-94. However during 1990-91 there was slight decline in the value added in which year it stood at Rs. 24 crore.

Gujarat

Introduction

The setting up of SLPEs in Gujarat begun with formulation of the state on 1st May, 1996 when the erst while Bombay state was bifurcated. The Gujarat State Financial Corporation and Gujarat State Warehousing Corporation came into being to fill in the void. After laying the necessary infrastructure the State Government moved on to promote industrialization in the state.

Profile

There are 45 SLPEs in Gujarat comprising 20 commercial, 17 commercial-cum-promotional and 8 promotional SLPEs. Out of these, 29 SLPEs (9 commercial, 19 commercial-cum-promotional and 3 promotional) form a part of this study since filed-in data sheets were not received from the rest of the SLPEs.

Total Investment

The Gujarat State SLPEs registered an increase in the total investment during the study period. The Commercial SLPEs had an investment of Rs. 249.81 crore in 1985-86 which increased to Rs. 1,839.12 crore in 1993-94. The highest increase in total investment was recorded in Promotional SLPEs from Rs. 84.82 crore in 1985-86 to Rs. 1,981.28 crore in 1993-94. The investment registered a CARG of 27%. The total investment was the maximum in Sardar Sarovar Narmada Nigam Ltd., a total of Rs. 1,837.42

Table 5. 6

Sector	*1985-86*	*1986-87*	*1987-88*	*1988-89*	*1989-90*	*1990-91*	*1991-92*	*1992-93*	*1993-94*
Comm	249.81	324.60	418.23	634.53	760.59	1038.97	1300.61	1591.01	1839.12
C-P	363.78	456.67	486.8.3	491.75	545.56	586.37	694.22	783.30	905.58
Prom	84.82	86.30	85.66	797.18	986.73	1384.02	1986.33	1988.55	1981.28
Total	698.41	867.57	990.72	1923.46	2292.88	3009.36	3981.16	4362.86	4725.28

Comm: Commercial, C-P: Commercial-cum-Promotional, Prom: Promotional.

crore in 1993-94. The Gujarat Civil Supplies Corporation Ltd. had a negative total investment throughout the period under study.

Net Worth

The 29 SLPEs in Gujarat showed an upward trend in net worth in aggregate. The Promotional SLPEs had the highest net worth of Rs. 2769.85 crore in 1993-94 mainly because of Sardar Sarovar Nigam Ltd. which had a net worth of Rs. 1,742.53 crore for the same year. The Commercial-cum-Promotional SLPEs in aggregate had negative net worth for the years 1988-89, 1989-90, 1990-91 and 1992-93. The Gujarat State Construction Corporation Ltd., Gujarat Tractor Corporation Ltd. and gujarat Trans Receivers Ltd. registered a negative net worth from 1985-86 to 1993-94. However in aggregate the net worth increased from Rs. 275.71 crore in 1985-86 to Rs. 3,148.74 crore in 1993-94 at a CARG of 35.6% over the above mentioned period.

Sales

The Commercial SLPEs of Gujarat accounted for the highest sales of Rs. 1,428.09 crore in 1993-94. The highest sales among the 29 SLPEs was recorded by the Gujarat State Fertilizer Company which increased its sales from Rs. 328.12 crore in 1985-86 to Rs. 1,151.60 crore in 1993-94. The Commercial-cum-Promotional SLPEs registered an increase in sales from Rs. 554.92 crore in 1985-86 to Rs. 887.89 crore in 1993-94. In aggregate the sales of the 29 SLPEs increased from Rs. 958.54 crore in 195-86 to Rs. 2,323.50 crore in 1993-94. A CARG of 11.7% in total net sales has been recorded.

Gross Profit

The Commercial SLPEs of Gujarat accounted for the highest gross profit throughout the period under study. Among the commercial SLPEs the highest gross profit was earned by Gujarat State Fertilizers Company Ltd., of Rs. 51.41 crore in 1985-86 which increased to Rs. 169.43 crore in 1993-94. The SLPEs in Gujarat mostly earned positive gross profits. Only 7 SLPEs earned negative gross profits but this also was only for about 3 to 4 years. In aggregate the gross profit increased from Rs. 109.11 crore in 1985-86 to Rs. 356.85 crore in 1993-94 recording a CARG of 16%. It was only the Gujarat Dairy Development Corporation Ltd. which earned negative gross profits for 6 years i.e.,from 198-89 to 1993-94.

Profit After Tax (PAT)

The Promotional SLPEs of Gujarat recorded a negative PAT throughout the period under study. These SLPEs accounted for negative PAT of Rs. 5.56 crore in 1985-86 which increased to Rs. 12.26 crore in 1993-94. The highest PAT of Rs. 75 crore was earned by the Gujarat State Textile Corporation Ltd. in 1993-94. The Gujarat State Fertilizer Company Ltd. also earned high profit upto 1991-92 after which the PAT of the Company started reducing upto 1993-94. None of the SLPEs Commercial and Commercial-cum-Promotional category have been at the top position.

Accumulated Losses

Out of the 29 SLPEs in Gujarat 11 of them had accumulated losses in 1985-86. By 1993-94 only 10 of the SLPEs had accumulated losses. The Commercial-cum-Promotional SLPEs registered highest accumulated losses of Rs. 412.73 crore mainly because of the Gujarat Textile Corporation Ltd. which has been accumulating losses throughout i.e., 1985-86 to 1993-94. In 1993-94 the accumulated losses of this unit alone accounted to Rs. 397.17 crore. The total accumulated losses increased from Rs. 28.36 crore in 1985-86 in Commercial-cum-Promotional units to Rs. 412.73 crore in 1993-94. Next came the promotional units which had accumulated losses of Rs. 18.43 crore in 1985-86 which increased to Rs. 68.51 crore

1993-94. In aggregate the 29 SLPEs of Gujarat recorded accumulated losses of Rs. 74.18 crore in 1985-86 which increased to Rs. 511.67 crore in 1993-94.

Return On Investment (ROI)

Out of 29 SLPEs of Gujarat 13 of them had positive ROI throughout the period of reference. The Gujarat State Civil Supplies Corporation Ltd. is the only unit which had negative ROI throughout from 1985-86 to 1993-94. Highest ROI has been earned by the Gujarat State Land Development Corporation from 1985-86 to 1993-94. On the whole the commercial, Commercial-cum-Promotional and Promotional units had a declining ROI. In aggregate also the same result has been observed. The total ROI which was 31.59% in 1985-86 declined to 17.76% in 1993-94. Out of the 29 SLPEs in Gujarat 7 SLPEs had recorded 0% ROI.

Return on Paid-Up Capital (ROPUC)

In Gujarat the promotional SLPEs registered a negative ROPUC throughout i.e., 1985-86 to 1993-94 mainly because of Gujarat water Resources Development Corporation Ltd. 6 of the SLPEs registered a zero ROPUC. On the whole 3 SLPEs recorded negative ROPUC from 1985-86 to 1993-94. From 1985-867 to 1988-89 the Gujarat State Civil Supplies Corporation earned highest ROPUC but from 1988-89 it went down drastically. By 1993-94 it was The Gujarat State Textile Corporation Ltd. which was earning highest return of 360.58%. The Commercial-cum-Promotional SLPEs recorded an increase in ROPUC from 25.82% in 1985-86 to 48.61% in 1993-94 whereas the Commercial SLPEs registered a reduction in ROPUC from 15.65% in 1985-86 to 9.92% in 1993-94. In aggregate there was only a meager increase in ROPUC from 12.91% in 1985-86 to 13.51% in 1993-94.

Return On Net Worth (RONW)

The Return on Net worth of the Commercial units had increased to a maximum of 21.39% in 1988-89 from 16.01% in 1985-86. But again it decreased to 14.25% in 1993-94. In the Commercial-cum-Promotional SLPEs the maximum RONW was earned in 1987-88 i.e, 273.38% from 26.79% in 1985-86. The promotional units registered a negative RONW throughout the period under study mainly because of Gujarat Water Resources Development Corporation Ltd., which earned negative RONW throughout. In aggregate the RONW decreased from 13.93% in 1985-86 to 6.03% in 1993-94 though the RONW decreased from 13.93% in 1987-88.

Gross Margin to Sales (GMS)

The maximum GMS was accounted for by the commercial SLPEs in Gujarat GMS it was 24.28% in 1985-86 which increased to 25.05% in 1993-94. The highest GMS was by Gujarat Tribal Development Corporation which is a promotional unit. Out of the 29 SLPEs in Gujarat 13 of them registered a 0% GMS. In aggregate the GMS increased from 12.80% in 1985-86 to 16.67% in 1993-94.

Debt-Equity Ratio (D/E Ratio)

The Debt-Equity Ratio of 12 SLPEs amongst the 29 SLPEs was zero. The commercial SLPEs registered a meager increase in D/E ratio from 0.29 in 1985-86 to 1.06 in 1993-94. There was a slight increase in D/E ratio of Commercial-cum-Promotional units from 4.81 in 1985-86 to 6.43 in 1993-94. The promotional units recorded a slight reduction in D/E Ratio from 1.31 in 1985-86 to 0.95 in 1993-94. Gujarat State Civil Supplies Corporation Ltd. registered highest D/E ratio in 1985-86 i.e., 14.27 but by 1993-94 The Gujarat State Textile Corporation Ltd. registered the highest D/E ratio of 11.5. In aggregate the D/E ratio was 1.41 in 1985-86 which very slightly increased to 1.84 in 1993-94.

Current Ratio

The current ratio in the Gujarat SLPEs in aggregate varied between 1.73 and 1.78 between 1985-86 to 1993-94. The Promotional units recorded the highest current ratio throughout the period of study. It varied between 2.97 and 4.41 for the period under study.

Value Added

The value added has been steadily increasing during the period under study. It has increased from Rs. 142 crore in 1985-86 to Rs. 731 crore in 1993-94 i.e., an increase by five times. Although in all the enterprises, there was continuous increase in value added, Gujarat State Fertilizers Company Limited's contribution was the highest during 1985-86. The value added of the company was Rs. 43 crore. This had increased to Rs. 243 crore in 1993-94.

Haryana

Introduction

Haryana, a late entrant on the political map of India was carved out of the undivided Punjab in 1967. Half of the SLPEs in Haryana were set up during the Fourth Plan Period alone. Trading and service and manufacturing enterprises were larger in number as compared to the enterprises in other categories. The SLPEs have become the engine of economic development in the state.

Profile

The Haryana State at present has 39 SLPEs, consisting of 19 Commercial, 16 Commercial-cum-Promotional and 4 Promotional SLPEs. Of these the filled-in data sheets were received from 27 SLPEs (Commercial 11, Commercial-cum-Promotional 13 and Promotional 3) The rest were not able to send their data sheets.

Table 5.7

Sector	1985-86	1986-87	1987-88	1988-89	1989-90	1990-91	1991-92	1992-93	1993-94
Comm	49.22	55.57	63.26	79.01	110.85	135.66	174.23	200.43	200.64
C-P	206.40	168.35	232.10	265.93	276.19	336.37	405.73	507.24	701.24
Prom	6.75	9.43	16.69	13.65	15.24	18.74	19.73	25.60	27.43
Total	262.37	233.35	312.05	358.59	402.28	490.77	599.69	733.27	969.31

Comm: Commercial, C-P: Commercial-cum-Promotional, Prom: Promotional.

Total Investment

The total investment of the 27 SLPEs in Haryana stood at Rs. 969.31 crore in 1993-94, compared to Rs. 262.45 crore in 1985-86. During this period under reference, it had a CARG of 17.74%. Table 5.7 gives data relating to the sector-wise total investment in the SLPEs.

Net Worth

The SLPEs in Haryana under study had a net worth of Rs. 298.39 crore in 1993-94 compared to Rs. 52.81 crore in 1985-86. During this period the net worth grew at a CARG of 42.16%. In absolute terms, it grew almost 6 times over the period. Out of the 27 enterprises 8 enterprises completely eroded their net worth.

Sales

During the period, the total sales of 27 SLPEs went up from Rs. 312.62 crore in 1985-86 to Rs. 1167.63 crore in 1993-94 registering a CARG of 17.90%. Haryana State Co-operative Supply & Marketing Federation had occupied the top position in terms of sales during the study period. Its sales had increased from Rs. 190.93 crore in 1985-86 to Rs. 722.26 crore in 1993-94. The Haryana Agro-Industries Corporation Ltd. stood in 2nd position from 1989-90 onwards. In 1993-94 its sales was Rs. 178.50 crore. As a whole the Commercial SLPEs had shown a better performance in sales compared to other SLPEs. Its sales had gone up from 214.89 crore to Rs. 907.23 crore during the study period. All Promotional SLPEs had zero sales throughout the study period.

Gross Profit

Out of 27 SLPEs in 1993-94, 17 earned gross profit and the rest had registered either zero or negative gross profit. The Haryana State Co-operative Supply & Marketing Federation had top position in gaining the gross profit in

1993-94. The Haryana State Cooperative Apex Bank Ltd. had been maintaining top position in gross profit throughout the study period expect 1993-94. Besides these two the following SLPEs also earned profits throughout the study period from 1985-86 to 1993-94.

1. The Sonepat Co-operative Sugar Mills

2. Haryana Concast Limited

3. Haryana Land Reclamation and Development Corporation

4. The Haryana State Co-operative Land Development Bank Ltd.

5. Haryana Backward Classes Kalyan Nigam

The Kaithal Co-operative Sugar Mills Limited and the Haryana Harijan Kalyan Nigam Limited had incurred losses thoughout the study period. The Haryana Hotels Limited, the Haryana Dairy Development Co-operative Federation, Housing Board, Haryana and Haryana Police Housing Corporation had secured zero profits throughout the study period. The aggregate gross profit of 27 SLPEs went up from Rs. 36.12 crore in 1985-86 to Rs. 258.96 crore in 1993-94, registering a CARG of 27.92%.

Profit After Tax (PAT)

In 1993-94 15 SLPEs had shown profit after tax and the rest registered losses or zero profits. The following SLPEs earned profits throughout the period 1985-86 to 1993-94:

1. Haryana State Electronics Development Corporation Ltd.

2. Haryana Concast Limited

3. The Haryana State Co-operative Apex Bank Ltd.

4. Housing Board, Haryana

5. The Haryana State Federation of Consumer's Co-operative wholesale

6. Haryana Financial Corporation

7. Haryana Backward Classes Kalyan Nigam.

The Haryana Dairy Development Co-operative Federation, Haryana Police Corporation and Haryana Women Development Corporation showed zero profit after tax throughout the study period. The Kaithal Co-operative Sugar Mills Limited, the Haryana Dairy Development Corporation Ltd. and the Haryana Harijan Kalyan Nigam Ltd. incurred losses throughout the study period. The aggregate profit of 27 SLPEs was Rs. 2.54 crore in 1985-86 and the figure turned to positive from the next year and in 1993-94 it had Rs. 54.14 crore profit.

Accumulated Losses

Among 27 SLPEs, 14 had accumulated losses in 1993-94, 19 SLPEs had accumulated losses in 1985-86. The Haryana Dairy Development Co-operative Federation was at the top in terms of accumulated losses throughout the study period except in 1993-94. In 1993-94, this position was occupied by the Kaithal Co-operative Sugar Mills Ltd. In aggregate, the accumulated losses of the SLPEs went up from Rs. 54.17 crore in 1985-86 to Rs. 102.12 crore with a CARG of 8.24%.

Return On Investment (ROI)

Twenty-seven Haryana SLPEs could generate 37.79% ROI in 1993-94 as compared to 13.53% in 1985-86. The Haryana Agro Industries Corporation Ltd. toped the list in terms of ROI in 1993-94. The Haryana Harijan Kalyan Nigam Limited earned negative ROI throughout the period of study.

Return On Paid-Up Capital

The equity share holders of the SLPEs as a whole earned 14.21% ROPUC in 1993-94. In 1985-86 it was –1.11%. The increase in ROPUC was mainly due to the Commercial SLPEs. The Palwal Co-operative Sugar Mills Ltd., Haryana State Co-operative Supply & Marketing Federation, Haryana Seeds Development Corporation Ltd. and the Haryana Minerals Limited earned more than 20% ROPUC in 1993-94. The Kaithal Co-operative Sugar Mills Limited, Haryana State Federation of Consumers' Co-operative Wholesale and Haryana Harijan Kalyan Nigam Limited earned negative ROPUC throughout the period under reference.

Return On Net Worth (RONW)

In aggregate the SLPEs earned 17.91% RONW in 1993-94 compared to –4.09% in 1985-86. This increase occurred mainly due to improvement in the performance of that commercial sector enterprise. The Kaithal Co-operative Sugar Mills Limited had highest RONW in 1993-94 with 64.19% and the lowest was in the case of the Haryana State Co-operative Land Development Bank Ltd. with –15.40%. The Haryana Harijan Kalyan Nigam Ltd. had negative RONW throughout the study period. The Haryana Dairy Development Co-operative Corporation, Haryana Dairy Development Co-operative Federation, Haryana Financial Corporation and Haryana Women Development Corporation and had zero RONW through out the study period.

Gross Margin to Sales (GMS)

The GMS of the SLPEs as whole has increased from 2.84% in 1985-86 to 19.85% in 1993-94. The Haryana Agro Industries Corporation Ltd. had highest GMS in 1993-94 with 67.27%. The Commercial-cum-Promotional SLPEs had higher GMS in 1993-94 as compared to the GMS earned in the other sectors. The Haryana State Handloom and Handicrafts Corporation Ltd. had a negative GMS throughout the study period. Among 27 SLPEs, 14 SLPEs had zero GMS in 1993-94.

Debt-Equity Ratio (D/E Ratio)

The overall D/E ratio increased from 3.84% to 4.67% during the period 1985-86 to 1993-94. The Commercial-cum-Promotional SLPEs had the highest D/E ratio throughout the study period. The Haryana State Co-operative Apex Bank Ltd. had highest D/E ratio since 1985-86. In 1993-94 its D/E ratio was 12.37%. Among 27 SLPEs, 9 SLPEs had zero D/E ratio in 1993-94.

Current Ratio

The overall liquidity seemed to be the satisfactory with the current ratio varying from 1.02 to 0.94 during the study. The Haryana Dairy Development Corporation had 60:1 Current ratio in 1993-94. The Promotional SLPEs had a high current ratio throughout the study period compared to the current ratio pertaining to the other categories.

Value Added

Total value added steadily increased during the period under study. It increased from Rs. 58 crore in 1985-86 to Rs. 316 crore in 1993-94. The Commercial-cum-Promotional enterprises were contributing more to the total value added compared to the Commercial and Promotional enterprises. Among the commercial-cum-promotional enterprises, the maximum value was added by the Haryana State Cooperative Apex Bank Ltd. The value added of the Haryana state Cooperative Apex Bank increased from Rs. 22 crore in 1985-86 in 1993-94.

Himachal Pradesh

Introduction

Keeping in view the state's resources endowment, geo, physical conditions, potentials and problems and soci-economic environment the areas of strength for growth in the state economy through the SLPEs have been identified as power, forests, mineral resources, horticulture and tourism. SLPEs of H.P. have been set up by the State Government to cater to the basic needs of its general public, industrialization of the state, providing infrastructural facilities and all round economic growth of the state.

Profile

The Himachal pradesh state has 16 SLPEs comprising 6 commercial, 7 Commercial-cum-Promotional and 3 promotional SLPEs. The filled-in data sheets were received from 13 SLPEs (4 commercial, 6 Commercial-cum-Promotional and 3 Promotional)

Total Investment

The total investment in the 13 SLPEs of Himachal Pradesh increased from Rs. 268.08 crore in 185-86 to Rs. 450.05 crore in 1993-94 showing a CARG of 6.69%. Table 5.8 gives data relating to the sector-wise total investment in the SLPEs.

Among Commercial SLPEs, The Himachal Pradesh State Cooperative Bank Limited had the largest share of 98%. In Commercial and Promotional The H.P. State Industries Development Corporation Ltd. had highest total investment throughout the study period. The Himachal Pradesh Housing Board stood in 1st position among Promotional SLPEs.

Table 5.8

Sector	*1985-86*	*1986-87*	*1987-88*	*1988-89*	*1989-90*	*1990-91*	*1991-92*	*1992-93*	*1993-94*
Comm	206.96	205.17	206.24	204.48	203.48	203.79	205.04	258.53	286.13
C-P	45.85	60.35	76.34	87.23	100.14	105.44	122.87	119.95	131.30
Prom	12..21	13.26	15.26	18.63	22.01	25.17	27.70	28.89	32.62
Total	268.02	278.78	297.84	310.34	325.63	334.40	355.61	407.37	450.05

Comm: Commercial, C-P: Commercial-cum-Promotional, Prom: Promotional.

Net Worth

The SLPEs in Himachal Pradesh under study had net worth of Rs. 119.07 crore in 1993-94 compared to Rs. 62.30 crore in 1985-86. It has almost doubled over the period under study. Out of 13 SLPEs the following SLPEs have already eroded their net worth since 1985-86 (or earlier)

1. H.P. General Industries Corporation

2. H.P Khadi and Village Industries Board

3. H.P Ex-servicemen Corporation

At the same time the H.P. Mahila Vikas Nigam turned around in 1989-90 and has been adding positively to its net worth.

Sales

In total the sales of the 13 SLPEs thesales figure had gone up from Rs. 104.73 crore in 1985-86 to Rs. 270.84 crore in 1993-94. H.P. Civil Supplies Corporation Ltd. came top among the SLPEs in terms of sales in all the years and it was followed by H.P. State Forest Corporation Ltd. The sales of Commercial and Promotional SLPEs showed better turnover compared to that of Commercial and Promotional enterprises. In 1993-94 the total sales stood at Rs. 270.84 crore, out of this the H.P. State Forest Corporation and H.P. Civil Supplies Corporation Ltd. contributed Rs. 241.10 crore.The H.P. State Industries Development Corporation Ltd. showed zero sales from 1988-89 on wards.

Gross Profit

Out of 13 SLPEs in 1985-86, 6 showed gross profit and rest had either zero or negative gross profit. In 1993-94 7 SLPEs showed gross profit. The Himachal Pradesh State Co-operative Bank Ltd. and H.P. State Forest Corporation had been maintaining the top position in gross profit throughout the period. These two SLPEs shared half of the total gross profit of SLPEs in the state. The aggregate gross profit of 13 SLPEs went up from Rs. 9.21 crore in 1985-86 to Rs. 18.61 crore in 1993-94.

Profit After Tax (PAT)

In 1993-94, 6 SLPEs had shown profit after tax and the rest showed loss or zero profit. Among the SLPEs, the following SLPEs earned profits throughout the period 1985-86 to 1993-94:

1. The H.P. State Co-operative Bank Ltd.
2. H.P. State Civil Supplies Corporation Ltd.
3. H.P. Forest Development Corporation Ltd.

The following SLPEs incurred losses from 1985-86 to 1991-92.

H.P. Tourism Development Corporation

H.P. Housing Board

Other SLPEs had a mixed performance during the period.

The H.P. State Co-operative Bank Limited earned profit of Rs. 5.70 crore in 1993-94 while the total figure was Rs. 8.25 crore. The aggregate profit of 13 SLPEs was Rs. 4.43 crore in 1985-86 and it went up to Rs. 8.25 crore in 1994-94.

Accumulated Losses

Among 13 SLPEs, 8 had accumulated losses in 1993-94, compared to 6 in 1985-86. The H.P. Horticultural

Produce Marketing and Processing Corporation was the highest in terms of accumulated losses in all the years of study and it was followed by Himachal Worsted Mills Limited and H.P. Tourism Development Corporation Limited. At the end of 1993-94, the H.P. Horticultural Produce Marketing & Processing Corporation showed accumulated losses of Rs. 19.55 crore in 1993-94 compared to Rs. 9.33 crore in 1985-86. In aggregate, the accumulated losses of the SLPEs went up from Rs. 17.32 crore in 1985-86 to Rs. 36.91 crore in 1993-94.

Return On Investment (ROI)

Thirteen SLPEs could generate 2.90% ROI in 1993-94 compared to4.52% in 1985-86. The H.P. State Civil Supplies Corporation Ltd., H.P. Tourism Development Corporation and the H.P. State Forest Corporation were at the top in terms of ROI in 1993-94. H.P. Horticulture Produce Marketing & Processing Corporation was prominent among the SLPEs earning negative ROI since 1987-88. All three promotional SLPEs had nil ROI throughout the study period.

Return On Paid-Up Capital

The equity shareholders of the SLPEs as a whole earned 7.44% ROPUC in 1985-86 and it declined to 7.40% in 1993-94. The H.P. State Co-operative Bank Ltd. earned ROPUC throughout the study period. The H.P. Housing Board which had negative ROPUC up to 1991-92 and started earning positive returns from 1992-93. In 1993-94 its ROPUC which had 73.54% was the highest ROPUC earning among all the SLPEs in the state throughout the study period.

The H.P. General Industries Corporation Limited showed nil ROPUC in all the years except 1988-89 and 1989-90 its ROPUC was zero. The following SLPEs had zero ROPUC in 1993-94.

1. H.P. Horticulture Produce Marketing and Processing Corporaiton
2. Himachal Worsted Mills Limited
3. Shimla Development Authority
4. Himachal Pradesh Khadi and Village Industries Board
5. Himachal Pradesh Mahila Vikas Nigam

The following SLPEs had earned negative ROPUC more than 5 years under the study.

1. Himachal Pradesh Tourism Development Corporaiton Ltd.
2. Himachal Pradesh Housing Board
3. H.P. Ex-Servicemen Corporation

Return On Net Worth (RONW)

In aggregate the SLPEs earned 6.98% RONW in 1985-86 and the same in 1993-94. In commercial slot only the H.P. State Co-operative Bank Ltd. had earned 14.16% RONW in 1993-94 and more than that in previous years.

The H.P. Tourism Development Corporation and Himachal Pradesh Housing Board showed negative RONW upto 1991-92 and turned to positive gain RONW from 1992-93. Seven SLPEs showed zero or negative RONW throughout the study period. These are the following:

1. H.P. General Industries Corporation Ltd.
2. H.P Horticulture Produce Marketing and Processing Corporation

3. Himachal Worsted Mills Limited

4. Shimla Development Authority

5. Himachal Pradesh Mahila Vikas Nigam

6. H.P. Ex-servicemen Corporation

7. H.P. Khadi & Village Industries Board

Gross Margin to Sales (GMS)

The GMS of the SLPEs as a whole has come down from 6.61% in1985-86 to 4.89% in 1993-94. The H.P. Horticultural Produce Marketing & Processing Corporation, Himachal Pradesh Tourism Development Corporation Limited had high GMS compared to the state total in the year 1993-94. The H.P. Horitcultural Produce Marketing and Processing Corporation earned a high GMS (44.02%) among all the SLPEs in the state. It followed by the Himachal Pradesh Tourism Development Corporation Ltd. whose GMS was 28.32% in 1993-94.

Out of 13 SLPEs, 5 had positive GMS, 1 had negative and rest had zero GMS throughout the study period except 1993-94. In 1993-94 the Himachal Khadi and Village Industries Board earned positive GMS after incurring losses in earlier years.

Debt-Equity Ratio (D/E Ratio)

The overall D/E ratio of H.P. SLPEs declined from 4.81 to 4.18 during 1985-86 to 1993-94. Among all the SLPEs, the Shimla Development Authority had an unusually high D/E ratio of 1258:1 followed by H.P. Housing Board (10:1) All the Commercial SLPEs enjoyed the high D/E ratio compared to otheRs. The following SLPEs had a zero D/E ratio:

1. Himachal Pradesh Khadi and Village Industries Board
2. H.P. State Forest Corporation Limited
3. H.P. Mahila Vikas Nigam
4. H.P. Ex-servicemen Corporation

Current Ratio

The current ratio of H.P. SLPEs had come down from 3.36 to 2.83 during the study period. The H.P.State Co-operative Bank Ltd. had highest Current ratio throughout the stuyd period. In 1993-94, it had a current ratio of 83.53.

Value Added

For all the SLPEs in Himachal Pradesh the value added as whole increased from Rs. 21.26 in 1985-86 to Rs. 50.86 in 1993-94. The Commercial-cum-Promotional SLPEs registered maximum value added through the period under study. It increased from Rs. 12.70 in 1985-86 to Rs. 31.34 crore in 1993-94. It was only the Himachal Pradesh Ex-servicemen Corporation that recorded negative value added among all the SLPEs upto 1988-89 i.e., Rs. -0.01 crore.

Jammu & Kashmir

Introduction

The growing realization of the part of the Indian Government for expanding the public sector as the medium of industrialisation and removing regional imbalances motivated the state of Jammu & Kashnir to set up the SLPEs.

Profile

The Jammu & Kashmir state has 10 SLPEs, comprising 7 Commercial, 2 Commercial-cum-Promotional and 1 promotional. Of these only 5 Commercial and 1

Table: 5.9

Sector	*1985-86*	*1986-87*	*1987-83*	*1988-89*	*1989-90*	*1990-91*	*1991-92*	*1992-93*	*1993-94*
Comm	60.69	55.28	50.75	48.94	40.66	31.81	27.55	19.71	6.44
C-P	0.00	0.00	0.00	0.00	0.00	0.00	0.00	0.00	0.00
Prom	0.00	0.00	0.00	0.00	0.00	0.00	0.00	0.00	0.00
Total	60.69	55.28	50.75	48.94	40.66	31.81	27.55	19.71	6.44

Comm: Commercial, C-P: Commercial-cum-Promotional, Prom: Promotional.

Commercial-cum-Promotional (total 6) SLPEs form a part of this study as the filled-in data sheets were not received from other SLPEs.

Total Investment

The Total Investment in the 6 of Jammu & Kashmir SLPEs stood at Rs. 60.69 crore in 1985-86 and it came down to Rs. 6.44 crore in 1993-94 mainly due to a negative investment of Jammu & Kashmir industries Limited. Its Total investment in 1985-86 was Rs. 13.64 crore and turned to negative from 1989-90 and in 1993-94 it was Rs. –36.97 crore. Table 5.9 gives data relating to the sector-wise Total Investment in the SLPEs.

Net Worth

The SLPEs in Jammu & Kashmir under study had a net worth of Rs. 26.51 crore in 1985-86 and decreased to Rs. –27.08 in 1993-94. Jammu & Kashmir Industries Ltd. eroded its net worth since 1990-91.

Sales

During the study period the total sales of 6 SLPEs went up from Rs. 40.08 crore in 1985-86 to Rs. 55.07 crre in 1993-94, registering a CARG of 4.05%. The Jammu & Kashmir Projects Construction Corporation Ltd. was on top among all the SLPEs and it was followed by J & K Cements Ltd. and by J & K Industries Ltd. in 1993-94.

Gross Profit

Out of 6 SLPEs, in 1993-94 showed a gross profit and the rest showed either zero or negative gross profit. Jammu & Kashmir Cements Limited had been maintianing the tip position in Gross Profit throughout the study period. The aggregate Gross Profit of 6 SLPEs decreased from Rs. 3.23 crore to Rs. –6.49 during the period 1985-86 to 1993-94.

Profit After Tax

In 1993-94, 2 SLPEs had shown Profit After Tax and the rest showed loss or zero profit. Among these SLPEs, the J & K Industries Ltd. earned profits throughout the period 1985-86 to 1993-94.

The following SLPEs incurred losses throughout the period:

1. J & K State Handloom Development Corporation Limited

2. Himalayan Wool Combers Ltd.

3. J&K Cements Limited

In aggregate the SLPEs had shown a better performance in profit. In 1985-86, the profit was Rs. -1.32 crore which increased to Rs. 12.03 crore in 1993-94.

Accumulated Losses

Among 6 SLPEs, 5 had accumulated losses in 1993-94. This number remained almost same throughout the period. The J & K Industries Ltd. was the highest in terms of accumulated losses from 1989-90 onwards. The J & K Cements Limited occupied this place of pride prior to this period. In aggregate the accumulated losses of the SLPEs went up from Rs. 15.57 crore in 1985-86 to Rs. 71.76 crore during to 1993-94.

Returns On Investment (ROI)

The SLPEs in Jammu & Kashmir could generate 128.72% ROI in 1993-94 compared to 11.59% in 1985-86. The J & K projects Construction Corporation Ltd. came topped the list in terms of ROI in 1993-94. It was followed by Himalayan Wool Combers with 28.89%. J & K State Handloom

Development Corporation Ltd. was prominent in earning negative ROI from 1992-93.

Return On Paid-Up Capital (ROPUC)

The equity shareholders of the SLPEs as a whole earned 46.32% in 1993-94 which in the year 1985-86 was –3.20%. Among these SLPEs J & K Industries Ltd. gained more ROPUC i.e., 78.57%. The J & K State Handloom Development Corporation Limited and the Himalayan Wool Combers Ltd. were prominent in securing negative ROPUC since 1985-86.

Return On Net Worth

In aggregate the SLPEs having negative RONW in 1985-86 and it went up to –44.42% in 1993-94. The J & K Projects Construction Corporation Limited earned 17.91% RONW in 1993-94 and rest had negative RONW.

Gross Margin to Sales (GMS)

The GMS of SLPEs as a whole is negative in 1993-94. It was 14.40% in 1985-86 and it decreased to –6.76% in 1993-94. The J & K Industries Ltd. and the J & K State Handloom Development Corporation Limited had negative GMS in 1993-94 and earlier. J & K Cements Limited showed top position with 18.67% GMS in 1993-94 and was followed by Himalayan Wood Combers Ltd. with 6.57% GMS.

Debt-Equity Ratio (D/E Ratio)

The overall D/E ratio of J & K SLPEs increased from 0.61% in 1985-86 to 1.71% in 1993-94. Himalayan Combers Ltd. had the highest D/E ratio in 1993-94 and was followed by J & K Industries Ltd. with 2.04 :1. J & K Cement Limited and J & K State Financial Corporation had a zero D/E ratio throughout the study period.

Current Ratio

The overall current ratio came down from 1.46 to 0.71 during the study period. The J & K Industries Ltd., the lowest current ratio throughout the study period with 0.43 in 1993-94. The J & K State Handloom Development Corporation Ltd. had highest current ratio throughout the study period.

Value Added

The total value added by all the SLPEs in Jammu and Kashmir as a whole increased consistently over the period under reference. The total value added went up almost five times from Rs. 9 crore in 1985-86 to Rs. 42 crore in 1993-94. Among the commercial SLPEs, Jammu and Kashmir Industries Limited contributed more value added compared to other SLPEs.

Karnataka

Introduction

The SLPEs are on the economic scene in Karnataka since 1920s. The erstwhile state of Mysore had sir M.Visveswaraya as the principal advisor to the Prince. Under his guidancea number of enterprises were set up to harness the abundant resources of raw material and power in certain localities thus creating pockets of industrialization. This ultimately gave rise to employment opportunities and created other economic avenues too. With the passage of time, the area of operations of the SLPEs changed from the state to national levels due to phenomenal growth in their size.

Profile

Karnataka state at present has 68 SLPEs, comprising 39 commercial, 22 commercial-cum-promotional and 7 promotional ones. Of these only 22 commercial, 14

Table 5.10

Sector	*1985-86*	*1986-87*	*1987-88*	*1988-89*	*1989-90*	*1990-91*	*1991-92*	*1992-93*	*1993-94*
Comm	1364.30	1466.40	1568.49	1667.00	1852.40	2012.82	2398.10	2715.43	3100.54
C-P	309.53	372.02	437.34	524.70	602.16	725.23	912.73	1122.92	1228.20
Prom	0.00	0.00	0.00	0.00	0.63	3.50	3.92	6.56	9.40
Total	1673.83	1838.42	2005.83	2191.70	2455.19	2741.55	3314.75	3844.91	4338.14

Comm: Commercial, C-P: Commercial-cum-Promotional, Prom: Promotional.

commercial-cum-promotional and 2 promotional SLPEs form a part of this study as the filled-in data sheets were not received from the remaining enterprises.

Total Investment

The Total Investment in the 38 SLPEs of Karnataka stood at Rs. 4,338 crore at the end of 1993-94 compared to Rs. 1, 673 crore at the end of 1985-86. During the period under reference, it had a CARG of 12.65%. Table 5.10 gives data relating to the sector-wise Total Investment in the SLPEs.

Net Worth

The SLPEs in Karnataka under study had a net worth of Rs. 1,354 crore in 1993-94 compared to Rs. 256 crore in 1985-86. During this period the net worth grew at a CARG of 23.15%. In absolute terms, it had grown almost 5 times over the period. Out of 38 enterprises, 9 enterprises had eroded their net worth. Among them the following SLPEs had eroded their net worth since 1985-86:

1. Karnataka Soaps and Detergents Limited
2. Karnataka State Textiles Limited
3. The Mysore Electrical Industries Limited
4. Karnataka Compost Development Corporation Limited
5. Karnataka Silk Industries Corporation Limited
6. Karnataka Film Industries Development Corporation Limited

The Karnataka Vidyuth Karkhane Limited and the Mysore Paints and Varnish Limited successfully turned around in 1989-90 and have been adding positively to their net worth.

Sales

During the study period the total sales of 38 SLPEs went up from Rs. 525 crore, registering a CARG of 8.28%. The Karnataka Food and Civil Supplies Corporation Limited acquired top slot among the SLPEs in terms of sales during all the years. In 1993-94 this SLPE had sales of Rs. 367 crore, followed by the NGEF Limited which had a turnover of Rs. 104 crore. The Karnataka Vidyuth Karkhane is the fastest growing SLPE in terms of annual rate of growth in sales which is 27.25%. Throughout the period of study promotional SLPEs showed better turnover in aggregate compared to commercial SLPEs, which happened due to inclusion of KRCSC in the former category.

Gross Profit

Out of 38 SLPEs, in 1993-94, 17 SLPEs recorded gross profit and the rest had either nil or negative gross profit. The Karnataka Power Corporation had been maintianing the top position in Gross Profit throughout the period. Its gross profit went up from Rs. 60.06 crore to Rs. 235.46 registering a Compound Annual Rate of Growth of 18.47%. The KSFC showed a whopping increase in gross profit from Rs. 18.28 crore to Rs. 119.55 crore in the same period, registering a CARG of 26.46%. Besides these two, Mysore Minerals Limited, Karnataka State Seeds Corporation Limited.

Profit After Tax

The Profit after Tax was Rs. 26.69 crores in 1985-86 fir commercial enterprises. It declined to Rs. 21.41 crore in 1993-94. During the intervening years, it had a tendency to fluctuate between loss making and profit making. The Commercil-cum-Promotional enterprises had the tendency to earn profit although while the promotional enterprises incurred losses between 1985-86 and 1991-92. They earned a small profit during the rest of the years of the study.

Accumulated Losses

Karnataka SLPEs in all the three categores showed the tendency to Accumulated Losses. This tendency was highly pronounced in case of commercial enterprises. Some of the enterprises that incurred vast maginitude of accumulated losses included Karnataka Composte Development Corproration Ltd., The Mysore Acetate & Chemicals Company Ltd., Karnataka Silk Industries Corporation Ltd., The Mysore Sugar Company Ltd., The Mysore Electrical Industries Limited, Karnataka State Textiles Limited, Karnataka Vidyuth Karkhane Limited, NGEF Limited, Karnataka Soaps and Detergents Limited, Karnataka State Handicrafts Development Corporation Ltd.

Return On Investment (ROI)

Thirty-four Karnataka SLPEs could generate 20.38% ROI in 1993-94 compared to 14.11% in 1985-86. The Commercial-cum-Promotional SLPEs as a whole generated more ROI in comparison with the commercial SLPEs. Karnataka State Agro Corn Products Limited, Mysore Paints & Vasrnish Limited, Karnataka Implements & Machineries Company Limited, Karnataka Small Industries Marketing Corporaiton Limited came at the tope level in terms of ROI in 1993-94. The SLPEs such as the Mysore Acetate & Chemicals Company Limited, Karnataka State Handicrafts Development Corporation Limited are prominent among the SLPEs earning negative ROI since 1985-86 or earlier.

Return On Paid-Up Capital (ROPUC)

The equity shareholders of the SLPEs as a whole earned a meager 2.21% of ROPUC in 1993-94 which was as high as 10.54% in 1985-86. The fall was caused mainly by the commercial SLPEs. In this case the average ROPUC came down from 11.22% to 1.74% during 1985-86 to 1993-94. The Karnataka Vidyuth Karkhane Limited, Jungle Lodges

& Resorts Limited, Karnataka Implements & Machineries Limited, D. Devaraj Urs Truck Terminals Limited earned more than 20% ROPUC in 1993-94. In that year Mysore Acetate & Chemicals Company Limited earned negative ROPUC (-19.16%) compared to 38.43% in the previous year. The Karnataka Soaps & Detergents Limited, Karnataka State Handicrafts Development Corporation Limited earned negative ROPUC throughout the period under reference.

Return On Net Worth (RONW)

In aggregate the SLPEs earned a 2.37% RONW which is very marginal. Although some of the SLPEs earned impressive RONW, due to loss making units the aggregate SLPEs showed a dismal picture. The Jungle Lodges and Resorts Limited and D.Devraj Urs Truck Terminals Limited showed high RONW of 31% and 27% than 10% of RONW in 1993-94. The prominent among them are the Mysore Paints and Varnish Limited (12%) and the Karnataka Vidyuth Karkhane Limited (25%).

Gross Margin to Sales (GMS)

The GMS of the SLPEs as a whole had come down from 11.10% in 1985-86 to 6.99% in 1993-94. Comparatively, the Commercial SLPEs showed higher decline in the GMS on an average than the commercial-cum-promotional SLPEs. The Mysore Acetate and Chemicals Limited leads the SLPEs with 95% GMS followed by Karnataka State Warehousing Corporation with 76%. The Karnataka Compost Development Corporation Limited was showing negative GMS till 1992-93 but it successfully showed 23% GMS in 1993-94. Similarly Karnataka Soaps and Detergents Limited recorded 4.67% GMS in 1993-94. Out of 38 SLPEs 16 had positive GMS 5 had negativoe and rest had zero GMS in 1993-94.

Debt-Equity Ratio (D/E Ratio)

The overall D/E Ratio of Karnataka SLPEs declined from 4.81 to 1.93 during 1985-86 to 1993-94. Among all the SLPEs, the Karnataka State Police Housing Corp. Ltd. had an unusually high D/E Ratio of 135:1 followed by KSFC (8.8:1). Commercial-cum-Promotional SLPEs enjoy high D/ E Ratio compapred to the SLPEs in the other categories.

Current Ratio

The overall liquidity, seems to be satisfactory with the current ratio varying from 1.5 to 1.74 during the period of study. The Karnataka Basin Lift irrigation Corporation had a current ratio of 121:1 in 1993-94 which is not a healthy sign. Otherwise except promotional SLPEs the current ratio varied from 0.12 to 3.3 in 1993-94.

Value Added

In Karnataka the value added by the SLPEs as an aggregate went up steadily from Rs. 175 crore in 1985-86 to Rs. 525 crore in 1993-94. Among the commercial enterprises maximum vlaue added was registered by the Karnataka Power Corporation Limited (KPCL). During 1985-86 the value added by KPCL was Rs. 68 crore, which went up to Rs. 203 crore in 1993-94.

Kerala

Introduction

The SLPEs as instruments of socio-economic development assumed significance, toa large extent, only after the formation of the Kerala State in 1956. Prior to this the Maharajas were concerned primarily about industrialization and agricultural development without equal concern for equity dimension of public investment. After 1956 the launching of public enterprises or corporations had tremendous appeal for the people of

Table 5.11

Sector	*1985-86*	*1986-87*	*1987-88*	*1988-89*	*1989-90*	*1990-91*	*1991-92*	*1992-93*	*1993-94*
Comm	320.30	335.33	345.50	356.13	378.64	392.00	376.68	413.43	410.24
C-P	67.28	122.08	99.70	133.09	135.11	129.46	146.98	197.92	208.12
Prom	11.13	12.13	12.35	15.93	16.85	18.36	18.97	18.19	17.61
Total	398.71	469.54	457.55	505.15	530.60	539.82	542.63	629.54	635.97

Comm: Commercial, C-P: Commercial-cum-Promotional, Prom: Promotionl

Kerala, as these created potential for getting employment opportunities. Kerala State stands in the forefront in the number of the SLPEs in a single state.

Profile

There are 104 SLPEs in Kerala, comprising 71 Commercial, 24 Commercial-cum-Promotional and 4 Promotional SLPEs (Total 73) form a part of this study as the filled-in data sheets were not received from the remaining SLPEs. Kerala has the largest number of SLPEs in the country. The response from the SLPEs of this state was quite enthusiastic and 70% of them responded to this study. Compared to other states, the audit and accounts of Kerala SLPEs are more or less complete and in better shape.

Total Investment

The total investment in the 73 SLPEs of Kerala stood at Rs. 636 crore at the end of 1993-94 compared to Rs. 399 crore at the end of 1985-86. During the period under reference, it had a CARG of 6.00%. Table 5.11 gives data on sector-wise total investment in the SLPEs. The growth in total investment of Commercial-cum-Promotional SLPEs as a whole was faster than that in other secrors.

The Kerala State Industrial Development Corporation Ltd. (KSIDC) topped in terms of total investment in 1993-94, in which year it had a total investment of Rs. 126.85 crore followed by Kerala State Electronics Development Corporation Limited (KELTRON) with Rs. 81.59 crore. The KSIDC registered a 19.01 Compound Annual Rate Growth, which is highest among all the SLPEs.

Net Worth

The SLPEs of Kerala under study registered negative growth in terms of net worth when it fell down from Rs. 102.40 crore in 1985-86 to Rs. 86.48 crore in 1993-94.

Although in case of Commercial-cum-Promotional the net worth went its rapid erosion in the case of SLPEs led to an aggregate decline in net worth. The KSIDC recorded a steady growth in net worth and came on the top in 1993-94. Its net worth grew at 21.69% CARG frin Rs. 14.73 crore in 1985-86 to Rs. 70.83 crore in 1993-94. Such high rate of growth was possible only due to infusion of large equity during various years. For example, the paid up capital of the KSIDC went up by Rs. 13.60 crore and Rs. 15.25 crore in 1992-93 and 1993-94 respectively. Out of 74 SLPEs, 16 have already eroded their net worth. Among them the following SLPEs eroded their net worth since 1985-86:

1. Keltron Power Limited
2. Keltron Rectifiers Limited
3. Kerala Garments Limited
4. Meat Products of India Limited
5. Sitaram Textiles Limited
6. Kerala State Drugs and Pharmaceuticals Limited
7. Kerala State Construction Corporation Limited
8. Kerala State Cashew Development Corporation Limited.

The Malbar Cements Limited, the Metal Industries Limited, United Electrical Industries Limited, Kerala Clays and Ceramic Limited, Kerala State Film Development Corporation Limited and State Farming Corporation of Kerala Limited turned around during different years due to either infusion of new equity or good profits earned.

Sales

The SLPEs of Kerala had a total turnover of Rs. 1,264.61 in 1993-94, compared to Rs. 682.60 crore thus registering

8.01% CARG. The growth rate in case of commercial SLPEs was higher as compared to the growth rate in commercial-cum-promotional SLPEs. The Kerala State Civil Supplies Corporation Limited (KSCSC) maintained its top position among the SLPEs in terms of sales throughout the study period. However its sales did not show an impressive growth rate compared to some other SLPEs. Among commercial SLPEs, Kerala State Beverages (Manufacturing and Marketing) Corporation showed highest turnover of Rs. 168.05 crore in 1993-94, followed by Rs. 130.78 crore of KELTRON.

Gross Profit

On an aggregate, the SLPEs of Kerala registered a high growth in gross profit, which turned out to be Rs. 113.62 crore in 1993-94 as compared to Rs. 12.50 crore in 1985-86. The CARG for increase in growth in gross profits amounted to 31.77%. The commercial-cum-promotional SLPEs as a whole incurred gross losses during the entire period under reference. However the gross loss of the SLPEs in this category came down from Rs. 13.14 crore in 1985-86 to Rs. 5.65 crore in 1993-94. The major contributor to this loss was KSCSC. Out of 74 SLPEs studied, 34 showed gross profit in 1993-94 and rest showed either no profit or gross loss. Among the gross profit making SLPEs, the following turned around and showed gross profit in different years.

1. Kerala State Textile Corporation
2. Steel and Industrial forgings Limited
3. United Electrical Industries Limited
4. Kerala Minerals and Metals Limited
5. Forest Industries (Travancore) Limited
6. Foam Mattings (India) Limited

Profit After Tax

Compared to 34 SLPEs showing gross profit in 1993-94, 31 SLPEs earned PAT during the same year. However the loss incurred by the other SLPEs outplaced the profits of the other enterprises, resulting in an aggregate negative PAT throughout except the last year of the study. The aggregate losses shot up from Rs. 6.47 crore in 1985-86 to Rs. 37.71 crore in 1991-92, and then subsequently declined to Rs. 30.36 crore during the following years. In 1993-94 the PAT was Rs. 4.03 crore. 28 SLPEs recorded negative or zero PAT during the period.

Accumulated Losses

Among 74 SLPEs in the state 44 SLPEs had accumulated losses. The Kerala State Cashew Development Corporation Limited had highest accumulated loss of Rs. 123.18 crore in 1993-94 followed by the Kerala Minerals and Metals Limited with Rs. 92.26 crore. The aggregate accumulated loss of the SLPEs grew at 14.45 (CARG) from Rs. 212.29 crore in 1985-86 to Rs. 624.99 crore.

Return On Investment

As a whole the SLPEs in Kerala generated surplus resulting in 24.58% ROI in 1993-94, which was 10.64% in 1985-86. The Commercial SLPEs showed a better ROI compared to other categories. 29 commercial and 5 commercial-cum-promotional SLPEs earned positive ROI in 1993-94. The SLPEs such as Keltron Component Complex Limited, Kerala Agro Machinery Corporation Limited, Kerala Minerals and Metals Limited earned a very high ROI.

Return On Paid-Up Capital (ROPUC)

In aggregate, the SLPEs under reference, SHOWED a return of 0.23% to the equity holders on their investment in 1993-94. It provided a bold relief as till 1992-93 the SLPEs as a whole registered to earn negative return on their equity capital. The following units earned positive ROPUC during all the years of study:

1. Keltron Component Complex Limited
2. Keltron Resistors Limited
3. Kerala Agro Machinery Corporation Limited
4. Kerala State Industrial Products Corporation Limited
5. Kerala Urban Development Finance Corporation Ltd.
6. Oil Palm India Limited
7. The Rehabilitation Plantations Limited
8. The Travancore Rubber Works Limited
9. Travancore Titnium Products Limited
10. Kerala State Film Development Corporation Limited.

Return On Net Worth (RONW)

In 1993-94, 30 SLPEs earned a positive RONW. There were SLPEs such as the Keltron Magnetics Limited, Kerala State Film Development Corporation, Steel Complex Limited which after registering negative RONW, turned around and earned positive RONW in different years. Out of 30 SLPEs as mentioned above 21 SLPEs earned more than 10% RONW. The following SLPEs turned out to be top five in terms of RONW in 1993-94:

1. Kerala State Film Development Corporation
2. Keltron Resistors Limited
3. Malabar Cements Limited

4. Keltron Crystals Limited
5. United Electrical Industries Limited

Twelve SLPEs earned RONW during all the years of the study.

Gross Margin to Sales (GMS)

The 74 SLPEs under study in aggregate earned 11.20% GMS in 1993-94 compared to 6.53% in 1985-86. The Rehabilitation Plantations Limited and Kerala Shipping and Inland Navigation Corporation Limited earned 54.27% and 44.83% GMS in 1993-94 respectively. During this year 31 SLPEs earned positive GMS while the rest earned negative or zero GMS. The commercial SLPEs as a category earned positive GMS. The Commercial-cum-Promotional SLPEs in aggregate recorded negative GMS.

Debt/Equity Ratio (D/E Ratio)

The overall D/E Ratio of kerala SLPEs varied from 1.33 to 1.74 during the period under study. The commercial SLPEs had a low level of long-term debt as compared to D/E Ratio obtained for commercial-cum-promotional SLPEs. In the former category, Kerala Urban Development Finance Corporation Limited (KUDFC) had a high D/E Ratio of 20.27 in 1993-94. In earlier years too KUDFC enjoyed high leverage in terms of D/E Ratio. Among all the SLPEs, 7 had D/E Ratio of 20.27 in 1993-94. In earlier years too KUDFCC enjoyed high leverage in terms of D/E Ratio. Among all the SLPEs, 7 had D/E Ratio exceeding 3.1 in 1993-94. Prominent among them were Kerala State Co-op. Agricultural and Rural Development Bank Limited, Keltron Resistors Limited and Kerala State Cashew Development Corporation Limited.

Current Ratio

The liquidity position of the SLPEs in Kerala was below the mark since the current ratio remained below 1.50 during all the years of the study. In case of commercial SLPEs, it was even lower than 1.50.

Value Added

In Kerala the total value added of the SLPEs as a whole was observed to be increasing steadily over the period under reference. The increase has been about two fold starting from Rs. 123 crore in 1985-86 to Rs. 245 crore in 1993-94. Among all the SLPEs, the Commercial ones, contribution to total value added was more. In this group The Kerala Mineral and Metals Limited was continuously creating the largest value added in all the years of study.

Madhya Pradesh

Introduction

Madhya Pradesh is endowed with abundant forest and mineral wealth. It is inhabited by a large tribal community. The SLPEs in the State have been set up to industrialise the state by using this resource base and promote the cause of the weaker sections of the society. The Promotional, welfare and manufacturing enterprises had lion's share in the total number of SLPEs set up in the state.

Profile

In the state of Madhya Pradesh, there are 11 Commercial, 13 Commercial-cum-Promotional and 2 Promotional enterprises and for the purpose of the analysis the data is available for 3 Commercial, 5 Commercial-cum-Promotional and 2 Promotional enterprises.

Total Investment

In terms of total investment, the SLPEs of M.P. had an investment of 509.77 crore at the end of 1993-94 which increased almost three fold to Rs. 186.28 crore at the end of 1985-86. At the end of 1993-94, the M.P. Financial

Table 5.12

Sector	*1985-86*	*1986-87*	*1987-88*	*1988-89*	*1989-90*	*1990-91*	*1991-92*	*1992-93*	*1993-94*
Comm	19.64	23.95	29.13	30.67	51.51	76.63	63.80	55.68	62.59
C-P	165.06	213.80	259.55	309.38	372.40	92.16	419.53	427.19	430.85
Prom	1.51	2.04	4.13	6.53	9.81	12.35	13.77	14.51	16.33
Total	186.21	239.79	292.81	346.58	433.72	181.14	497.10	497.38	509.77

Comm: Commercial, C-P: Commercial-cum-Promotional, Prom: Promotionl

Corporation topped the list with Rs. 355.62 crore followed by the M.P. Rajya Van Vikas Nigam Ltd. with Rs. 61.44, crore and the M.P State Warehousing Corporation with Rs. 3,416 crore.

Net Worth

In terms of net worth, if the SLPEs of M.P are analysed, then we would observe feature which in most of the states we do not find. All the enterprises reporting were showing a positive net worth. The total net worth of the enterprises at the end of fiscal 1993-94 was Rs. 201.01 crore which when compared with that of 1985-86 was more by three and a half times, i.e., it was Rs. 55.61 crore at the end of fiscal 1985-86. In Commercial enterprises the net worth increased more than five times, whereas in Commercial-cum-Promotional and in promotional enterprises it increased by nearly three times. In Commercial enterprises the net worth increased from Rs. 14.47 crore at the end of 1985-86 to Rs. 78.12 crore at the end of fiscal 1993-94.

Sales

In terms of sales the growth was not very much appreciable, the sales increased only by 42 per cent when compared to the figures of 1985-86. The size of sales increased from Rs. 113.77crore at the end of fiscal 1985-86 to Rs. 161.71 crore at the end of fiscal 1993-94. The trend was same with the commercial, Commercial-cum-Promotional and promotional enterprises with the mean difference of a little over five per cent. The sales had increased from Rs. 83.08 at the end of fiscal 1985-86 to Rs 114.02 crore at the end of fiscal 1993-94 in the case of the Commercial-cum-Promotional enterprise whereas in the case of the commercial enterprises it stood at the figures are Rs. 30.40crore in 1985-86 to Rs. 43.43 crore in 1993-94

Gross Profit (GP)

In terms of gross profit too, the SLPEs of M.P were showing a positive trend. Only one enterprise was showing negative Gross Profit is enterprise was from the promotional group viz., M.P Audyogik Kendra Vikas Nigam (Jabalpur) Ltd. The total Gross Profit of the SLPEs was Rs. 39.85 crore at the end of fiscal 1993-94. It was Rs. 18.39 crore in 1985-86. The G.P increased by 2.17 times during the period of the study.

Profit After Tax (PAT)

In terms of Profit after Tax, the SLPEs of M.P were showing a mixed performance. The Profit After Tax at the end of fiscal 1985-86 was Rs. 4.11 crore and went to a negative of Rs. 4.75 crore in 1993-94. The decline was noticed in the case of the Commercial-cum-Promotional enterprise whereas the Promotional enterprise and the Commercial enterprises where showing a positive trend. The overall figure of –4.75 included Rs. –12.82 crore PAT of MPSFC

Accumulated Losses

The total accumulated losses for the enterprises of Madhya Pradesh stood a Rs. 32.51 crore as at the end of fiscal 1993-94. The Madhya Pradesh Financial Corporation Ltd. had topped the list of enterprises reportaccumulated losses. The accumulated losses for the enterprises was just Rs. 1.86 crore at the end of fiscal 1985-86. Over 90% of accumulated losses enlarged to the Commercial-cum-Promotional enterprises whereas in the case of the Commercial enterprises 3 enterprises reported nil accumulated losses.

Return On Investment (ROI)

The ROI in the enterprises of M.P. came down from 10.61 in 1985-86 to 8 at the end of the year 1993-94. Out of the 11 enterprises 8 enterprises reported a positive ROI and the remaining three reported nul or negative ROI. In terms of ROI, the M.P. Laghu Udyog Nigam Ltd. topped the list with 94.20 percent followed by M.P. State Warehousing Corporation with 27.98 percent and the M.P. Rajya Pashudhan Evam Kukkut Vikas Nigam Ltd. recorded an ROI of 19.77 percent.

Return On Paid-Up Capital (ROPUC)

The ROPUC in the SLPEs of M.P. was negative at the end of the year 1993-94 with –2.17 per cent. The ROPUC was a positive of 6.89% in 1985-86. Thus it is clear that the enterprise performance in overall terms declined. In the case of the Commerical enterprises the ROPUC was positive, whereas in the case of the Commercial-cum-Promotional enterprise it was negative.

Return On Net Worth (RONW)

In terms of RONW too the SLPEs of M.P. were showing a negative RONW of –2.36 per cent in 1993-94 whereas the RONW was positive at the end of year 1985-86 with 7.48 per cent. It declined to 3.86 and 3.85 in 1990-91 and 1991-92, respectively and then shot up to 6.60 per cent in 1992-93. In terms of RONW the M.P. State Warehousing Corporation had topped the list with22.66% per cent followed by the Madhya Pradesh Laghu Udyog Nigam Ltd. with 8.15 per cent. The RONW was positive in Commercial enterprises whereas in the case of the Commercial-cum-Promotional and Promotional enterprise it was negative.

Gross Margin to Sales (GMS)

The Gross Margin to Sales in the SLPEs was ranging between 17.24 and 35.97 per cent. The enterprises that topped in terms of GMS are the M.P. State Electronics Development Corporation with 248.98 per cent followed by M.P Rajya Pashudhan Evam Kukkut Vikas Nigam with

170.00 per cent. At the end of 1993-94 the commercial enterprises had 41.45 per cent GMS whereas in the Commercial-cum-Promotional and Promotional enterprise the GMS was 20.11 and 19.95 respectively.

Debt-Equity Ratio (D/E Ratio)

In terms of Debt-Equity ratio in the SLPEs of M.P. it may be stated that the ratio was ranging between 1.72 and 2.69 during the period of study. In terms of Debt-equity ratio, Madhya Pradesh Rajya Van Vikas Nigam Ltd. had a high D/E Ratio of 3.72 . In the case of the Commercial enterprises the Debt-Equity ratio was only 0.06 and in the case of the Promotional enterprise only 0.25 whereas in the case of Commercial-cum-Promotional enterprise the D/E ratio was 2.85.

Current Ratio (C/R Ratio)

Out of the 11 enterprises considered for the study of SLPEs M.P., the current ratio for one Commercial-cum-Promotional enterprises i.e., the M.P. Rajya Matsya Vikas Nigam Ltd. and one Promotional enterprise i.e., the M.P. Urja Vikas Nigam Ltd. was less than 1.33:1 whereas in the case of all the other enterprises at the end of 1993-94, in terms of current ratio, the M.P State Electronics Development Corporation was leading the table with a ratio of 67.79 followed by the M.P. Audyogik Kendra Vikas Nigam (Jabalpur) Ltd. with a ratio of 8.2.

Value Added

The SLPEs of Madhya Pradesh registered a total value added of Rs. 24 crore in 1985-86, which went up to Rs. 50 crore in 1989-90. In 1993-94 the total value added was Rs. 54 crore

Table 5.13

Sector	1985-86	1986-87	1987-88	1988-89	1989-90	1990-91	1991-92	1992-93	1993-94
Comm	55.03	72.60	77.11	113.32	129.53	153.50	156.79	179.33	211.41
C-P	1294.17	1536.47	1672.26	2408.56	2408.56	3627.98	4040.45	4941.76	4699.95
Prom	7.32	8.91	10.46	11.87	11.87	19.37	18.31	15.36	30.25
Total	1356.52	1617.98	1759.83	2533.75	2533.75	3800.85	4215.55	5136.45	4941.61

Comm: Commercial, C-P: Commercial-cum-Promotional, Prom: Promotional.

Maharashtra

Introduction

Maharashtra always has been the vanguard of industrial development. Though representing only 9% of the total population of India, it accounts for nearly 16% of the fixed investment, 21% of the industrial labour and 25% of the total value of industrial output. prior to 1960 there was no state undertaking incorporated as such. State undertakings in Maharashtra are characterised by being predominantly promotional and developmental in nature.

Profile

In the state of Maharashtra there are around 12 Commercial enterprises, 17 Commercial-cum-Promotional and 14 Promotional enterprises. Out of which the data available for our analysis is for 10 Commercial, 15 Commercial-cum-Promotional and 10 Promotional enterprises.

Total Investment

The investment in all the SLPEs together as at the end of 1993-94 stood at Rs. 5,048.18 crore which was almost three times than that of the total investments in Andhra Pradesh. In terms of total investment, the Maharashtra State Co-operative Bank Ltd. topped the list with Rs. 2,637.96 crore followed by Maharashtra Industrial Development Corporation with Rs. 1,024.67 crore. The Investment in the Maharashtra Cooperative Bank Ltd. was almost twelve and half times that of total investment in Commercial enterprises, i.e., Rs. 211.41 crore. In the Commercial enterprises the Maharashtra state Textile Corporation Ltd. topped the table with Rs. 105.27 crore which was again 50% of the total investment in all the commercial enterprises in Maharashtra. The total investment over the period had increased four fold from Rs.

1,358.76 crore in1985-86.One more interesting feature that can be observed in the given information is that out of the total investment the promotional enterprises contribute only 0.59 per cent.

Net Worth

The SLPEs in Maharashtra had been showing a very good picture. There were 3 enterprises showing negative net worth. These enterprises included:

1. Maharashtra State Farming Corporation Limited.
2. Maharashtra State Co-operative Oil Seeds Growers Federation Ltd.
3. Maharashtra Land Development Corporation Ltd.

Sales

In terms of sales the overall sales recorded an increase Rs. 402.53 crore at the fiscal 1985-86 to Rs. 960.45 crore at the end of fiscal 1993-94. The sales shoot up by 2.38 times over the period of study for all the SLPEs taken together. But the Promotional enterprises showed a different trend.

Gross Profit

In terms of gross profit seven enterprises were showing a negative figure or gross loss out of 34 enterprises. The enterprises showing gross loss came from one Commercial, 2 from Commercial-cum-Promotional and 4 from Promotional enterprises. One enterprise which was showing negative gross profit till the previous year i.e., 1992-93 had turned around and showed a positive gross profit of Rs. 1.69 crore. The Maharashtra State Cooperative Bank Ltd. which topped the table in terms of Gross Pofit with Rs. 388.67 crore was followed by the Maharashtra State Financial Corporation with Rs. 78.81 crore of the GP earned.

Profit After Tax (PAT)

The SLPEs of Maharashtra had shown a mixed performance in terms of profit earning . Out of 10 Commercial enterprises there were 2 enterprises showing profit negative similarly in the category of the Commercial-cum-Promotional enterprise also out of 14 enterprises 2 showed negative PAT in the Promotional enterprises, 3 out of 10 were showing a negative profit after tax. The profit after tax increased for the half time from Rs. 10.37 crore at the end of fiscal 1985-86 to Rs. 48.48 crore at the end of 1993-94 .There were three enterprises which were making losses continuously which comprise one from each i.e., Commercial, Commercial-cum-Promotional and the Promotional categories. These were:

1. Maharashtra State Co-operative Oilseeds Growers Federation Ltd.
2. The Maharashtra Fisheries Development Corporation Ltd.
3. Likshahir Annabhau Sathe Development Corporation Ltd.

Accumulated Losses

The losses accumulated the enterprises stood at Rs. 160.63 crore at the end of 1993-94 the losses were Rs. 53.56 crore at the end of 1985-86. Thus, there was a three fold rise in the accumulated losses during 1985-86 to 1993-94 topped the table followed by the Maharashtra State textile Corporation Ltd. topped the table followed by Maharashtra State Co-operative Oilseeds Growers Federation Ltd.

Return On Investment (ROI)

In terms of ROI, the SLPEs of Maharashtra were showing a 14.84 per cent Return a their investment at the end of 1993-94, in Kinwat Roofing Tiles Ltd. the ROI was

100% and in Maharashtra State Financial Corporation is around 4.65 per cent. In Maharashtra State Mining Corporation Ltd. ROI was negative and showing –229.12 per cent. Also, in another three enterprises the ROI was negative.

Return On Paid-Up Capital (ROPUC)

In terms of Return on paid-up capital the return ranged between 1.07 and 2.80 in the SLPEs of Maharashtra during the period of study. In terms of ROPUC The Maharashtra State Financial Corporation Ltd. topped the list with 142.91 per cent followed by Kinwat Roofing tiles Ltd. with 35.14% and Maharashtra State Handlooms Corporation Ltd. with 39.42 per cent. On the average the ROPUC of all the enterprises put together for the period of study was 1.58 per cent.

Return on Net Worth

On an average the SLPEs of Maharashtra were showing a RONW of 9.57 per cent during the period of study. The RONW was of 11.43 per cent as at the end of 19933-94. In terms of RONW, the Maharashtra State Handloom Corporation Ltd. topped the list with 35.56 per cent followed by MAFCO Ltd. with 2.81 and the Commercial enterprises were showing an average RONW of 13.24 per cent.

Gross Margin to Sales (GMS)

The GMS in the SLPEs in Maharashtra was 5.97 per cent in 1985-86. The GMS increased to 8.27 per cent in 1993-94. Whereas on average the Commercial enterprises were showing a 11.33 per cent of GMS and the Commercial-cum-Promotional enterprises showed a GMS of 4.91 per cent, the Promotional enterprises showed a GMS of 10.05 per cnet. In terms of GMS, the Parbhani Krushi Gosamvardhan

Ltd. topped the list with 266.67 followed by the Kolhapur Chitrangari Mahamandal Ltd. with 214.29 and the Forest Development Corporation of Maharashtra Ltd. with 76.16 per cent.

Debt-Equity Ratio

In the SLPEs of Maharashtra, the Debt-Equity ratio was fluctating between 2.14 and 2.37 during the period of study. In three of the Commercial enterprises the D/E ratio exceeded 2. The Maharashtra State Farming Corporation Ltd. topped the list of the enterprises Commercial enterprises with a 9.75 Debt-Equity ratio of the Commercial-cum-Promotional enterprises the ratio exceeded 2:1 in 4 enterprises. The Maharashtra Land Development Corporation Ltd., Maharashtra State Co-operative Band Ltd. and Maharashtra State Financial Corporation respectively.

Current Ratio

In the SLPEs of Maharashtra, the current ratio fluctuated between 1.53 and 2.72 during 1986-87 to 1993-94. In Vasantrao Naik Vimukta Jatis and Nomadic Tribal Development Corporation the ratio was as high as 64:1 followed by the Maharashtra State Co-operative Sugar Ltd. with 10.99 and the Maharashtra Industrial Development Corporation with 7.18.

Value Added

The total value added by the SLPEs in the State increased gradually from Rs. 206 crore in 1985-86 to Rs. 636 crore in 1993-94. The maximum value added belonged to the the Maharashtra State Cooperative Bank Limited. During 1985-86 the value added by this SLPE was Rs. 113 crore and it shoot up to Rs. 360 crore in 1993-94.

Table 5.14

Sector	*1985-86*	*1986-87*	*1987-88*	*1988-89*	*1989-90*	*1990-91*	*1991-92*	*1992-93*	*1993-94*
Comm	0.03	-0.02	-0.10	-0.19	-0.03	-0.13	0.03	0.37	0.55
C-P	0.38	1.05	8.29	11.19	17.10	20.19	21.81	9.18	18.01
Prom	0.00	0.00	0.00	0.00	0.00	0.00	0.00	0.00	0.00
Total	0.41	1.03	8.19	11.00	17.07	20.06	21.84	9.55	10.56

Comm: Commercial, C-P: Commercial-cum-Promotional, Prom: Promotional.

Manipur

Introduction

The objective of the SLPEs in Manipur included exploitation of industrial resources development of agro-based production, promotion of small and medium industries, provision of economic support to weavers and artisans and improvement in this economic and living of the tribals in the state. Manipur has only 8 SLPEs

Profile

There were 15 SLPEs in Manipur comprising of 10 Commercial, 3 Commercial-cum-Promotional, 2 Promotional SLPes. The response from these SLPEs was very poor to the data sheet . Only 2 SLPEs namely, the Manipur Industrial Development Corporation and the Manipur Agro-Industries Corporation Limited are covered in this study.

Total Investment

The total investment of the two SLPEs grew up substantially from Rs. 0.41 crore in 1985-86 to Rs. 18.56 crore in 1993-94, thus showing 61% CARG. The major shift in investment occurred in 1987-88.

Net Worth

The total net worth of these two SLPEs went up from Rs. 0.73 crore in 1985-86 to Rs. 12.71 crore in 1993-94. Till 1990-91, the Manipur Agro Industries Corporation Limited had eroded its net worth. Afterwards it had shown positive net worth due to such equity investments.

Sales

The total turnover of the SLPEs went up from Rs. 0.43 crore in 1985-86 to Rs. 1.22 in 1993-94. The Manipur

Industrial Development Corporation contributed more than the Manipur Agro Industries Corporation towards the total turnover.

Gross Profit

It is peculiar to observe that the total gross profit of the two SLPEs was more than the total turnover of the same. tHis arised due to non inclusion of service income (which is major source of income) of Manipur Industries Development Corporation in the sales. The total gross profit went up from Rs. 0.33 crore to Rs. 2.12 crore during the study period.

Profit After Tax

The aggregate PAT of the two SLPEs came down from 0.03 crore to –0.56 crore during the period under reference. Neither of the SLPEs started consistency in earningprofits.

Accumulated Losses

The total accumulated losses stood at Rs. 2.90 crore at the end of 1993-94 as compared to Rs. 0.62 crore at the end of 1985-86. The Manipur Industries Development Corporation contributed almost 70% of the total accumulated losses at the end of 1993-94.

Return On Investment

The average ROI of the two SLPEs was not consistent in the years under reference. It increased from 17.86% in 1985-86 to 31.19% in 1988-89 to come down to 15.50% in 1993-94. The Manipur Industrial Development Corporation showed positive ROI in all the years under reference whereas in case of Manipur Agro Industrial Corporation Limited consistant trend was seen in regard to the ROI.

Return On Paid-Up Capital (ROPUC)

The SLPEs due to continuous losses in the years under reference there occurred a declined trend in ROPUC. The ROPUC of the two SLPEs on an average came down from 3.12% in 1985-86 to –4.14% in 1993-94. In 1993-94, the Manipur Agro Industries Corporation earned 2.63% ROPUC as compared to –5.00% attained by the Manipur Industrial Development Corporation.

Return On Net Worth (RONW)

In terms of RONW, the Manipur Agro Industries Corporation showed a better performance as compared to the Manipur Industrial Development Corporation. However the average RONW of the two SLPEs fell from 4.11% to –4.41% during 1985-86 to 1993-94. Latest in 1992-93 both the SLPEs were able to show a positive RONW of 16.22% and 11.60%, respectively.

Gross Margin To Sales (GMS)

The two SLPEs of Manipur earned 235.45% GMS as a whole in 1993-94 as compared to 11.63% in 1985-86. The Manipur Industrial Development Corporation showed more than 100% GMS in all but 3 years. This was possible since it had nominal sales but higher other income in the years under reference.

Debt-Equity Ratio

Comparatively Manipur Industrial Development was highly levered than Manipur Agro-Industries Corporation. Its D/E ratio fell from 2.92 in 1985-86 to 0.89 in 1993-94. At the end of 1993-94 the Manipur Agro Industries Corporation had a D/E ratio of 0.21 only. Both the SLPEs could take the advantage of their low leverage and go in for debt financing.

Table 5.15

Sector	*1985-86*	*1986-87*	*1987-88*	*1988-89*	*1989-90*	*1990-91*	*1991-92*	*1992-93*	*1993-94*
Comm	17.05	16.94	20.19	12.35	9.86	9.65	12.12	18.61	18.24
C-P	6.99	8.42	8.65	12.65	14.50	16.50	19.48	22.86	25.10
Prom	0.00	0.00	0.00	0.00	0.00	0.00	0.00	0.00	0.00
Total	24.04	25.36	28.84	25.00	24.36	26.15	31.60	41.47	43.30

Comm: Commercial, C-P: Commercial-cum-Promotional, Prom: Promotional.

Current Ratio

Both the Manipur Agro Industries Corporation and Manipur Industrial Development Corporation enjoyed better liquidity since they had current ratio of 2.00 and 2.57 respectively, in 1993-94. Overall current ratio improved from 1.38 in 1985-86 to 2.55 in 1993-94.

Value Added

The value added increased from Rs. 0.15 crore in 1985-86 to 1993-94.

Meghalaya

Introduction

Meghalaya is a fast developing State of the North-East Region with great potential for making further advancement. The State is endowed with natural resources and good industrial climate infrastructuraly it is well connected by roads to the plains and it has surplus power supply. However, entrepreneurship is lacking in the State and the private sector is kept away. In such a situation the state Government had to assume of entrepreneurial role.

Profile

There are 12 SLPEs in Meghalaya State comprising 7 Commercial and 5 Commercial-cum-Promotional SLPEs. Only 7 Commercial and 4 Commercial-cum-Promotional SLPEs responded to the data sheet and form therefore, a part of this study.

Total Investment

The total investment in the 11 SLPEs of Meghalaya went up from Rs. 24.04 crore in 1985-86 to Rs. 43.34 crore in 1993-94 registering 7.65% CARG. The total investment in Meghalaya Industrial Development Corporation Limited was more than 50% of the total investment in all the SLPEs.

The next SLPE having higher investment was Mawaluh Cherra Cements Limited.

Net Worth

The SLPEs of Meghalaya under study registered a 12.41% CARG. Out of 11 SLPEs, 4 SLPEs namely Meghalaya Government Construction Corporation Limited, Meghalaya Watches Limited, Meghalaya Apex Handloom Weavers & Handicrafts Corporation and Meghalaya Tourism Development Corporation Limited had negligible or zero net worth in all the years under study. Meghalaya Industrial Development Corporation showed a growth rate of 16.66% (CARG) in net worth. It contributed almost 50% of the total net worth of all the SLPEs.

Sales

The SLPEs of Meghalaya had a total turnover of Rs. 30.99 crore in 1993-94 compared to Rs. 12.91 crore in 1985-86 thus registering 11.00 CARG. The Commercial SLPEs contributed almost 100% of the total turnover of SLPEs as a whole. The Commercial-cum-Promotional SLPEs had a turnover of Rs. 0.17 crore in 1985-86, which went up to Rs. 0.5' crore in 1993-94. The turnover of Mawaluh Cherra Cements Limited contributed 74% if the total turnover of all the SLPEs in 1993-94.

Gross Profit

On an aggregate the SLPEs of Meghalaya registered a good growth in gross profit during the period under study. In 1985-86, the SLPEs in aggregate incurred a gross loss of Rs. 0.036 crore. However in 1993-94 the SLPEs showed Rs. 2.45 crore of gross profit. Like other parameters as mentioned above, Mawaluh Cherra Cement Limited earned the highest profit of Rs. 2.33 crore in 1993-94, which was more than the total gross profit of all SLPEs in the State.

Profit After Tax

The SLPEs of Meghalaya on a whole earned a profit of Rs. 1.02 crore in 1993-94 compared to net loss of Rs. 1.92 crore in 1985-86. The Mawaluh Cherra Cements Limited showed net loss up to 1988-89 and turned around in 1989-90. Afterwards it showed net profit continuously. In 1993-94 it earned a PAT of Rs. 1.144 crore. Two SLPEs namely the Meghalaya Watches Limited and the Meghalaya Handloom and Handicrafts Development Corporation incurred net losses in all the years under reference.

Accumulated Losses

Among 11 SLPEs of Meghalaya, 6 had accumulated losses aggregating Rs. 21.68 crore in 1993-94. The corresponding number for 1985-86 were 7 and Rs. 16.27 crore respectively. The accumulated loss of Mawaluh Cherra Cement Limited came down slowly from Rs. 14.95 crore in 1989-90 to Rs. 8.25 crore in 1993-94. Meghalaya Government Construction Corporation Limited and the Meghalaya Apex Handloom Weavers & Handicrafts Cooperative had accumulated losses in none of the years under reference.

Return On Investment (ROI)

Unlike other states, the ROI of the SLPEs in Meghalaya as a whole increased from 8.81% in 1985-86 to 27.75% in 1993-94. Meghalaya Handloom & Handicrafts Development Corporation earned highest ROI of 37.5% in 1993-94 followed by the Mawaluh Cherra Cements Limited with 29.46%. Meghalaya Bamboo Chips Limited showed a negative ROI through the period under study.

Return On Paid-Up Capital (ROPUC)

In aggregate the SLPEs under reference, showed a return of 2.43% to the equity holders on their investment compared to negative ROPUC of 10.87%. in this case,

Mawaluh Cherra Cements Limited was the second highest among the SLPEs to show 6.70% ROPUC in 1993-94, after the Meghalaya Government Construction Corporation with 11.05%.

Return on Net Worth

In 1993-94, only 2 SLPEs viz., the Mawaluh Cherra Cements Limited and the Meghalaya Industrial Development Corporation Limited showed positive RONW. The remaining SLPEs under study showed zero or negative RONW. Overall, the SLPEs earned 2.73% RONW in 1993-94 compared to –12.92% in 1985-86.

Gross Margin to Sales

On an aggregate the SLPEs earned 15% GMS in 1993-94 which was as high as 21.57% in 1989-90 and as low as 8.13% in 1985-86. The Mawaluh Cherra Cements Limited's GMS was 160% in 1993-94. The Gross Margin turning not to be more than the sales itself was due to the fact the company earned more other income compared to sales. The Commercial-cum-Promotional SLPEs earned more GMS compared to the Commercial ones.

Debt-Equity Ratio (D/E Ratio)

The overall D/E ratio of Meghalaya SLPEs varied from 0.32 to 0.91 during the various years of the study. The D/E ratio was very low as compared to D/E ratio of the other SLPEs. Meghalaya Bamboo Chips Limited enjoyed D/E ratio of more than 2:1 in most of the years. In 1993-94 it had the highest D/E ratio of 3.75 : 1.

Current Ratio

The liquidity position of the SLPEs in Meghalaya was satisfactory. The current ratio flucutated between 0.85 in 1985-86 to 1.57 in 1993-94. However the Commercial

Table 5.16

Name of the SLPEs	*1990-91*	*1991-92*	*1992-93*	*1993-94*
Mizoram State Co-operative Fruit Forestry & Vegetable Federation	0.00	0.00	0.00	0.12
Mizoram Food & Allied Industries Limited	1.98	2.61	3.66	3.66
Total'	1.98	2.61	3.66	3.78

SLPEs, except the Meghalaya State Warehousing Corporation had low current ratio. The liquidity position of the Mawaluh Cherra Cements Limited remained satisfactory during the later half of the study period.

Value Added

The value added registered many fluctuations during the period under reference. It was Rs. 2 crore during 1985-86. During 1986-87, it was Rs. 3 crore. In 1991-92 the total value added declined to Rs. 1 crore. However, it again shootup to Rs. 6 crore in 1993-94.

Mizoram

Introduction

Mizoram came on to the political map of India very recently. It has only one enterprise in the financial sector which is involved in the promotion of small and medium industries in the state. The enterpreneurship in the state is hampered by infastructural bottlenecks, on the one hand and lack of entrepreneurship, on the other.

Profile

There are 5 SLPEs in Mizoram comprising 3 Commericial and 2 Commercial-cum-Promotional SLPEs. Of them only 2 SLPEs viz., the Mizoram State Co-operative Fruit Forestry the Vegetable Federation and Mizoram Food and Allied Industries Limited are covered by this study. The Mizoram State Cooperative Fruit Forestry & Vegetable Federation set up on 1989 started commercial operation only in 1993. Similarly the Mizoram Food and Allied Industries Limited set up in 1989. The company started its operations in 1989.

Total Investment

The total investment in Mizoram Food and Allied industried Limited increased from Rs. 1.98 crore in 1990-

91 to Rs. 3.66 crorein 1992-93 at 22..73% CARG. With the addition of the Mizoram State Co-operative Fruit Forestry & Vegetable Federation in 1993-94 the total investment in these two SLPEs stood at Rs. 3.78 crore at the end of 1993-94.

Net Worth

The net worth of Mizoram Food and Allied Industries Limited went up from Rs. 1.98 crore in 1990-91 to Rs. 3.66 crore during 1992-93. This was possible not only due to creation of reserves but infusion of more equity into this SLPE. The total net worth of the two SLPEs was Rs. 3.78 in 1993-94.

Sales

The sale of the Mizoram Food and Allied Industries Limited went up from Rs. 0.12 crore in 1990-91 to Rs. 0.54 crore in 1992-93 registering a more than 4 fold growth. The total sales of the two SLPEs was 0.65 crore in 1993-94.

Gross Profit and Profit After Tax

The Mizoram Food and Allied Industries Limited has been incurring gross losses since its commencement of business operations. Its gross loss went up from Rs. 17 lakh to Rs. 46 lakh during 1990-91 to 1992-93. During 1993-94, Mizoram State Co-operative Fruit Forestry & Vegetable Federation was able to earn a gross profit of Rs. 0.22 crore. The PAT was of the level of the GP as there did not happens to be any outgo on the interest account.

Accumulated Losses

With continuous loss is incurred by the Mizoram State Food & Allied Industries Limited, an accumulated loss shoot at Rs. 0.92 crore in 1992-93.

Return On Investment (ROI)

The Mizoram State Food & Allied Industries Limited earned an ROI of 4.55% in 1993-94 whereas the Mizoram State Co-operative Fruit Forestry and Vegetable Federation earned negative ROI in all the 4 years of its operation. It showed a decline in its performance in terms of the ROI continuously.

Return On Paid-Up Capital (ROPUC)

The Mizoram State Co-operative Fruit Forestry & Vegetable Federation earned a return of 3.89% on its paid-up capital in 1993-94. The Mizoram Food & Allied Industries Limited showed ROPUC of –7.71% in 1990-91 and 10.07% in 1992-93. In 1993-94, both the SLPEs together recorded an ROPUC of –9.82%. In fact, even with an increase in equity capital the Mizoram Food & Allied Industries Limited, registered a negative ROPUC.

Return On Net Worth (RONW)

Although lower, the Mizoram State Fruit Forestry & Vegetable Federation was able to earn 2.79% RONW in 1993-94. As usual, the Mizoram Food & Allied Industries Limited was ailing in its operations and showed negative FONW in all the years of the study.

Gross Margin to Sales (GMS)

The Mizoram Food & Allied Industries Limited was not able to have recorded sales more than its cost of goods sold in any of the year of the study. In 1990-91 it recorded 100% gross loss to sales, which came down to 70.37% in 1992-93. However, Mizoram Food & Allied Industries Limtied earned 9.09 GMS in 1992-93.

Debt-Equity Raito

During 4 years of its operations, the Mizoram Food & Allied Industries Limited had Rs. 15 lakh long-term loans

Table 5.17

Sector	*1985-86*	*1986-87*	*1987-88*	*1988-89*	*1989-90*	*1990-91*	*1991-92*	*1992-93*	*1993-94*
Comm	33.40	16.67	-1.40	-17.50	-43.63	-60.13	-04.14	-115.67	-131.02
C-P	9.06	13.20	9.25	14.22	12.93	15.07	14.79	14.65	13.16
Total	42.46	29.95	7.85	3.28	-30.70	-45.06	-69.62	-101.02	-117.86

Comm: Commercial, C-P: Commercial-cum-Promotional, Prom: Promotional.

only in 1991-92. Otherwise in none of the years it had any long-term debt. The Mizoram State Co-operative Fruit Forestry & Vegetable Federation also had no long-term debt in 1993-94. Hence in these cases, the D/E ratio turned out to be nil. It shows that the SLPEs could take the advantage of their leverage and access debt market.

Current Ratio (C/R Ratio)

The Mizoram State Co-operative Fruit Forestry & Vegetable Federation had an unsastifactory liquidity position with a current ratio of 1.38 in 1993-94. In the case of the Mizoram Food & Allied Industries Limited, the current ratio was as high as 36.33 in 1990-91 which came down to 4.81 in 1992-93.

Value Added

In 1985-86 the value added was zero which turned out to be negative at Rs. 0.13 crore in 1993-94 for the two SLPEs in the State.

Nagaland

Introduction

Nagaland was born on the Indian map as a political entity in 1967. The commercial activities and trade practices were neglacted in this region by the BritisheRs. The economy of the State is agrarian though the state has vast mineral resources. After the dawn of independence and the formation of the State in order to throw the shackles of poverty and under development, the policy makers chose SLPEs as a major instrument of development.

Profile

In Nagaland there are 6 SLPEs comprising 4 Commercial, one each from Commercial-cum-Promotional and Promotional enterprises. Only 3 enterprises responded to be data sheet queries.

Total Investment

The total investment in the 3 SLPEs shows an entirely different trend compared to other states. The total investment came down to Rs. -117.86 crore in 1993-94 from Rs. 42.46 crore during 1985-86. This was possible due to negative total investment in the Nagaland Pulp & Paper Company Limited. It shows that the net working capital of Nagaland Pulp & Paper Company Limited was highly negative, which could cancel the in the net fixed assets. The total investment in the Nagaland Industrial Development Corporation Limited increased from Rs. 9.06 crore in 1985-86 to Rs. 13.16 in 1993-94.

Net Worth

The Nagaland Pulp & Paper Company Limited eroded its net worth since 1985-86. Up to 1993-94 it eroded its net worth by Rs. 201.53 crore. The net worth of the Nagaland Industrial Development Corporation went up from Rs. 6.54 crore at the end of 1985-86 to Rs. 9.76 crore at the end of 1993-94.

Sales

The total sales of the SLPEs in Nagaland came down substantially from Rs. 6.58 crore in 1985-86 to Rs. 0.74 crore in 1993-94. This decline in sales was caused due to deteriorating sales position of the Nagaland Pulp & Paper Co. Ltd. In 1993-94, the Nagaland Pulp & Paper Co. Ltd. made no sales. In contrast, it had made sales amounting Rs. 6.13 crore in 1985-86.

Gross Profit

Nagaland Pulp & Paper Company Limited and the Nagaland Industrial Development Corporations are making gross losses since 1985-86. Whereas the Nagaland State Mineral Development Corporation Limited made no profit or loss in all the years, the total gross loss of SLPEs in Nagaland came down from Rs. 19.23 crore in 1985-86 to Rs. 9.63 crore in 1993-94.

Profit After Tax (PAT)

The net loss of SLPEs in Nagaland as a whole increased from Rs. 21.43 crore in 1985-86 to Rs. 25.60 crore in 1993-94. Out of the total loss in various years the Nagaland Pulp & Paper Company Limited contributed to the extent of more than 90% on this score.

Accumulated Losses

The total accumulated losses of the Nagaland SLPEs went up from Rs. 69.91 crore to Rs. 256.75 crore during 1985-86 to 1993-94. The corresponding figures for the Nagaland Pulp & Paper Company Limited were Rs. -69.31in 1985-86 and Rs. 250.40 crore in 1993-94. This makes it clear as to what extent the Nagaland Pulp & Paper Company Limited contributed to the total accumulated losses.

Return On Investment (ROI)

The Nagaland SLPEs had a negative total investment as a whole. Hence the ROI cannot be interpreted. However, the Nagaland Industrial Development Corporation earned a positive ROI in all but 3 years of this study .

Return On Paid-Up Capital (ROPUC)

The SLPEs as a whole recorded –50.92% ROPUC in 1993-94 as compared to –45.56% in 1985-86. The Nagaland Industrial Development Corporaiton showed –1.51% ROPUC in 1993-94 as compared to –0.39% in 1985-86.

Return On Net Worth (RONW)

The Nagaland Industrial Development Corporation showed negative RONW in all the years under study. In the other two cases th interpretation is not possible, since their net woth was negative too. In 1993-94, the Nagaland Industrial Development Corporation showed –7.55% RONW as compared to –10.20% in the previous year.

Gross Margin To Sales (GMS)

In terms of GMS, the SLPEs of Nagaland depict a poor picture. For instance the GMS of the Nagaland Paper & Pulp Company Limited was –603.5% in 1992-93. This shows how the SLPEs were unable to meet their expenses out of its own revenue. The Nagaland Industrial Development Corporation's GMS came down from 40% in 1985-86 to 3.08% in 1993-94.

Debt-Equity Ratio (D/E RATIO):

On an average, the SLPEs of Nagaland were low-levered enterprises. The overall D/E ratio varied from 1.11 to 1.27 during the various years of the study. The Nagaland Industrial Development Corporation was low levered as compared to the than Nagaland Pulp & Paper Company Limited. It has a good scope to access debt finances.

Current Ratio

The Nagaland State Mineral Development Corporation Limited enjoyed high liquidity, measured in terms of the current ratio. However the current ratio of the Nagaland State Mineral Development Corprоaiton declined from 34.75 to 11.87 during the study period. The Nagaland Pulp & Paper Company Limited was suffering from liquidity crisis since it had a very low current ratio 0.03 at the end of 1993-94.

Value Added

The SLPEs in Nagaland showed negative value added throughout the period under study. It was Rs. -8.94 crore in 1985-86 which became Rs. -3.96 crore in 1993-94. This

Table 5.18

Sector	1985-86	1986-87	1987-88	1988-89	1989-90	1990-91	1991-92	1992-93	1993-94
Comm	11.05	14.09	16.67	17.42	16.73	13.00	14.41	14.73	15.6
C-P	427.18	432.12	489.7.3	542.56	615.03	677.97	746.39	806.66	568.32
Prom	1.85	2.34	2.39	3.04	3.32	3.48	3.60	3.70	4.76
Total	440.08	448.55	508.79	563.02	635.08	695.25	764.40	825.09	588.68

Comm: Commercial, C-P: Commercial-cum-Promotional, Prom: Promotional.

trend was mainly beacause the Nagaland Pulp and Paper Company Ltd., registered a negative value added throughout the period under study.

Orissa

Introduction

Orissa is one of the relatively less developed states in the country. The most important challenge faced by the state during the four decades of post independence era is stepping up the rate of growth in the state to overcome stagnation. In the pursuit of achieving this end, the state Government has opted for the SLPEs as a means of economic development. The investments in Public Enterprises as well as their assets have registered phenomenal growth. But these enterprises have lagged behind anticipation in terms of financial performance.

Profile

In the State of Orissa there were 43 SLPEs in overall. These comprised of 16 Commercial, 26 Commercial-cum-Promotional and 1 Promotional. The data reported for the purpose of this study was for only 17 enterprises comprising five Commercial, 11 Commericla-cum-Promotional and 1 Promotional enterprises.

Total Investment

In the SLPEs of Orissa the total investments stood at Rs. 588.68 crore as at the end of 1993-94. When compared with the figures of 1985-86, the investments grew at a CARG of 3.7%. In terms of total Investment, Orissa State Finance Corporation topped the list which is followed by the Industrial Development Corporation of Orissa Ltd., Industrial Promotion and Investment Corporaiton of Orissaand Orissa State Co-operative Agricultural and Rural Development with Rs. 150.59 crore, Rs. 107.67 crore and

Rs. 101.15 crore respectively. Out of the Total investment, the Commercial-cum-Promotional enterprises had a 96% share and the remaining investment was made with the Commercial and Promotional group of enterprises.

Net Worth

The total net worth of the SLPEs of Orissa reported as at the end of fiscal 1993-94 was Rs. 262.31 crore which when compared to that of the figures of 1985-86 had increased by 62%. In terms of Net Worth the Industrial Development Corporation of Orissa Ltd. tops with Rs. 88.93 crore followed by the Industrial Promotion and Investment Corporation of Oriss Ltd., with Rs. 67.02 crores and Orissa Testile Mills Ltd. with Rs. 57.73 crore. In the case of the Orissa State Financial Corporation, the net worth which has increased from Rs. 9.05 crore in 1985-86 to Rs. 58.48 crore in 1992-93 immediately dropped down to Rs. 3.35 crore by the next year. In the case of the Orissa Industrial Infrastructure Development Corporation the net worth was negative till 1992-93 and it turned out to be positive in 1993-94.which was 0.29 crore. Whereas, in case of Orissa State Seeds Corporation Ltd. the net worth was positive till the end of 1992-93, but it had eroded wholly and became negative in the succeding year. All the other enterprises were showing a positive net worth in 1993-94.

Sales

In all the SLPEs of Orissa reproted during the period, sales showed a positive growth rate and had increased by 72% in overall, representing a CARG of 7.04%. In terms of sales, Orissa State Civil Supplies Corporation Ltd., was leading the table with Rs. 205.60 crore closley followed by the Industrial Development Corporaiton of Orissa Ltd., with Rs. 137.44 crore. Both these enterprises represent Commercial-cum-Promotional group and the Commerical enterprise category was the Orissa Textile Mills and which was on top with Rs. 47.08 crore sales.

Gross-Profit

In terms of Gross Profit all the SLPEs reproted barring 5 enterprises are showing a positive Gross Profit in the year 1993-94. The 5 enterprises showing negaitve Gross Profit are from Commercial-cum-Promotional group. They included:

1. Orissa State Financial Corporation
2. Orissa State Lether Corporation Ltd.
3. Orissa Film Development Corporation Ltd.
4. Orissa State Police Housing and Welfare Corporation Ltd.
5. Orissa State Seeds Corporation.

The Gross Profit which was Rs. 34. 14 crore in 1985-86 had increased to Rs. 74.39 crore in the year 1992-93 and declined to Rs. 1.13 crore in the year succeding year i.e.,1993-94. In terms of Gross Profit, the Orissa State Financial Corporation was topping the list in 1992-93 with Rs. 31.48 crore closely followed by Industrial Development Corporation of Orissa Ltd.

Profit After Tax (PAT)

The PAT in the SLPEs of Orissa was negative throughout the period under study. It had increased in negative terms from Rs. 6.49 crore at the end of the year 1985-86 to Rs. 73 23 crore at the end of the fiscal 1993-94. The Oriss State Financial Corporation has topped in terms of negative PAT and registered a loss of Rs. 57.61 crore in the year 1993-94. Out of 17 enterprise reproted eight enterprises showed a negative PAT, two enterprises showed zero PAT and all other show positive PAT.

Accumulated Losses

The Accumulated Losses in the SLPEs reported from Orissa stood at Rs. 174.15 crore at the end of the financial year 1993-94, when compared to the figures of 1985-86 in this regard, the accumulated losses increased three fold. All the enterprises reproted for the study have accumulated losses excepting three enterprises, namely the Industrial Development Corporation of Orissa Ltd., the Orissa Film Development Corporation and Orissa State Co-operative Agricultural and Rural Development Corporation. In almost all the enterprises accumulated losses were showing an increasing trend.

Return On Investment (ROI)

In terms of ROI, the SLPEs of Orissa, have shown a ROI of 5.81% at the end of fiscal 1993-94 which when compared with the fitures of 1985-86 had come down four fold. It was 22.46% in 1985-86 incresed to 34.51% at the end of the year 1992-93 and declined to 5.81%. This may be the impact of Orissa state Financial Corporation's ROI, where the Orissa State Financial Corporation was showing the ROI of 5437.9% in the year 1992-93 the ROI declined to –28.03.%, because of this the overall Commercial-cum-Promotional enterprise ROI too declined from 39.15% in 1992-93 to 1.17% in 1993-94. In the case of the Commercial and Promotional enterprises the ROI increased from 18.49% in 1985-86 to 27.02% in the year 1993-94 in the case of the Commercial-cum-promotional -15.14% to 1985-86 to 13.42% in 1992-94 in promotional enterprises.

Return On Paid-Up Capital

In terms of ROPUC too, the SLPEs of Orissa were showing negative figure of –23.24%, when compared to that of 1985-86 it went negative for about six times, as it was –4.14% in the fiscal 1985-86. There were only six enterprises showing positive ROPUC, represented by 2 in

Commercial enterprises out of 5 enterprises, 3 enterprises in Commercial-cum-Promotional out of 11 enterprises and 1enterprise in promotional enterprises. In terms of ROPUC Orissa Industrial Infrastructure Development Corporation Ltd., topped the list with 329.41% followed by Orissa Maritime & Chilka Area Development Corporation Ltd.

Return On Net Worth

In terms of Return on Net Worth too the SLPEs of Orissa were showing a negative return of 27.81% at the end of fiscal 1993-94 which was 3.99% at the end of fiscal year 1985-86. This shows that the return generated was very poor. A positive RONW was observed in only 7 enterprises and all the remaining enterprises earned a negative RONW. These 7 enterprises comprised 2 Commercial, 4 Commercial-cum-Promotional and 1 from Promotional enterprises.

Gross Margin to Sales

In terms of Gross Margin to Sales the SLPEs of Orrisa earned 5.60% GMS at the end of financial year 1993-94 which was 6.98% at the end of financial year 1985-86. Excepting in the Orissa State Leather Corporation Ltd., in all the SLPEs of Orissa there was a positive Gross Margin to Sales. In terms of Gross Margin the Aska Cooperative Sugar Industries Ltd. tops the list with 43.28% followed by the Orissa State Cashew Development Corporation Ltd. with 38.53% and the Orissa Film Development Corporation Ltd. with 26.67%. The average Gross Margin in all the enterprises over the years or the period of study was 5.64%.

Debt-Equity Ratio (D/E Ratio)

The Debt-Equity Ratio in all the SLPEs reproted ranges from 1.97 to 3.20 over the period of the study. In all the enterprises the debt-equity ratio was not exceeding 2:1 barring 4 enterprises. In the Orissa Textile Mills Ltd. it was

Table 5.19

Sector	*1985-86*	*1986-87*	*1987-88*	*1988-89*	*1989-90*	*1990-91*	*1991-92*	*1992-93*	*1993-94*
Comm	44.11	57.04	69.20	71.04	90.20	81.48	118.63	132.73	157.06
C-P	-14.52	-90.49	-79.34	8.91	6.83	34.70	56.60	48.76	58.50
Prom	6.67	7.71	9.37	9.02	8.63	6.64	-2.31	1.70	2.28
Total	36.26	-25.74	-0.77	88.97	105.66	122.82	172.92	183.19	2177.92

Comm: Commercial, C-P: Commercial-cum-Promotional, Prom: Promotional.

38.66 which was very high and in Orissa State Co-operative Agricultural & Rural Development Corporation and in Orissa State Financial Corporation and Orissa State Seeds Corportion Ltd. it was 7.79, 4.74 and 4.18 respectively which was also above the normal standard norms.

Current Ratio

The Current ratio in all the enterprises reported during the study was ranging between 1.20 and 2.03. Only 7 enterprises had reproted current ratio of more than 1.33 and all the other reproting enterprises holdes the ratio below the norm. In Industrial Promotion & Investment Corporation of Orissa Ltd., had a current ratio exceeding to 23.39 followed by the orissa Film Developemnt Corporation Ltd., with 12.07.

Value Added

The value added of the SLPEs increased from Rs. 47 crore to Rs. 130 crore between 1985-86 and 1992-93. However during 1993-94 there was tremendous declined in the value added which amounts to Rs. 41 crore. The Industrial Development Corporation of Orissa Limited, which was the major contributor to value added since the beginning of the study.

Punjab

Introduction

In the pre-independence era, some of the princely states in punjab used to operate a few state enterprises, mainly to distill and distribute liquor. The state enterprises were organised by the departmental undertakings and not as companies. In order to promote faster economic development in accordance with the national policy and for achieving other socio-economic objectives, the public sector was assigned an important role by the State.

Profile

The Punjab State has 30 SLPEs, consisting 7 Commercial, 19 Commercial-cum-Promotional and 4 Promotional. The filled-in data sheets were received from 26 SLPEs comprising 13 Commercial, 10 Commercial-cum-Promotional and 3 Promotional.

Total Investment

The Total Investment in the 26 SLPEs of Punjab stood at Rs. 213.65 crore at the end of 1993-94 compared ot Rs. 36.26 crore at the end of 1985-86. During the period under reference, it had a CARG of 24.82%. Table 5.19 gives data relating to the sector-wise Total Investment in the SLPEs.

Net Worth

The SLPEs in Punjab under study had a net worth of Rs. 51.94 crore at the end of 1985-86 and it shoot up to Rs. 143.12crore at the end of 1993-94. During this period the net worth grew at a CARG of 13.35%. out of 26 SLPEs, 7 enterprises had eroded their net worth. The following SLPEs eroded their net worth since 1985-86:

1. The Kothapura Co-operative Spinning Mills Limited
2. Punjab State Electronics Development & Production Corporation
3. The Tarn-Taran Co-operative Sugar Mills Limited
4. The Gurdaspur Co-operative Sugar Mills Ltd.
5. Punjab Housing Board
6. The Punjab State Civil Supplies Corporation Ltd.
7. Punjab Police Housing Corporation

The Faridkot Co-operative Sugar Mills Ltd. had zero net worth up to 1990-91 and from 1991-92 onwards it had been adding positively to its net worth.

Sales

During the study period, the total sales of the 26 SLPEs increased from Rs. 426.29 crore in 1985-86 to Rs. 1,596.09 crore in 1993-94 registering a CARG of 17.95%. The Punjab State Civil Supplies Corporation Limited topped the SLPEs in terms of sales during all the years. In the year 1993-94 the SLPEs sales by this corporation amounted to Rs. 1,054.16 crore followed by Punjab Agro-Industries Corporation Limited with Rs. 168.83 crore. Through out the period of study, the Commercial and Promotional SLPEs showed better turnover in aggregate compared to commercial SLPES.

Gross Profit

Out of 26 SLPEs in 1993-94, 16 SLPEs showed gross profit and the rest had either zero or negative gross profit. Among these 16 enterprises, 11 SLPEs had earned gross profit throughout the study period. The Punjab State Civil Supplies Corporation Limited maintained a top position in terms of gross profit throughout the period, followed by the Punjab Communications Limited. The Mirinda Co-operative Sugar Mills, Punjab State Warehousing Corporation Ltd., the Punjab State Handloom Weavers Apex Co-operative Society and Punjab Women & Childern Development and Welfare Corporation earned gross profit during the study period. The aggregate gross profit of 26 SLPEs went up from Rs. 341.46 crore in 1985-86 to Rs. 201.87 crore in 1993-94.

Profit After Tax

In 1993-94, 19 SLPEs had shown profit after tax and the rest loss or zero profit throughout the period from 1985-86 to 1993-94. The following enterprises earned PAT continuously:

1. Punjab Communications Limited

2. Punjab State Warehousing Corporation Ltd.
3. Punjab Women & Children Development & Welfare Corporation

The Gurdaspur Co-operative Sugar Mills Limited and the Fazilka Co-operative Sugar Mills Limited had incurred losses up to 1992-93 but turned around earning profits in 1993-94. The Punjab Communications Limited gained profits and was at top among all the SLPEs in 1993-94 with profit of Rs. 18.33 crore it was followed by the Punjab State Civil Supplies Corporation Ltd. which had Rs. 14.06 crore. The aggregate profit of 26 SLPEs did not show a steady trend. In 1985-86 there was an aggregate loss of Rs. 22.98 crore and in 1993-94 the SLPEs as a whole earned profit of Rs. 69.56 crore.

Accumulated Losses

Among 26 SLPEs, 12 had accumulated losses throughout the study period. The Punjab State Civil Supplies Corporation Ltd. was leading in terms of accumulated losses in all the years of study. At the end of 1993-94 it showed accumulated losses of Rs. 123.26 crore as compared to Rs. 99.40 crore of accumulated loosesin 1985-86. In aggregate the accumulated losses of the SLPEs shot up from Rs. 131.34 crore in 1985-86 to Rs. 215.53 crore in 1993-94.

The following enterprises have zero accumulated losses throughout the study period.

1. Punjab Communications Ltd.
2. Punjab Police Housing Board
3. Punjab Scheduled Castes Land Development & Finance Corporation

Return On Investment (ROI)

The 26 Punjab SLPEs could generate 30.70% ROI in 1993-94 as compared to 5.28% generated in 1985-86. The Batala Co-operative Sugar Mills Ltd. and The Morinda Co-operative Sugar Mills Ltd. earned the highest ROI in 1993-94. The Punjab State Forest Development Corporation Limited and the Gurdaspur Co-operative Sugar Mills Limited were prominent among the SLPEs earning negative ROI in 1993-94.

Return On Paid-Up Capital (ROPUC)

The equity shareholders of the SLPEs as a whole earned 18.21% of ROPUC in 1993-94. The Punjab State Civil Supplies Corporation Limited topped the SLPEs in the state with 391.42% ROPUC in 1993-94. It was followed by the Morinda Co-operative Sugar Mills Ltd. with 102.18% of ROPUC. There were 5 SLPEs in which ROPUC was higher than the state average. The Kothapura Co-operative Sugar Mills alone had a negative ROPUC in 1993-94. In 1985-86 was seven such enterprises were in the category of earning negative ROPUC.

The SLPEs which had a negative ROPUC up to 1992-93 and turned to positive were-

1. The Batala Co-operative Sugar Mills Ltd.
2. The Barnala Co-operative Sugar Mills Ltd.
3. The Morinda Co-operative Sugar Mills Ltd.
4. The Gurdaspur Co-operative Sugar Mills Ltd.
5. The Fazilka Co-operative Sugar Mills Ltd.

Return On Net Worth

In aggregate, the SLPEs earned a 14.42% RONW in 1985-86. At the end of 1993-94, SLPEs recorded 46.84%

RONW. The Faridkot Co-operative Sugar Mills Ltd. had the highest RONW in 1993-94 with 64.03%, followed by Punjab Women & Children Developemtn and Welfare Corporation with 40.08%. In 1993-94, 3 SLPEs had a negative RONW whereas in 1985-86 RONW was negative in 5 SLPEs.

Gross Margin to Sales

The GMS of the SLPEs as a whole, increased from 0.71% in 1985-86 to 5.58% in 1993-94. The Punjab Women & Children Development and Welfare Corporation had the highest GMS throughout the study period and in 1993-94 it was 650.00%. in 1993-94 there were 14 SLPEs which had positive GMS, and 2 SLPEs had negative GMS and the rest had nil GMS.

Debt-Equity Ratio (D/E Ratio)

The overall D/E Ratio of Punjab SLPEs declined from 5.45 to 1.20 during 1985-86 to 1993-94. The Punjab State Civil Supplies Corporation Limited had an unusually high D/E Ratio of 86.54 in 1993-94. There were 8 SLPEs which had zero D/E Ratio in 1993-94. Commercial-cum-Promotional SLPEs showed a lower current ratio compared to that of the other sectors throughout the study period.

Current Ratio

The overall current ratio increased from 1.01 to 1.25 during the period of study. In 1993-94 the Budhewal Co-operative Sugar Mills Limited registered highest current ratio with 10.02. The Commercial-cum-Promotional SLPEs showed a lower current ratio compared to that of the other sectors throughout the study period.

Value Added

The value added incresed from Rs. 61 crore in 1985-86 to Rs. 292 crore in 1993-94.

Table 5.20

Sector	*1985-86*	*1986-87*	*1987-88*	*1988-89*	*1989-90*	*1990-91*	*1991-92*	*1992-93*	*1993-94*
Comm	38.60	43.24	42.95	57.72	86.42	120.82	156.39	206.46	230.00
C-P	121.92	137.18	152.78	159.98	180.39	207.14	258.81	308.09	33.00
Prom	37.93	45.36	48.85	53.35	55.50	59.15	63.07	67.40	69.00
Total	198.15	225.78	244.58	271.05	322.31	387.11	478.27	581.95	633.00

Comm: Commercial, C-P: Commercial-cum-Promotional, Prom: Promotional.

Rajasthan

Introduction

The State of Rajasthan was carved out by integrating 19 princely states and 3 chiefships. Most of the princely states were performing the functions of a welfare state. They took keen interest in development of industry agriculture, banking and railways. The Public Enterprises spurred the economic prosperity in the princely states. They were run on the principle of making profits and organised in the departmental form.

Profile

In the State of Rajasthan there were 27 Commercial, 12 Commercial-cum-Promotional and 4 Promotional enterprises and the data was available for analysis only for 11 Commercial, 7 Commercial-cum-Promotional and 2 Promotional enterprises, which formed 5% of the total SLPEs in the State.

Total Investment

In the SLPEs of Rajasthan the total investment stood at Rs. 633.58 crore at the end of 1993-94 as compared to the investment in 1985-86. More than 50% of the Total Investment is held in Commercial-cum-Promotional enterprises and around 40 percent belonged to the with Commercial enterprises. In terms of total investment, the Rajasthan State Industrial Development & Investment Corporation Ltd. topped the list with Rs. 264.56 crore followed by Rs. 168.53 crore in the Rajasthan State Mines & Minerals Ltd.

Net Worth

The net worth of the enterprises reported as at the end of fiscal 1993-94 was Rs. 300.67crore when compared to the same as at the end of 1985-86 which was Rs. 70.95 crore it had increased four fold. In the Commercial enterprises the net worth had increased almost around seven times, whereas in Commercial-cum-Promotional enterprises it increased around three and a half times and the same in Promotional enterprises had increased by two and a quarter times. In two enterprises one from Commercial Rajasthan Electronics Ltd. and the other from Commercial-cum-Promotional, Rajasthan State Agro-Industries Corporation Ltd. the net worth had totally eroded and were showing a negative net worth of Rs. 1.59 and Rs. 8.91 respectively at the end of fiscal 1993-94.

Sales

The total sales of SLPEs reported stand at Rs. 436.16 crore at the end of fiscal 1993-94 when compared to that of the year 1985-86 it increased five times and it was only Rs. 96.25 crore. Rajasthan State Mines and Minerals Ltd. topped the list with Rs. 100.85 crore in sales followed by Rajasthan State Bridge & Construction Corporation Ltd. with Rs. 87.96 crore followed by Rajasthan State Ganganagar Sugar Mills Ltd. with Rs. 70.82 crore where all the three were from commercial enterprises. Whereas in Commercial-cum-Promotional enterprises Rajasthan State Agro Industries Corporation Ltd. topped the list and had sales of Rs. 31.05 crore at the end of fiscla 1993-94.

Gross Profit (G.P.)

All the enterprises excepting Government Salt Works, didwâna and the Rajasthan Tribal Area Developemnt Co-operative Federaiton Ltd. were showing positive gross profit which was a very impressive feature of the SLPEs reported in the study. In terms of Gross Profit, The Rajasthan State Industrial Development & Investment Corporation Ltd. topped the list with Rs. 25.59 crore followed by the Rajasthan State Mines & Minerals Ltd. and the Rajasthan State Financial Corporation with Rs. 23.01 and Rs. 20.31

crore, respectively. The Rajasthan State Agro Industries Corporation Ltd. which was making loss till the year 1991-92 had turned around in 1992-93. It recorded a gross profit of Rs. 0.43 crore a the end of fiscal 1993-94. The same was the case with Sri Keshoraipatnam Sahakari Sugar Mills Ltd. which recorded a positive gross profit of Rs. 2.31 crore at the end of fiscal 1993-94.

Profit After Tax (PAT)

In terms of profit, the SLPES of Rajasthan had shown a mixed performance. Out of 11 Commercial enterprises, 2 categories of enterprises were showing negative PAT, whereas in Commercial-cum-Promotional and Promotional there were 2 out of 7 and 1 out of 2 enterprises were showing negative PAT respectively. The Rajasthan Electronics Ltd. which was showing positive PAT till 1991-92 had started showing negative PAT this could because of liberalisation. Leaving the Rajasthan Electronics Limited all other 'enterprises were showing a positive PAT excepting the Rajasthan State Mineral Development Corporation Ltd. which was also showing negative PAT in 1993-94, whereas the Rajasthan Paryatan Vikas Nigam Ltd. it was reverse, as it recorded positive PAT from 1989-90.

Accumulated Losses

In the SLPEs of Rajasthan, the accumulated losses declined from Rs. 13.75 crore in 1985-86 to Rs. 8.95 crore in 1993-94 in the Commercial enterprises. However as the accumulated losses had increased from Rs. 31.19 crore in 1985-86 to Rs. 39.32 crore in 1993-94.

Return On Investment

In terms of ROI, the Commercial SLPEs were showing an average ROI of 27 per cent in 1993-94 whereas in the Commercial-cum-Promotional enterprise it was 1.90 per cent during the same period.but it started improving from 1991-92 when we observe the data.

Return On Paid-Up Capital

Return as a percentage of paid-up capital in the SLPEs of Rajasthan was on average 6.25% in Commercial enterprises, 2.75% in Commercial-cum-Promotional, and in the case of the promotional enterprise it was negative and increased around 3 per cent in 1993-94. But, in overall it had increased from 0.94 in 1985-86 to 5.50% in 1993-94.

Return On Net Worth

When return is compared as a percentage of net worth it could be observed that on an average it was 8.74 per cent in the case of Commercial enterprises 3.26% in case of Commercial-cum-Promotional and 6.94% in the case of Promotional enterprises. The following enterprises had a positive RONW throughout the period of the study:

1. Rajasthan State Mineral Development Corporation Limited from Commercial
2. Rajasthan Small Industries Corporation Ltd. from Commercial-cum-Promotional
3. Rajasthan Tribal Areas Development Co-operative Federation Limited from Promotional.

In the case of the Rajasthan State Seeds Corporation Ltd., the RONW declined from 63.99% in 1986-87 to 23.62% in 1993-94. Whereas in the case of the Rajasthan Paryatan Vikas Nigam Ltd. it showed positive trend from the year 1989-90 onwards.

Gross Margin to Sales (GMS)

Gross Margin as a percentage to sales was increasing on the whole in SLPEs of Rajasthan. It had increased to 11.67% in 1993-94 from 7.67 in 1985-86. On an average the SLPEs they were showing a 9.37% of gross margin to sales. In the case of Rajasthan State Agro Industries Corporation

Table 5.21

Sector	*1985-86*	*1986-87*	*1987-88*	*1988-89*	*1989-90*	*1990-91*	*1991-92*	*1992-93*	*1993-94*
Comm	0.55	0.45	0.41	0.39	1.52	3.70	4.03	4.32	4.39
C-P	4.44	6.06	9.84	11.47	13.69	15.22	16.81	18.42	17.03
Prom	0.00	0.00	0.00	0.00	0.00	0.00	0.00	0.00	0.00
Total	4.99	6.51	10.25	11.86	15.21	18.92	20.84	22.74	21.42

Comm: Commercial, C-P: Commercial-cum-Promotional, Prom: Promotional.

Ltd. it was negative till 1990-91, but from the year 1991-92 it became positive.

Debt-Equity Ratio

The D/E ratio in SLPEs of the Rajasthan during the period under study fluctuated between 0.79 to 0.83. But in some enterprises the ratio was more than 2 and in the Rajasthan Electronics Limited it was 6.17. In Rajasthan State Seeds Corporation Ltd. it was 7.56.

Current Ratio (C/R Ratio)

The Current Ratio for the of SLPEs in Rajasthan for all the enterprises taken together fluctuated between 1.57 and 1.85 during the period of the study. Out of 20 enterprises reproted for the study, there were only two enterprises showing a ratio of less than 1.33, The Government Salt Works (Didwana) topped the list with 37.55 closely followed by Crude Sodium Sulphate Works (Didwana) with 30.44 and Rajasthan Electronics Ltd. with 6.00 percent at the end of 1993-94. The remaining enterprises recorded current ratio between 1.00 and 3.62 at the end of the year 1993-94.

Value Added

The value added increased gradually from Rs. 32 crore to Rs. 124 crore between 1985-86 and 1993-94. During the period 1985-86 the maximum value added came from the Rajasthan State Industrial and Investment Corporation Limited. Its percentage contribution to the total value added declined from 26 per cent in 1985-86 to 21 per cent in 1993-94.

Sikkim

Introduction

Sikkim become a state of the Indian Union under the constitution (38 Amendment) Act, 1975, which came into force with restrospective effect from 26th April, 1975. Sikkim has been declared industrially backward. The main industrial units are the Food Preservation Factory at Singtam, Sikkim Tanneries Ltd. at Majitar, Sikkim Flour Mills at Tadong, Sikkim Distilleries at Rongpo. HMT watch assembly unit, Sikkim Time Corporation and Yoksum Breweries. Sikkim tea estate at Temi and Kewzing extends over an area of 200ha. Tea is exported to USSR and West Germany. A coffee plantation has also been started at Majitar on an experimental basis with commendable results.

Profile

At present there were 9 SLPEs comprising 6 Commercial, 2 Commercial-cum-Promotional and 1 Promotional SLPEs. Out of them only 4 SLPEs, two each from Commercial and Commercial-cum-Promotional category and included in this study.

Total Investment

The total investment in the 4 SLPEs of Sikkim went up from Rs. 4.99 crore in 1985-86 to Rs. 21.42 crore in 1993-94, thus registering 20% CARG. The Temi Tea Estate (TTE) formerly knowed as Sikkim Tea Board had only fixed investment in terms of grants from the state government instead of equity or long-term loans. The major SLPE in terms of total investment was the Sikkim Industrial Development & Investment Corporation.

Net Worth

The aggregate net worth of Sikkim SLPEs rose from Rs. 3.48 crore in 1985-86 to Rs. 12.67 in 1993-94 . The net worth of Sikkim Industrial Development & Investment Corporation shot up from Rs. 2.91 crore in 1985-86 to Rs. 17.11 crore in 1992-93 to come down to Rs. 7.26 crore in 1993-94.

Sales

The aggregate sales of Sikkim SLPEs moved up by more than 5 times from Rs. 0.66 crore in 1985-86 to Rs. 3.43 crore in 1993-94. The Sikkim Jewels Limited and The Temi Tea Estate were major SLPEs in terms of the turnover.

Gross Profit

The gross profit of Sikkim SLPEs under study, as a whole, increased from Rs. 0.01 crore in 1985-86 to Rs. 2.26 crore in 1993-94. Except the Sikkim Mining Corporation (SMC), all the SLPEs were earning gross profits during the period under reference. In 1993-94, Sikkim Industrial Development & Investment Corporation was at top in terms of gross profit earned.

Profit After Tax (PAT)

The total PAT of the SLPEs in the State went up from Rs. 0.01 crore in 1985-86 to Rs. 0.49 crore in 1991-92. Then it declined to –1.75 crore in 1993-94. The Temi Tea Estate was the only SLPE to earn net profits during the entire period of study. Sikkim Industrial Development & Investment Corporation earned profits till 1988-89 and afterwards it started incurring losses.

Accumulated Losses

The Accumulated losses went up from Rs. 0.65 crore in 1985-86 to Rs. 4.52 crore in 1993-94.

Return On Investment (ROI)

The SLPEs of Sikkim under study generated 9.75% ROI in 1993-94 as compared to 2.75% generated in 1985-86. In 1993-94, the Sikkim Industrial Development & Investment Corporation earned highest ROI of 11.51% followed by the Sikkim Minning Corporation with 7.35%. Sikkim Mineral Corporation after showing positive ROI in the first two years of the study, recorded negative ROI for 4 years and then turned around to exhibit positive ROI continuously for next three years.

Return On Paid-Up Capital (ROPUC)

The average ROPUC for the SLPEs as a whole came down from 1.15% to 0.44% during the period under reference. This indicates to the excessive interest burden shared by the SLPEs. The Sikkim Jewels Limited recorded 2.55% ROPUC in 1993-94 whereas the other SLPEs showed zero ROPUC.

Return On Net Worth (RONW)

Like ROPUC, only one SLPE i.e., Sikkim Jewels Limited could show return on the net worth since 1989-90. However its RONW fell down from 3.24% to 1.29% during the study period . The Sikkim Industrial Development & Investment Corporation was showing RONW till 1988-89. The aggregate RONW came down from 1.15% to 0.55% during the study period.

Gross Margin to Sales (GMS)

The Sikkim Jewels Limited showed GMS of 23% in 5 years of its operations, The Sikkim Industrial Development & Investment Corporation showed unusually high GMS of 196.00% in 1993-94.

Debt/Equity Ratio (D/E Ratio)

The SLPEs of Sikkim were found out to be low levered firm. Having scope to tap debt finances for any capital expenditure project. In case of Sikkim Jewels Limited, the D/E ratio came down from 0.88 to 0.36 during 1989-90 to 1993-94. Sikkim Industrial Development & Investment Corporation had D/E ratio ranging from 0.83 to 1.31 in various years. Hence it too has to scope of tapping debt finance.

Table 5.22

Sector	*1985-86*	*1986-87*	*1987-88*	*1988-89*	*1989-90*	*1990-91*	*1991-92*	*1992-93*	*1993-94*
Comm	238.28	241.01	228.74	219.33	225.68	224.82	319.23	409.92	692.98
C-P	36.62	39.66	47.90	51.86	52.55	55.87	58.97	57.97	72.12
Prom	0.00	0.00	0.00	0.00	0.00	0.00	0.00	0.00	0.00
Total	274.90	280.67	276.64	271.59	278.23	280.69	378.20	467.89	768.27

Comm: Commercial, C-P: Commercial-cum-Promotional, Prom: Promotional.

Current Ratio

The Sikkim Jewels Limited maintained a moderate liquidity position with a current ratio of a 1:! In all the years of its operation. The Sikkim Industrial Development & Investment Corporation had a high current ratio of 12.20 in 1993-94 compared to 2.41 in 1985-86. The Sikkim Mining Corporation's current ratio remained below or little more than 1 in all but one year of the study period.

Value Added

The value added had increased from Rs. 0.36 crore to Rs. 1.28 crore during the period from 1985-86 to 1993-94.

Tamil Nadu

Introduction

Tamil Nadu did not have any industry, excepting a few textile mills at the dawn of independence. The first state level financial corporation, the Madras Industrial Investment Corporation was incorporated and registered on 26th March, 1949. This Corporation now called the Tamil Nadu Industrial Investment Corporation triggered the development of the engineering and foundry industry which laid the foundation for the automobile industry in Tamil Nadu.

Profile

Out of the 68 SLPEs in Tamil Nadu only 18 enterprises sent the filled-in data sheet. 10 Commercial, 6 Commercial-cum-Promotional and 2 Promotional units form a part of the study.

Total Investment

The investment in the Commercial SLPEs in Tamil Nadu dominated the total investment. It increased from Rs. 238.28

crore in 1985-86 to Rs. 692.98 crore in 1993-94 registering a CARG of 14.3%. The maximum total investment in the Commercial SLPEs of Tamil Nadu was from the Tamil Nadu News Print and Papers Ltd. which increased from Rs. 196.65 crore in 1985-86 to Rs. 333.56 crore in 1993-94. The promotional SLPEs which numbered two did not have any total investment up to 1993-94. The Madras Metropolitan Water Supply and Sewerage Board had an investment of Rs. 3.17 crore. In aggregate the 18 SLPEs registered an increase in total investment from Rs. 274.90 crore in 1985-86 to Rs. 768.27 crore in 1993-94 with a CARG of 13.7%.

Net Worth

In Tamil Nadu out of 10 Commercial SLPEs, 5 had eroded their net worth by 1993-94 and recorded a negative net worth. The Pallavan Transport Corporation Ltd. registered a negative net worth through out the period of the study. However the net worth of 10 Commercial SLPEs was Rs. 16.51 crore in 1985-86 which increased to Rs. 113.39 crore in 1993-94. In aggregate the total net worth which was Rs. 288.94 crore increased to Rs. 151.71 crore between 1985-86 to 1993-94 accounting for a CARG of 23%.

Sales

Ten Commercial SLPEs in Tamil Nadu accounted for the highest sales of the 18 SLPEs under study. The maximum of sales were recorded by Tamil Nadu New Print and Papers Ltd. which increased from Rs. 147.57 crore in 1985-86 to Rs. 204.91 crore in 1993-94. The Pallavan Transport Corporation was recorded with Rs. 67.09 crore and Rs. 114.40 crore in 1985-86 and 1993-94 respectively. The sales 10 Commercial SLPEs accounted for sales worth Rs. 330.64 crore in 1985-86 which increased to Rs. 556.98 crore in 1993-94. The Commercial-cum-Promotional SLPEs accounted for Rs. 41.28 crore in 1985-86 which increased to Rs. 122.43 crore in 1993-94. In aggregate the 18 SLPEs registered a rise in sales from Rs. 371.92 crore in 1985-86 to Rs. 679.41 crore in 1993-94. for the same period with a CARG of 7.82%.

Gross Profit

In Tamil Nadu, out of 18 SLPEs, only 4 of them were earning a negative gross profit. By 1993-94, the gross profit of the 10 commercial units had increased from Rs. 28.51 crore in 1985-86 to Rs. 93.82 crore in 1993-94. The maximum gross profit was earned by the Tamil Nadu News Print and Papers Limited worth Rs. 19.72 crore in 1985-86 and Rs. 67.49 crore in 1993-94. 10 commercial SLPEs registered an increase from Rs. 28.51 crore in 1985-86 to Rs. 93.82 crore in 1993-94 recording a CARG of 16.05%. The Commercial-cum-Promotional SLPEs increAWS the gross profits recorded a minimum increased in gross profit from Rs. 4.22 crore in 1985-86 to Rs. 5.70 crore in 1993-94. In aggregate the gross profit increased from Rs. 35.54 crore in 1985-86 to Rs. 103.76 crore in 1993-94.

Profit After Tax (PAT)

Though the Commercial SLPEs of Tamil Nadu earned negative PAT from 1985-86 to 1988-89, but later they made it up and earned the highest PAT during 1993-94 of Rs. 49.13 crore. The Tamil Nadu News Print and Papers Limited earned the maximum PAT of Rs. 54.05 crore in 1993-94. The Commercial-cum-Promotional SLPEs reccorded a slight declined in PAT from Rs. 2.59 crore in 1985-86 to Rs. 2.30 crore in 1993-94. In aggregate the 18 SLPEs which had a negative PAT up to 1988-89 registered an increase in PAT to Rs. 51.43 crore in 1993-94 registering a CARG of 15.5% between 1989-90 and 1993-94.

Accumulated Losses

The highest accumulated losses were recorded by the Tamil Nadu News Print and Papers Ltd. in 1985-86 of Rs. 49.95 crore but this was eliminated to zero in 1989-90 .

However the maximum accumulated losses of Rs. 91.81 crore were recorded by Pallavan Transport Corporation Ltd. by 1993-94. The Commercial SLPEs as such had the maximum of accumulated losses through out the period under study. The accumulated losses increased from Rs. 94.18 crore in 1985-86 to Rs. 124.79 crore in 1993-94. The accumulate losses of both the Commercial-cum-Promotional and the Promotional SLPEs were comparatively very much lower. In aggregate the accumulated losses of the 18 SLPEs increased from Rs. 110.88 crore in 1985-86 to Rs. 124.93 crore in 1993-94.

Return On Investment (ROI)

The Return on Investment in aggregate for 18 SLPEs was very meager. The promotional SLPEs recorded zero ROI. The Commercial SLPEs which earned ROI of 33.68% in 1985-86 reduced and the Commercial-cum-Promotional SLPEs became 19.45%. The Pallavan Transport Corporation Ltd. recorded a negative ROI throughout the period of study. The Tamil Nadu Forest Plantation Corporation Ltd. recorded the highest ROI of 364.18% in 1985-86 which declined to 43.73% in 1993-94. In aggregate the ROI registereda a decline of from 28.11% to 16.72% between 1985-86 to 1993-94.

Return On Paid-Up Capital (ROPUC)

The Negative ROPUC of 6.55% in 1985-86 in Commercial SLPEs was converted to a positive ROPUC of 21.13% in 1993-94. It was the Pallavan Transport Corporation Ltd. which had a negative ROPUC almost throughout the period under study i.e., 1985-86 to 1993-94. The Tamil Nadu Forest Plantation Corporation Ltd. recorded negative ROPUC from 1988-89 to 1993-94. In aggregate the ROPUC of –3.10% in 1985-86 was converted to a positive ROPUC 10.65% in 1993-94.

Return On Net Worth (RONW)

The RONW which was negative for the 10 Commercial SLPEs i.e, -47% in 1985-86 recoreded an increase to 43.33% by 1993-94. But the Commercial-cum-Promotional SLPEs which earned 22.28% of RONW in 1985-86, saw it declining reduced to 6% in 1993-94. In aggregate, the RONW which was –17.24% in 1985-86 increased to 33.90% in 1993-94.

Gross Margin by Sales (GMS)

The Commercial SLPEs recorded the highest GMS through out the period of study. The GMS recorded for Commercial SLPEs in 1985-86 was 24.09% which declined to 22.16% in 1993-94. The Overseas Manpower Corporation Ltd. registered a highly fluctuating GMS. It started with a GMS at 33.33% in 1985-86 which turned to nil in 1986-87 and next shoot up to 91.67% in 1987-88. The GMS was 5% in 1993-94 for this enterprise. The Commercial-cum-Promotional SLPEs showed a very slight increase in GMS from 8.72% in 1985-86 to 9.00% in 1993-94. In aggregate, the GMS which was 22.38% in 1985-86 declined to 20.17% in 1993-94.

Debt-Equity Ratio (D/E Ratio)

10 Commercial SLPEs of Tamil Nadu increased their D/E ratio from 1.61 in 1985-86 to 2.41 in 1993-94, whereas the 2 Promotional SLPEs showed a downward trend from 3.74 in 1985-86 to 2.04 in 1993-94. In aggregate, the debt-equity ratio was 1.78 in 1985-86 which increased to 2.12 in 1993-94. In 1993-94, the maximum D/E ratio of 29.97 was recorded by the Tamil Nadu Power Finance and Infrastructure Development.

Current Ratio

The Tamil Nadu SLPEs recorded 1.32 and 2.32 current ratio between 1985-86 to 1993-94. The Tamil Nadu Power

Table 5.23

Sector	*1985-86*	*1986-87*	*1987-88*	*1988-89*	*1989-90*	*1990-91*	*1991-92*	*1992-93*	*1993-94*
Comm	0.00	0.00	0.00	0.00	0.00	0.00	0.00	0.00	0.00
C-P	1.74	2.51	3.36	4.93	5.04	6.57	7.14	7.63	8.56
Prom	0.00	0.00	0.00	0.00	0.00	0.00	0.00	0.00	0.00
Total	1.74	2.51	3.36	4.93	5.04	6.57	7.14	7.63	8.56

Comm: Commercial, C-P: Commercial-cum-Promotional, Prom: Promotional.

Finance and Infrasturcture Developemnt recorded the highest current ratio of 106.82 in 1991-92 which declined to 37.26 by 1993-94.

Value Added

The value added has been increasing constantly over the period under study. The increase had been about three fold starting from Rs. 126 crore in 1985-86 to Rs. 365 crore in 1993-94. Each category was showing a continuous increase in the total value added during the period of study. Among the commercial enterpriese, The Pallavan Transport Corporation Limted was constantly contributing more to the total value added. During 1985-86, the total value added was Rs. 37 crore which increased to Rs. 75 crore in 1993-94.

Tripura

Introduction

The political ideology in Tripura has mainly been responsible for the growth and development of the SLPEs in terms of investment and number. Tripura has a locational disadvantages and the underdeveloped infrastructure has thwarted the attempts of private sector entrepreneurs to set up industries in the state. However, the state is characterised by two features conducive to growth of industry viz., internal demand and resources. This prompted the state government to set up SLPEs in an increasing number.

Profile

There are 10 SLPEs in the State of Tripura comprising 4 Commercial and 3 Commercial-cum-Promotional and 3 Promotional category enerprise to SLPEs, Out of them, only 2 SLPEs namely Tripura Industrial Development Corporation Limited and Tripura Tea Development Corporaiton Limited form a part of this study. No other SLPE has responded to our data sheets sent.

Total Investment

The aggregate investment showed a stupendous growth (36% CARG) during the study period. It went up from Rs. 2.61 crore to Rs. 31.70 during 1985-86 to 1993-94. Tripura Industrial Development Corporation shared more than 70% of the total investment in 1993-94. It had a CARG of 50% compared to 22% in the case of the Tripura Tea Development Corporation.

Net Worth

The two SLPEs under study had a total net worth amounting Rs. 16.48 crore in 1993-94, which grew at 27.29% CARG from Rs. 2.39 crore in 1985-86. The growth in net worth was mainly accounted by infusion of net equity capital. Both the SLPEs had almost same net worth during the various years under study.

Sales

The two SLPEs achieved a total sales of Rs. 2.04 crore in 1993-94 compared to Rs. 0.03 crore in 1985-86. Normally Tripura Tea Development Corporation showed higher sales compared to Tripura Industrial Development Corporation in most of the years. In 1993-94 Tripura Industrial Development Corporation had a slaes of Rs. 0.68 crore compared to Rs. 1.36 crore of the Tripura Tea Development Corporation.

Gross Profit

The two SLPEs of Tripura showed gross loss in aggregate in all but one year out of 9 years under study. The gross loss went up from Rs. 0.05 crore in 1985-86 to 0.70 crore in 1993-94. The Tripura Tea Development Corporation made both gross profts and gross loss during the study period. Whereas the Tripura Tea Development Corporation is continuously incurred gross losses during the period of the study.

Profit After Tax (PAT)

The SLPEs of Tripura incurred net loss of Rs. 71.97 lakh in 1993-94 as compared to Rs. 2.58 lakh in 1985-86. The major contributor to such loss making was the Tripura Industrial Development Corporation. In 1993-94 its net loss went up to Rs. 70.69 lakh from Rs. 6.97 lakh incurred during the previous year. The Tripura Tea Development Corporation showed a declining trend in the net loss incurred in the same period.

Accumulated Losses

The Tripura Industrial Development Corporation contributed more than 9.55% of the total accumulated losses of Rs. 0.96 crore in 1993-94. The total accumulated loss stood at Rs. 0.05 crore at the end of 1985-86.

Return On Investment (ROI)

This was negative for commercial enteprises althrough whereas it had a mixed trend in the case of the Commercial-cum-Promotional enterprises. The promotional enterprises were in the mould of commercial enterprises.

Return On Paid-Up Capital (ROPUC)

The Tripura enterprises incurred losses althrough. Hence the return on equity wasnegative in case of Commercial & Commercial-cum-Promotional and promotional enterprises.

Return On Net Worth (RONW)

As net profit was negative throughout the period of study, the return on net worth in terms of percentage was also negative althrough.

Gross Margin to Sales (GMS)

The Gross Margin divided by sales was althrough

Table 5.24

Sector	*1985-86*	*1986-87*	*1987-88*	*1988-89*	*1989-90*	*1990-91*	*1991-92*	*1992-93*	*199-94*
Comm	147.74	147.85	100.63	122.04	98.81	81.13	85.43	51.37	-2.52
C-P	179.62	209.86	257.98	312.23	369.75	421.79	476.91	505.52	553.74
Prom	36.54	40.19	47.86	76.00	71.55	74.15	80.72	86.88	92.85
Total	363.90	397.90	406.47	510.35	540.11	577.07	643.06	643.77	643.27

Comm: Commercial, C-P: Commercial-cum-Promotional, Prom: Promotional.

negative for the commercial and promotional enterprises and also for the commercial-cum-promotional for th year 1985-86, 1986-87. However, it was positive during 1987-88 and 1993-94.

Debe Equity Ratio (D/E Ratio)

The coverage of total long term of loans by equity was inadequate. The Commercial, Commercial-cum-Promotional and Promotional enterprises.

Current Ratio

Theoretically the SLPEs of Tripura were found to have high liquidity. In fact, the Tripura Industrial Development Corporation had an unusual high current ratio of 580:1 in 1993-94. This was possible due to sudden fall in its current liabilities from Rs. 1.97 lakh in 1985-86 to Rs. 3.91 lakh in 1993-94.

Value Added

Value added constituted Rs. 0.03 crore in 1985-86 and increased to Rs. 0.86 crore in 1990-91 and it declined to Rs. 0.84 crore in 1991-92 and further came down to Rs. 0.79 crore in 1993-94.

Uttar Pradesh

Introduction

U.P. is the most populated state in India. A rapid elimination of Poverty in this state as well as a higher rate of growth in its State gross domestic product would help transform rapidly the entire economic scene of the country. The SLPEs have been selected as an instruments of public policy in this state to achieve these ends.

Profile

Uttar Pradesh had a total of 74 SLPEs out of which 24 are Commercial, 22 Commercial-cum-Promotional and 28 were Promotional units. Only 25 SLPEs had submitted the data required.

Total Investment

In Uttar Pradesh the total Investment in the Commercial-cum-Promotional SLPEs was the maximum throughout the period under study. It was Rs. 179.62 came in 1985-86 increasing to Rs. 553.74 crore in 1993-94. In the category of the Commercial SLPEs the Uttar Pradesh State Cement Corporation Ltd. claimed the highest total investment of Rs. 75.73 crore in 1985-86.

The promotional SLPEs registered an increase in the total investment from Rs. 36.54 crore in 1985-86 to Rs. 92.05 crore in 1993-94. By 1993-94, the U.P. Scheduled Castes Finance and Development Corporation claimed the highest total investment of Rs. 48.22 crore among the promotional units. In aggregate the total investment for the 25 SLPEs in U.P. stood at Rs. 363.90 crore in 1985-86 which increased to Rs. 643.27 crore in 1993-94 recording a CARG of 7.38%.

Net Worth

The net worth of the SLPEs in U.P. showed an upward trend. Only 2 out of the 25 SLPEs eroded their net worth by 1993-94. The U.P. State Cement Corporation Ltd. and the U.P. State Food and Essential Commodities Corporation Ltd. were the two SLPEs which eroded their net worth. Among these the U.P. State Cement Corporation Ltd. accounted for the highest negative networth with Rs. -251.97 crore which forced the aggregate Commercial SLPEs net worth to be negative in 1993-94 i.e., Rs. -85.20. The Commercial and Promotional units recorded the highest net worth of Rs. 139.73 crore in 1993-94. In aggregate the net worth reduced from Rs. 186.53 crore in 1985-86 to Rs. 132.07 crore in 1993-94.

Sales

Out of the 25 SLPEs the sales by the U.P. State Food and Essential Commodities Corporation Ltd. were the maximum i.e, Rs. 246.59 crore in 1993-94. The Commercial-cum-Promotional SLPEs recorded the highest sales through out the period under study. The 8 Commercial-cum-Promotional units had sales worth Rs. 103.55 crore in 1985-86 which increased to Rs. 409.32 crore in 1993-94. The sales of the U.P. State Cement Corporation Ltd. was the maximum among the Commercial SLPEs in 1993-94 i.e., Rs. 107.03 crore. In aggregate the sales of the 25 SLPEs increased from Rs. 250.35 crore to Rs. 714.11 crore recording a CARG of 14%.

Gross Profit

The Commercial SLPEs had a positive gross profit only up to 1986-87 after which in aggregate the 8 Commercial SLPEs recorded a negative gross profit till 1993-94. The highest gross profit was recorded by the 8 Commercial-cum-Promotional units i.e., Rs 68.13 crore in 1993-94. In aggregatethe 25 SLPEs accounted for a gross profit of Rs. 22.24 crore in 1985-86 which increased slightly to Rs. 37.62 crore in 1993-94 registering a CARG of 6.8%.

Profit After Tax (PAT)

The PAT of the 8 commercial SLPEs in U.P. was negative from 1986-87 to 1993-94. The U.P. State Cement Corp. Ltd. had a negative PAT through out the period under study. It accounted for a PAT of Rs. 60.36 crore in 1993-94. The other Commercial units which had a negative PAT in 1993-94 were the U.P. State Warehousing Corporation and U.P. Development Systems Corporation Ltd.. The PAT of the Commercial-cum-Promotional units kept fluctuating between and negative balances. In 1985-86 the PAT of the 8 Commercial-cum-Promotional units was Rs. 0.59 crore which increased to Rs. 6.24 crore in 1993-94. In aggregate the PAT was positive only in 1985-86 after that it turned negative and by 1993-94 it turned worth Rs. 51.03 crore.

Accumulated Losses

The accumulated losses of 8 commercial SLPEs dominated the scenario throughout the period under study. It increased from Rs. 51.47 crore in 1985-86 to Rs. 375.70 crore in 1993-94. The main loss making units including the 8 was the U.P. State Cement Corporation Ltd. which accounted for Rs. 319.81 crore of accumulated losses out of the Rs. 375.70 crore incurred in 1993-94. The Commercial-cum-Promotional SLPEs increased their accumulated losses from Rs. 2.44 crore in 1985-86 to Rs. 27.21 crore in 1993-94. There was a moderate increase in accumulated losses of the promotional units from Rs. 1.79 crore in 1985-86 to Rs. 2.60 crore in 1993-94. In aggregate the accumulated losses of the 25 SLEs were Rs. 55.70 crore in 1985-86 which increased to Rs. 405.59 crore in 1993-94.

Return On Investment (ROI)

The Return on Investment of the 8 commercial SLPEs increased from 11.43% to 43.78% between 1985-86 and 1993-94. The ROI for these 8 SLPEs was negative for three years i.e, 1988-89, 1989-90 and 1991-92. The ROI of the 8 Commercial-cum-Promotional SLPEs declined from 16.24% in 1985-86 to 15% in 1993-94. In 1993-94 the U.P. State Food and Essential Commodities Corporation Ltd. recorded a 1353.3% of ROI. The ROI of promotional units also decreased from 3.42% in 1985-86 to 0.80% in 1993-94. In aggregate the ROI of the 25 SLPEs which was 12.92% in 1985-86 declined to 9.78% in 1993-94.

Return On Paid-Up Capital (ROPUC)

The ROPUC of the 8 Commercial SLPEs was negative from 1986-87 to 1993-94. This was mainly because the U.P.State Cement Corporation Ltd. recorded a high negative ROPUC of 0.11% in 1985-86 which became –21.60% in 1993-94. The Commercial-cum-Promotional SLPEs ROPUC increased from 0.83% in 1985-86 to 4.51% in 1993-94 In aggregate, the 25 SLPEs had negative ROPUC from 1986-87 to 1993-94. It was 0.61% in 1985-86 which rose to –10.12% in 1993-94.

Return On Net Worth (RONW)

Eight Commercial SLPEs recorded a 66.58% of RONW in 1993-94 which is the maximum among the three categories of SLPEs in 1993-94. Though the Commercial SLPEs recorded a negative RONW in 1985-86 i.e., -1.40%, in RONW increased to 66.58% in 1993-94. The RONW Commercial-cum-Promotional units increased from 1.22% in 1985-86 to 4.23% in 1993-94. In aggregate the RONW was negative through out the period of study except in 1985-86.

Gross Margin to Sales (GMS)

The Commercial SLPEs had a positive GMS for the first three years of the study but later recorded a negative GMS. The GMS which was 14.52% in 1985-86 turned –10.05% in 1993-94. The Commercial-cum-Promotional SLPEs in U.P. recorded a decline from 20.43% in 1985-86 to 4.12% in 1993-94. The U.P. Seeds and Tarai Development Corporation Ltd., a Commercial-cum-Promotional SLPE recorded the highest GMS from 1985-86 to 1992-93 i.e., 108.30% to 108.14%. but in 1993-94 it declined drastically to 9.15% in 1993-94. The promotional SLPEs also showeed a decline in GMS from 5.17% in 1985-86 to 1.51% in 1993-94. In aggregate the 25 SLPEs registered a decline in GMS from 16.01% in 1985-86 to –0.91% in 1993-94.

Table 5.25

Sector	*1985-86*	*1986-87*	*1987-88*	*1988-89*	*1989-90*	*1990-91*	*1991-92*	*1992-93*	*1993-94*
Comm	-26.85	-4.83	-1.68	-0.04	2.17	5.75	6.24	2.80	-15.48
C-P	173.73	211.42	247.73	293.35	342.54	408.57	456.38	490.69	503.78
Prom	0.00	0.00	0.00	0.00	0.00	0.00	0.00	0.00	0.00
Total	146.88	206.59	246.05	293.31	344.71	414.32	462.62	493.49	488.30

Comm: Commercial, C-P: Commercial-cum-Promotional, Prom: Promotional.

Debt-Equity Ratio

The D/E ratio of the 8 Commercial SLPEs remained almost constant over the period under study as it was 0.59 in 1985-86 and 0.60 in 1993-94. For the Commercial-cum-Promotional SLPEs the D/E ratio which was 1.92 in 1985-86 incurred to 3.13 in 1993-94. The U.P Pashudhan Udyog Nigam Ltd. recorded a declined D/E ratio from 1985-86 to 1989-90. The 9 promotional SLPEs also registered a decrease in D/E ratio from 0.79 in 1985-86 to 0.52 in 1993-94. In aggregate, the 25 SLPEs registered an increase in D/E ratio from 0.97 in 1985-86 to 1.35 in 1993-94.

Current Ratio

The Commercial-cum-Promotional SLPEs registered the highest Current ratio of 5.24 in 1985-86 which declined to 4.07 in 1993-94. The U.P. (Paschim) Ganna Beej Evam Vijas Nigam Ltd. registered a 219.25:1 current ratio in 1993-94.

Value Added

The value added registered many fluctuations. It was Rs. 52 crore during 1985-86. During 1986-87, it was Rs. 49 crore. In the following year it went up to Rs. 55 crore. During 1988-89, it declined to Rs. 47 crore. Again from the year 1989-90 value added demonstrate has shown an increasing trend and touched to Rs. 115 crore during 1993-94. Among all the enterprises, the maximum value was added by the Commercial-cum-Promotional enterprises.

West Bengal

Introduction

West Bengal has been a front line State in terms of industrial development. In recent years, the state of economic growth of the state has suffered a set back. It is alleged that the SLPEs accounting for a good deal of investment there in contributed sustantially to this downturn. West Bengal has the distinction of having the third largest number of the SLPEs. The SLPEs in the State are the planned era phenomenon. The government here have all along been in favour of achieving aims of public policy through these enterprises.

Profile

The SLPEs in West Bengal numbered 37 out of which 29 were Commercial, 8 Commercial-cum-Promotional and no promotional unit. The response has been received from 22 SLPEs only out of which 15 were Commercial and 7 were Commercial-cum-Promotional enterprises.

Total Investment

Out of the 15 Commercial SLPEs, 6 SLPEs had a negative total investment in 1993-94. Out of the 6 SLPEs, 3 of them had negative investment through out the period under study. The three units were, West Bengal Sugar Industries Development Corporation Ltd., Durgapur Chemicals Ltd., West Bengal Ceramic Development Corporation Ltd. The Kalyani Spinning Mills Ltd. accounted for a negative total investment from 1985-86 to 1990-91. In aggregate, the 15 Commercial SLPEs had a negative total capital employed of Rs. -26.85 crore in 1985-86 which became a positive sum of Rs. 2.1 crore in 1989-90. In aggregate, 22 SLPEs saw their total investment increasing from Rs. 146.88 crore in 1985-86 to Rs. 430.30 crore in 1993-94 registering a CARG of 16.2%.

Net Worth

Out of the 15 Commercial SLPEs in West Bengal 7 of them had eroded their net worth. The Greater Calcutta Gas Supply Corporation Ltd. and Lily Biscuit Company Private Ltd. also did not have their net worth. Amongst the Commercial SLPEs which eroded their net worth by 1993-

94, 4 of them had negative net worth through out the period under study. The Commercial SLPEs in aggregate accounted for net worth of Rs. -99.95 crore in 1985-86 which increased to Rs. -235.17 crore in 1993-94. The Commercial-cum-Promotional units has net worth of Rs. 46.50 crore in 1985-86 which increased to Rs. 67.28 crore in 1993-94. In aggregate the 22 SLPEs had net worth of Rs. 53.45 crore in 1985-86 which declined to Rs. -167.81 crore in 1993-94.

Sales

The WEBEL Nicco Electronics Ltd. accounted for the maximum of sales of Rs. 4.81 crore in 1985-86 and remained in the top position among the Commercial SLPEs in West Bengal up to 1989-90 with a turnover of Rs. 10.63 crore. But in 1990-91, The Kalyani Spinning Mills occupied the top position with Rs. 11.24 crore of sales which increased to Rs. 18.38 crore in 1993-94. In aggregate the commercial SLPEs accounted for Rs. 23.15 crore of sales in 1985-86 which increased to Rs. 70.96 crore in 1993-94. Amongst the commercial-cum-promotional units the West Bengal Forest Development Corporaiton Ltd. which recorded the maximum sales in 1985-86 of Rs. 7.77 crore increased the sales gradually to Rs. 12.29 crore in 1993-94 whereas the West Bengal Handloom and Powerloom Development Corporation Ltd. which occupied the 2nd position in 1985-86 with sales worth Rs. 7.31 crore increased to its turnover Rs. 22.76 crore in 1993-94. In aggregate the sales of the Commercial and Promotional SLPEs increased from Rs. 25.85 crore in 1985-86 to Rs. 56.35 crore in 1993-94. In aggregate, 22 SLPEs registered an increase in sales from Rs. 49 crore in 1985-86 to Rs. 127.31 crore with a CARG of 12.68%.

Gross Profit

The Gross Profit of the 15 Commercial SLPEs was negative throughout the period under study. It was Rs. -

10.38 crore in 1985-86 and Rs. -11.46 crore in 1993-94. In the Commercial-cum-Promotional SLPEs, the West Bengal Tourism Development Corporation Ltd. recorded a negative gross profit of Rs. –0.24 crore in 1985-86. The negative trend of the unit continued up to 1991-92 after which the gross profit became positive. It was Rs. 0.18 crore in 1993-94. The West Bengal Industrial Development Corporation Ltd. recorded a negative gross profit from 1986-87 to 1993-94. In aggregate the 7 Commercial-cum-Promotional SLPEs registered an increase in gross profit from Rs. 8.94 crore in 1985-86 to Rs. 23.99 crore in 1993-94 with a CARG of 13.13%. Taken as a whole, the 22 SLPEs accounted for negative gross profit in 1985-86 of Rs. 1.44 crore which declined to Rs-0.41 crore in 1992-93. In 1993-94 the gross profit of 22 SLPEs was positive Rs. 12.53 crore.

Profit After Tax (PAT)

The PAT of the 15 Commercial SLPEs was negative from 1985-86 to 1993-94. It was Rs. -14.51 crore in 1985-86 and Rs. -27.50 crore in 1993-94. Out of the 15 SLPEs, 12 of had negative or nil PAT in 1993-94. The Lily Biscuit Company Ltd., Durgapur Chemicals Ltd. and Kalyani Spinning Mills Ltd. were the 3 SLPEs which earned negative PAT throughout the period under study. The Commercial-cum-Promotional SLPEs, in aggregate had Rs. 2.58 crore of PAT in 1985-86 which increased to Rs. 7.73 crore in 1993-94 though for a period between 1988-89 and 1992-93, 7 SLPEs earned negative PAT. In aggregate the 22 SLPEs had a negative PAT throughout Rs. 11.93 crore in 1985-86 and Rs. 19.77 crore in 1993-94.

Accumulated Losses

The Commercial SLPEs of West Bengal accounted for the highest accumulated losses through out the period under study. The accumulated losses which amounted to Rs. 118.79 crore in 1985-86 increased to Rs. 339.27 crore in

1993-94. The Durgapur Chemicals Ltd. accounted for the maximum accumulated losses from 1985-86 which increased to Rs. 128.29 crore in 1993-94. In the Commercial-cum-Promotional SLPEs the accumulated losses accounted to Rs. 2.21 crore in 1985-86 which increased to Rs. 64.75 crore in 1993-94 the maximum accumulated losses were recorded by the West Bengal Industrial Development Corporation through out the period under study. The losses which were Rs. 0.23 crore in 1985-86 increased to Rs. 33.65 crore in 1993-94. In aggregate the 22 SLPEs recorded accumulated losses of Rs. 121 crore in 1995-96 which increased to Rs. 404.02 crore in 1993-94.

Return On Investment (ROI)

The ROI of 15 Commercial SLPEs was a positive 134.65% in 1985-86 which decreased to a –79.36% in 1993-94. This was mainly because 6 of the 15 SLPEs were having negative ROI by 1993-94. The Commercial-cum-Promotional SLPEs registered positive ROI through out the period under study of the 9.99% in 1985-86 and 14.32% in 1993-94. In aggregate, the 22 SLPEs registered a negative ROI of –0.80% in 1985-86 and –0.95% in 1991-92. However, during 1993-94, registered a positive ROI of 0.28% and 5.36% respectively.

Return On Paid-Up Capital (ROPUC)

Twelve out of the 15 Commercial SLPEs had earned negative a ROPUC by 1993-94. The 15 units in aggregate earned negative ROPUC of –142.9% in 1985-86 which became –128.3% in 1993-94. The Durgapur Chemicals Ltd. and Kalyani Spinning Mills Ltd. recorded negative ROPUC through out the period under study. The Commercial and Promotional SLPEs registered a positive ROPUC of 5.14% in 1985-86 which became –8.84% in 1988-89 which continued as negative up to 1992-93 and became a positive of 5.57% in 1993-94. In aggregate the ROPUC was negative from 1985-86 to 1993-94. It was –18.48% in 1985-86 and –11.13% in 1993-94.

Return On Net Worth (RONW)

Fifteen Commercial SLPEs recorded a negative RONW during 1985-86. The aggregate RONW of the 15 SLPEs was –13.63% in 1985-86 which increased to –9.10% in '93-94. 7 SLPEs under the Commercial and Promotional category registered on ROI 5.55% in 1985-86 which turned –11.47% in 1988-89 and 11.49% in 1993-94. In aggregate, the 22 SLPEs registered a negative RONW of –20.65% in 1985-86 and –8.15% in 1993-94.

Gross Margin to Sales (GMS)

The GMS was negative for the 15 Commercial SLPEs through out the period under study, 7 SLPEs in Commercial-cum-Promotional category registered a positive GMS only in 1985-86. The GMS of the Commercial SLPEs was –39.78% in 1985-86 which further declined –20.53% in 1993-94. In aggregate, the 22 SLPEs earnd a negative GMS through out i.e., -13.65% in 1985-86 and –12.25% in 1993-94.

Debt-Equity Ratio (D/E Ratio)

The D/E raito of the 15 Commercial SLPEs increased from 9.52 in 1985-86 to 13.72 in 1993-94. The Commercial-cum-Promotional SLPE registered a decline in D/E ratio from 2.69 in 1985-86 to 2.46 in 1993-94. In aggregate the D/E ratio increased marginally from 3.78 in 1985-86 to 3.86 in 1993-94. The Kalyani Spinning Mills Ltd which accounted for highest D/e ratio in 1985-86 with 24.19 continued the same trend of highest D/E ratio up to 1991-92 after which the National Iron and Steel Company Ltd took over and in 1993-94 with a D/E ratio of 24.75.

Current Ratio

In aggregate, the SLPEs in West Bengal recorded a Current raito between 1.29 and 1.60 under the period of study. The Commercial SLPEs had minimum current ratio of 0.56 in 1985-86 and 0.93 in 1993-94. The Commercial-cum-Promotional units registered a current ratio of 2.20 in 1985-86 which declined to 1.50 in 1993-94.

Value Added

The value added increased from Rs.15.86 crore in 1985-86 to Rs. 81.31 crore in 1993-94. Among The Commercial-cum-Promotional enterprises West Bengal Finance Corporation's contribution to value added was the maximum.

CHAPTER 6

CAPOOR COMMITTEE REPORT

CHAPTER 1

APPOINTMENT

1.1 The conference of Chief Secretaries held in New Delhi in May 1976 discussed certain measures for implementing the quality of public administration in the various sectors of Government activity in the States. The conference recognised that the management of public enterprises has come to be an important area of Government responsibility in the states, as in the centre. This sector had many special features.

1.2 While it was outside the main system the Government administration, it was subject to close control and guidance of the State. It had become a significant instrument for achieving economic and social objectives of the stage. The range, complexity and size of operations as well as inter-face with other sectors of the economy made managemetn of the sector a challenging task.

1.3 Being relatively recent, the State Governments' experience of functioning in these non-traditional areas are limited. The demands of maangement of public sector were varied and unusual, making the mechanics of its administration complicated.

1.4 The sector has accounted for an increasing share of the scarce resources of the State in men, material and money. There was a growing concern at the lack of adequate return from these investment, which jeopardised the State and national plans for economic development. The conference of Chief Secretaries, therefore, recognised that any small improvement in the functioning of this sector would mean a greater capacity for the State Governments to change the economic and social conditions of the people.

1.5 The views of the conference of Chief Secretaires were taken up for further consideraiton by the conference of State Secretaries of Personnel and Administrative Reforms which met in december 1976. A sub-Group was set uup to study the situation and report to the conference. On receiving the Group's reprot, the conference decided that the nature of the problems entrusted for study to the Group called for deeper examination before reliable conclusions and practical recommendations could be made. Accordingly, the conference decided that the Group should function as a Standing Group to study the subject in depth and give its recommendations:

1.6 The Standing Group was set up in June 1977 with the following composition:-

1. Shri H.K.L. Capoor —Chairman
   Chief Secretary to the Government of Gujarat

2. Shri R.N. Maldipur, —Member
   Director
   Indian Institute of Publi Administration,
   New Delhi

3. Shri P.L. Sivaram, —Member
   Secretary,
   Administrative Reforms,
   Government of Andhra Pradesh, Hyderabad.
   (now Zonal Manager, Food Corporation of India)

4. Shri V.T. Chari, —Member
Secretary,
(General administration Deptt),
Bombay
(now Vice-Chairman, Maharashtra State Road Trnasport Corp.)

5. Shri S.M.Patankar, —Member
Adviser (Finance),
Bureau of Public Enterprises,
Ministry of Finance
New Delhi

6. Shri Manik Wadhwani, —Member
Secretary,
Department of Personnel & Director General,
Bureau of State Enterprises,
Government of Uttar Pradesh,
Lucknow.

7. Shri K.C. Sharma, —Member
Director (now Joint Secretary),
Department of Personnel & Administrative Reforms,
Government of India,
New Delhi

8. Shri A. Bhattacharjya, —Member
Secreatry,
Department of Public Enterprises
Government of Assam, Dispur
(now Joint Secretary, Union Public Service Commission)

9. Shri A.P. Saxena, —Member
Consultant,
Indian Institute of Public Administration,
New Delhi

10. Shri C.R.Venkataraman, —Member
Secretary of Personnel and Administrative
Reforms,
Government of Bihar,
Patna

11. Shri Radhakanta Nayak, —Member
Secretary,
Administrative Reforms,
Government of Orissa,
Bhubaneswar.

12. Shri T.M.C.Menon, —Convener
Joint Director,
Bureau of Public Enterprises,
Ministry of Finance.
New Delhi

1.7 A copy of the Government order constituting the Group is given as Appendix I.

1.8 S/Shri C.R. Venkataraman, Radhakanta Nayak and A.P. Saxena could not participate in the work of the Group.

1.9 The Group had the benefit of consultations with Shri G.C. Baveja, till recently Director-General, Bureau of Public Enterprises and Additional Secretary to the Government of India in the Ministry of Finance Shri B.C. Mathur, Additional Secretary to the Government of India in the department of Personnel and Administrative Reforms participated closely with the work of the Group and also joined in the visits to the State of Gujarat and Uttar Pradesh.

Terms and References

1.10 It was recognised that the area to be covered was extensive. Not only was the gamut of public sector operations wide-ranging but their geographical spread as well as technological and environmental differences were so great that it was impractical to do justice to the job except by adopting a selective approach.

1.11 The Group was, therefore, to examine crucial areas of publci sector managemnet with a view to recommending measures for imporoving policies, practices and organisations. While taking into account the special problems of the different States, it was to consider praticularly the need for and functions of a nodal organisation, scope for improvements in top management prolices, evaluation of performance and relationship with supervisory bodies.

Method of Enquiry

1.12 A serious handicpa faced by the Group was the alck of information on many improtant aspects of public sector managmenet in the States. This gap data had to be made up first.

1.13 A questionnaire was accordingly issued to the State Governments seeking information on the following matters:-

(a) Nodal Organisation:
(b) Delegation of Powers:
(c) Forms of Organisation:
(d) Relationship with Government and Legilature
(e) Personnel Management Policy:
(f) Management Information System:
(g) Annual Reporting to Government and Legislature; and
(h) Investment Appraisal.

1.14 The questionnaire is reproduced as Appendix II.

1.15 After considering the factual information obtained through replies to the questionnaire, the Group felt that it would be necessary to strengthen the data base by seeking the views of senior persons with considerable experience of the working of public sector in the States. A supplementary questionnaire was sent for this purposoe. This is given as Appendix III. Simultaneously, information was gathered on investment and performance of individual public enterprises in the States during the preceding three years.

1.16 The Group also visited selected States for discussions with Chief Executives and top management personnel of the public enteprises, the Chief Secretaries and Secretaries to Government dealing with public enterprises, in order to have the benefit of their experience and insights into the peculiar problems of public sector mangement in different States.

1.17 The Group collectively visited the States of Karnataka, Gujarat, Uttar Pradesh, Assam and Meghalaya. To obtain a wider coverage, the Group broke into smaller teams and visited Maharashtra, Orissa and Tamil Nadu. The persons met and the organisation visited are listed in Appendix IV.

CHAPTER 2

THE ROLE AND GROWTH OF PUBLIC SECTOR

2.1 Introduction

The history of public enteprises everywhere began with the utilities. The generation and distribution of electricity, provision of road and other modes of transmission were generally the first attempts of Government outside its traditional law and order activities. Its intervention to promote economic development and achieving other national objectives the public sector was assigned an improtant place. The utilities wer floowed by insitutions for providing infra-structure facilities for the development of industry and agriculture. Financial institutions, industrial estates, corporations for promotiong the production and marketing of agricultural produce were the main directions in the Government's activities expanded. More recent direct participation by Government in industrial and commercial activities, which were hitherto considered to be the domain of private entrepreneurial effort, increased.

2.2 Main Objectives

Organisations have to interpret their roles and aims to determine the directions of their activities. In the case of public enteprises the primary responsibility for this vests with Government whos etu up the enterprises. There is no doubt that the objectives and role of organisations were considered before they were set up, but unfortunately, very fote, these considerations do not come out in precise and clear terms so as to provide an aid to Management and subsequent evaluation.

In the case of publci enterprises economic and social development is perhaps the single most important purpose, for which they were established. These enterprises were expected to encourage industrialisation, redress regional imbalances, exploit local resources generate employment, develop technical manpower etc.

In quite a few cases, Government activities were hived off to public enteprises. This was done, mostly, to take advantage of financial faciltiies which would not have been otherwise available. Under the present system, financial institutions do not lend to departmental undertkaings. In many States, therefore, quite a few departmental activities were transferred to publci sector organisations in order to take advantage of institutional finance. This is a special feature of the public enterprises system in the States. Unlike the Central Government enterprises, the financing of the State Government enterprises is done to a large extent, both in terms of equity and loan, through institutional funds.

Public enterprises have also been set up to achieve fiscal, monetary and economic objectives of the Government. Control inflation, equitable distribution of scare commodities, mopping up to monopoly profits and raising of revenues have provided some of the justification for the setting-up of many public enterprises.

It is also true that the common belief that for purposes of efficiency and effectiveness, the corporate form of organisation was mot suitable has led Govenrments to adopt this form for many of their new activities.

In recent times, a striking feature has been the use of the public sector to develop backward regions and weaker sections of society. This objective has induced many States particularly, the Northern States such as Uttar Pradesh, Madhya Pradesh, Bihar and Assam to establish corporations for promotional of the interest of Scheduled Castes and Scheduled Tribes development of hill areas etc.

2.3 Limitations of Data

The Standing Group was faced with inadequate data on many important matters of public sector management in the State.s the Group covered this gap to a considerable extent by direct correspondance with the State Governments. Substantial information was obtained in regard to the names of enterprises, the investments made in them, their performance etc., from the State Governments. Other sources like the Central Electricity Authority (for information on Electricity Boards), the Ministry of Labour (for data on employment) etc., were also tapped. The information covered in respect of enterprises set up as departmental undertakings, statutory corporations and companues registered under the Companies Act is quite good. There are however some gaps even here. In some of thes organisations the financial accounts were not up-to-date. The arrears were even as much as three to four years. In respect of co-operatives and companies set up by State Governments as joint ventures with private/Central public sector organisations also, the coverage of information is meagre. Strictly, only co-operatives which have industrial and commercial activities would come within the purview of the Standing Group's work. It was difficult to get precise information in regard to these co-operatives. Similarly, quite a few States have established companies jointly with private sector organisation and in some cases with Central Government companies. Mainly, these have been under the aegis of the Industrial Development Corporaitons or the Industrial Investment Corporations. Participation of the State Governments in these ventures vary both financially and managerially. The growing importance of these companies in some States, particularly in Gujarat, is signifcant. In terms of their managerial requirements and relationship with Government they are perhaqps more remote from State influence than the other publci sector organisations.

2.4 An Overview of Performance

2.4.1 According to the replies received from the 17 major State governments, there are 588 enterprises (including Electricity Boards) in existence. However, data on investment and turnover were available only in respect of 545 of these enterprieses. Information in respect of each enterprise in the state is given in Appendix VI. These 545 enterprises acounted for an investment of Rs. 9575.92 crores as on 31.3.1977. state-wise investment, turover and employment in these enterprises were as follows:-

2.4.2 The investment figures as on 31-3-1977 are, unfortunately, not related to the same year as turnover which is for the year 1975-76. Some allowance has to be made for this while studying the statement.

2.4.3 What stands out as most significant is the low turnover compared to investment in th epublic enterprises in the States. Against an aggregate investment of Rs. 9600 croes the turnover was only Rs.3000 crores giving a capital/ turnover ratio of 3.2:1. In the Central Public Sector for aunit of investment, the turnover amounted to 1:1.31. Even the Central companies ratio is unfavourable as compared to the private sector. There are of course, several reasons for the low capital turnover ratio in the States. The price of products and services particularly Electricity and Transportation (which account for the bulk of investment) might contain a high element of subsidy. There are also many enterprises which have been set up for promotional purposes like those for developing backward areas and backward sections of society where turnover figures are not valid. Some of the investments may be new and yet to yield their returns. Even so, the position is disquieting.

2.4.4 It is diffiuclt to make inter-firm comparisons. This difficulty is compounded in the case of public enterprises operating in the States. Their diverse objectives and economic and other environmental constraints add to the usual problems of inter-industry comparisons. The social obligations, pricing policies, historical features and the characteristics of the industry influence performance as much as managerial competence.

2.4.5 However, for the Purposes of comparing the performance of these companies the financial results of their operations in terms of profit/loss during the last three years have been examined. The overall position regarding the number of companies makinmg profits and incurring losses each year would give a general idea of the financial health of these enterprises in the different States though this need not necessarily reflect the quality of management. The financial results may also be affected by government subventions which will not be relfected in the accounts. The

Table 2.1
Statement Showing Investment, Turnover and Employment of State Enterprises

S.No.	State	Total No. of Public Enterprises reported	No.of enterprises for which data available	Investment as on 31-3-77 (Rs. in crores)	Turnover in Public 1975-76 (Rs. in crores)	Employment sector as on 30-6-77 (Number)
1.	Assam	29	29	189.83	54.00	18988
2.	Andhra Pradesh	19	19	690.05	300.80	151591
3.	Bihar	33	33	464.97	99.40	45995
4.	Gujarat	28	28	668.76	274.23	68063
5.	Haryana	23	23	387.10	113.02	34779
6.	Himachal Pradesh	11	11	81.29	22.38	18352
7.	J & K	7	7	29.46	9.35	2582
8.	Karnataka	70	63	733.98	281.83	91653
9.	Kerala	51	51	383.31	132.47	91219
10.	Madhya Pradesh	19	12	549.17	117.48	48268
11.	Maharashtra	33	33	1031.61	356.54	116575
12.	Orissa	67	42	247.51	97.45	18658

(Contd.)

S.No	State	Total No. of Public Enterprises reported	No.of enterprises for which data available	Investment as on 31-3-77 (Rs.in crores)	Turnover in Public 1975-76 (Rs.in crores)	Employment sector as on 30-6-77 (Number)
13.	Punjab	23	23	744.40	209.55	32658
14.	Rajasthan	27	27	387.36	128.18	45654
15.	Tamil Nadu	59	55	691.92	522.86	179464
16.	Uttar Pradesh	55	55	1777.44	292.28	117552
17.	West Bengal	34	34	517.76	NA	66918
	Total	588	545	9575.92	3011.82	1148959
	Central Public Sector as on 1-4-1977		145	11097.00	14592.23	1575067

Note: Figure of Turnover in respect of States includes total operating revenue from State Electricity Boards.

Source: (i) State Governments

(ii) Central Electricity Authority-in respect of Investment/Turnover figures of State Electricity Boards.

(iii) DGET Ministry of Labour-Employment State-wise

(iv) BPE Annual Report on the working of Industrial & Commercial Undertakings of the Central Government 197 77-information relating to Central Public Sector following statement gives the number of enterprises which made profits and losses during each of the last three years in the different States:-

Table 2.2
Statement Showing Number of State Enterprises Making Profits/ Losses in Different States

Sl.No.	1974-75			1975-76			1976-77		
	Profit	Loss	NA*	Profit	Loss	NA*	Profit	Loss	NA*
01. Andhra Pradesh	9	12	8	12	11	6	9	3	17
02. Assam	14	2	3	12	5	2	11	6	2
03. Bihar	2	13	13	2	13	16	6	10	21
04. Gujarat	12	8	4	11	12	5	3	4	4
05. Haryana	7	11	4	7	12	3	9	9	4
06. Himachal Pradesh	6	5	..	5	5	1	4	3	1
07. J & K	3	3	1	3	3	1	4	2	24
08. Karnataka	25	20	18	21	25	17	23	19	12
09. Kerala	21	17	12	18	25	7	15	23	7
10. Madhya Pradesh	3	3	7	4	4	7	4	5	9
11. Maharashtra	19	14	2	20	13	2	16	10	52
12. Orissa	21	3	39	18	5	40	10	5	6
13. Punjab	8	9	8	6	11	8	10	9	5
14. Rajasthan	13	9	5	14	10	3	11	11	7
15. Tamil Nadu	22	26	7	21	32	2	25	23	4
16. Uttar Pradesh	18	10	27	29	12	14	30	11	14
17. West Bengal		N.A		9	13	12	4	18	12

Source: State Governments.
* Number of companies for which data is not available.

2.4.6 Owing to the information gaps and the difficulties of making comparisons which were mentioned earlier it is not possible to draw many reliable conclusions from the above statement in regard to the comparative performance of the public sector in the different States.

2.5 Pattern of Financing

2.5.1 Out of the investment of Rs. 9,575.92 crores, the Electricity Boards accounted for Rs. 6,664.04 crores which was financed through loans, bonds and debentures.

2.5.2 The investment of Rs. 2,911.88 crores in enterprises other than Electricity Boards was financed 41.3% by equity capital and 58.7% by loans. The details are given in Appendix V. The debt:equity ratio of these enterprises varied considerably as can be seen from the statement at Table 2.3.

Table 2.3
Statement Showing Financial Structure of State Enterprises (Other than Electricity Boards) as on 31st March, 1977

Sl.No.	*State*	*Debt Equity Ratio*
01.	Andhra Pradesh	1:0.54
02.	Assam	1:0.97
03.	Bihar	1:0.88
04.	Gujarat	1:0.36
05.	Haryana	1:0.87
06.	Himachal Pradesh	1:1.40
07.	J & K	1:5.13
08.	Karnataka	1:0.71
09.	Kerala	1:1.12
10.	Madhya Pradesh	1:1.87
11.	Maharashtra	1:0.61
12.	Orissa	1:1.42
13.	Punjab	1:1.12
14.	Rajasthan	1:0.64
15.	Tamil Nadu	1:0.46
16.	Uttar Pradesh	1:0.89
17.	West Bengal	1:0.34

Source: State Governments

2.5.3 Generally, the debt equity ratio is less than 1:1 which is the norm being followed by Central Government companies. The high equity financing in Jammu & Kashmir, Madhya Pradesh, Orissa, Himachal Pradesh.

2.6 Sectoral Pattern of Investment in the States

The investment in the public sector has been classified under 13 heads, viz.,

1. Industrial Development and Financial Institutions.
2. Trading and marketing.
3. Contract and Construction services.
4. Transportation.
5. Development of small industries .
6. Consumer goods.
7. Agro-based industries.
8. Minerals and metals.
9. Engineering industry.
10. Tourism.
11. Development of backward regions and weaker sections of the society.
12. Electricity Boards
13. Others.

2.6.2 In respect of technology, management and other aspects, these sectors vary considerably. Any comparative study of the performance of the public enterprises in the different states would, therefore, have to take into account the distinguishing features of the different sectors. In the following paragraphs, therefore, such a comparative study of the major sectors in the different states is attempted. The statement at Table 2.4 gives the sectoral pattern of investment in different states.

2.7 Electricity Boards

2.7.1 The Electricity Boards account for the biggest chunk of the public sector investment in all the states. This

Table 2.4
Statement showing Investment by Sectors in the States as on 31st March, 1977

Classification of enterprises	A.P	Assam	Bihar	Gujara	Haryana	H.P	J.K	Karnata	Keral
1	2	3	4	5	6	7	8	9	10
Ind.Dev&	49.79	17.45	18.11	123.90	17.64	6.16	12.47	17.90	8.64
Fin Institutions	(21.2)	(17.7)	(30.4)	(42.3)	(21.3)	(28.6)	(43.8)	(3.3)	(7.8)
Trading and	0.16	19.69	3.63	11.39	3.25	1.35	0.34	13.34	13.74
Marketing	(neg)	(19.9)	(3.0)	(3.9)	(3.9)	(6.3)	(1.2)	(2.4)	(12.4)
Contract &	4.59	1.48	4.69	45.67	...	2.66	...	...	0.59
Const. Services	(2.0)	(1.5)	(7.9)	(15.5)	...	(12.3)	...	....	(0.5)
Transportation	34.85	9.07	9.88	41.32	19.04	3.49	...	62.18	7.20
	(14.8)	(9.1)	(16.7)	(14.1)	(23.0)	(16.1)	...	(11.4)	(6.5)
Development of	5.95	2.97	5.47	1.50	...	...	0.48	0.92	6.45
Small Industries	(2.5)	(8.0)	(9.2)	(0.5)	...	...	(1.7)	(0.2)	(5.8)
Consumer goods	10.74	39.57	4.79	3.99	9.53	...	5.53	50.36	15.35
	(4.6)	(39.7)	(8.0)	(1.3)	(11.5)	...	(19.9)	(9.3)	(13.9)
Agro-based	2.62	7.07	2.80	6.40	24.68	3.87	...	4.6	14.14
Industries	(1.1)	(7.2)	(4.7)	(2.2)	(29.8)	(18.0)	...	(0.8)	(12.8)

Minerals & Metals	61.74	0.23	1.23	5.70	0.48	1.98	9.02	7.9	1.65
	(20.2)	(neg)	(2.1)	(1.9)	(0.6)	(9.2)	(27.7)	(1.8)	(1.5)
Engg.	64.93	...	...	52.03	3.78	1.14	...	385.00	33.85
Enterprises	(27.6)	...	...	(17.8)	(4.6)	(4.9)	...	(70.0)	(30.7)
Tourism	...	...	0.11	1.47	0.88	1.62	0.9	2.05	1.11
			(neg)	(1.8)	(4.6)	(5.7)	(0.2)	(1.9)	
Backward	...	1.35	8.90	1.12	2.52	...	...	...	6.56
Region & Backward	(1.4)	(15.0)	(0.4)	(3.0)	...	...	....	(5.9)	
Societies Dev Ent.									
Electiricty Boards	454.6	90.57	405.4	375.63	304.33	59.76	NA	190.12	272.7
Others	...	0.38	...	....	0.38	...	0.91	0.32	6.96
		(0.5)			(0.5)		(0.2)	(0.3)	
Total	690.0	189.83	464.9	668.76	387.10	81.29	29.46	733.98	383.3

Source: State Governments, Note: Figures in brackets indicate percentage to total investment (excluding Electricity Board
*Denote information not available in respect of all Public Enterprises in the State.

Table 2.4
Statement showing Investment by Sectors in the States as on 31st March, 1977

Classification of enterprises	*M.P.**	*Orissa**	*T.N.*	*U.P.*	*W.B.*	*Rajasth*	*Punjab*
1	*11*	*12*	*13*	*14*	*15*	*16*	*17*
Ind.Dev&	102.1	31.53	108.9	62.77	19.03	12.93	30.58
Fin Institutions	(32.3)	(39.7)	(47.2)	(21.5)	(9.3)	(16.8)	(15.9)
Trading and	5.10	0.88	19.72	8.21	4.78	5.67	36.94
Marketing	(1.6)	(1.1)	(8.5)	(2.8)	(2.4)	(7.4)	(19.2)
Contract &	7.76	1.08	...	37.73	...	...	13.41
Const. Services	(2.4)	(1.4)	...	(13.0)	...	...	(7.0)
Transportation	56.37	18.82	38.10	50.34	74.61	15.73	57.63
	(17.7)	(23.7)	(16.5)	(17.2)	(36.4)	(20.4)	(30.0)
Development of	13.51	3.67	21.48	6.42	13.88	2.14	8.98
Small Industries	(4.3)	(4.6)	(9.3)	(2.2)	(6.8)	(2.8)	(4.7)
Consumer goods	10.94	6.42	23.73	58.49	2.05	5.97	13.95
	(3.4)	(8.1)	(10.3)	(20.0)	(1.0)	(7.8)	(7.3)
Agro-based	39.35	3.07	8.63	16.96	7.95	9.17	27.48
Industries	(12.4)	(3.8)	(3.7)	(5.8)	(3.9)	(11.8)	(14.3)

Minerals & Metals	0.71	10.81	0.37	0.92	0.47	17.25	...
	(0.2)	(13.6)	(0.2)	(0.3)	(0.2)	(22.4)	...
Engg.	67.40...	3.95	39.26	75.40	...	1.13	
Enterprises	(21.2)	...	(1.8)	(13.4)	(36.8)	...	(0.6)
Tourism	1.11	...	2.18	0.92	0.93	0.54	...
	(0.3)	...	(0.9)	(0.3)	(0.4)	(0.7)	...
Backward	6.22	...	3.67	8.71	0.94	2.99	0.10
Region & Backward	(2.0)	...	(1.6)	(2.9)	(0.4)	(8.9)	(Neg)
Societies Dev Ent.							
Electiricty Boards	714.0	168.07	461.1	1484.8	312.9	310.30	552.37
Others	6.96	3.16	...	1.86	4.74	4.67	1.83
	(2.2)	(4.0)		(0.6)	(2.4)	(6.0)	(1.0)
Total	1031.	247.51	691.8	1777.4	517.7	387.36	744.40

Source: State Governments, Note: Figures in brackets indicate percentage to total investment (excluding Electricity Board
*Denote information not available in respect of all Public Enterprises in the State.

sector accounts for as much as 92% in Madhya Pradesh and even in Karnataka where its shared is the lowest, it accounts for 26% of the total investment in the public sector. The statement below gives the investment in respect of Electricity Boards and its percentage share to total investment in public sector in the different states.

Table 2.5
Statement Showing Investment in Respect of State Electricity Board as a Percentage to Total Investment

Sl.No.	*States*	*Investment as on 31.3.1977 (Rs.in crores)*	*Investment in Electricity Boards as % of total investment in public sector*
01.	Andhra Pradesh	454.68	65.9
02.	Assam	90.57	47.2
03.	Bihar	405.47	87.2
04.	Gujarat	375.63	56.2
05.	Haryana*	304.33	78.6
06.	Himachal Pradesh*	59.76	73.5
07.	J & K	NA	NA
08.	Karnataka*	190.15	25.9
09.	Kerala	272.77	71.2
10.	Madhya Pradesh	507.00	92.3
11.	Maharashtra	714.01	69.2
12.	Orissa*	168.07	67.6
13.	Punjab	552.37	74.2
14.	Rajasthan	310.30	80.1
15.	Tamil Nadu	461.10	66.6
16.	Uttar Pradesh	1484.85	83.5
17.	West Bengal	312.98	60.5
	Total	6664.04	

* Investment as on 31.3.76
Source: Central Electricity Authority.

2.7.2 If these investments are reckoned at current prices, their share would be considerably higher than what is indicated in the statement above. This is particularly true in the Electricity Boards where much of the investments took place many years ago.

2.7.3 The performance of the Electricity Boards based on the latest available information which is for the year ending 31st March, 1976 is given in Table 2.6

Table 2.6
Performance of State Electricity Boards on 31st March, 1976

Sl.No.	*State*	*Total operating Revenue (Rs. In Lakhs)*	*Net Profit (after charging interest) (Rs. In Lakhs)*	*Employment (Numbers)*
A.	*Northern Zone*			
1.	Haryana	3915.9	(-)734.7	19919
2.	Punjab	4837.7	(-)1213.6	29843
3.	Rajasthan	5772.3	204.0	17827
4.	Uttar Pradesh	16608.0	(-)9194.6	NA
B.	*Western Zone*			
1.	Gujarat	9026.9	(-)1.1	19253
2.	Madhya Pradesh	7763.8	651.6	33658
3.	Maharashtra	14267.4	194.8	48951
C.	*Southern Zone*			
1.	Andhra Pradesh	9054.1	351.0	51065
2.	Kerala	3453.5	(-)762.0	22494
3.	Karantaka	6183.7	614.6	31230
4.	Tamil Nadu	16871.0	1099.0	97325
D.	*Eastern Zone*			
1.	Bihar	7394.2	(-)1187.5	40350
2.	Orissa	3653.9	(-) 118.6	5824
3.	West Bengal	5630.8	(-) 930.5	23655

Source: Central Electricity Authority
Note: Information in respect of Assam, Himachal Pradesh and Jammu & Kashmir is not available.

2.7.4 The significant feature that emerges from the statement is the widespread losses suffered by the Electricity Boards in all the States except Rajasthan, Madhya Pradesh, Maharashtra, Andhra Pradesh, Karnataka and Tamil Nadu.

2.7.5 Given the importance of power for economic development, this is admittedly the most important sector in the States which requires urgent attention. The Governments of the States and the Central Government are seized of this matter. In their organisational and managerial features, as much as in their relationship with the State Governments, the Electricity Boards are on a different footing than other public sector enterprises.

2.8 Transportation Corporation

2.8.1 This is perhaps the second most imporotant activity in the public sector under the State Governments. It accounts for oa substantial portion of the total investment ranging from as much as 30% of the total investment in Punjab to 15% or more in the States of Andhra Pradesh, Bihar, Gujarat, Haryana, Himachal Pradesh, Maharashtra, Orissa, Tamil Nadu, U.P., West Bengal and Rajasthan. The performance of the Transportation Corporations in the different States is given in Table 2.7.

2.8.2 It is noteworthy that the Transport Corporations have been able to achieve a high turnover: investment ratio in a few States. This is true in Andhra Pradesh, Gujarat, Haryana, Himachal Pradesh, Karnataka, Maharashtra, Madhya Pradesh, Rajasthan and Tamil Nadu. In some of the States the turnover figures may be low, though the State Governments may be getting additional revenue by way of passenger tax.

2.9 Industrial Development and Financial Institutions

2.9.1 This sector consists of the institutions providing financial and other types of assistance to industry and agriculture. The Industrial Development Corporations generally provide long-term finance and infrastructural facilities. They develop industrial estates and other facilities required for setting up industries as well as provide assistance in the selection of technical collaboration, purchase of plant and machinery, prparation of Feasibility Reports etc. The Industrial Finance Corporations limit their role mainly to the provision of medium and short-term loans, underwriting of shares, assistance in preparing and evaluating project reports etc.

Table 2.7
Performance of State Road Transport Corporations as on 1-4-1977

Sl. No.	*State*	*Investment*	*Turnover*	*Profit/Loss*		
				1976-77	*1975-76*	*1974-75*
01.	Assam	792.96	620.00	1.01	(-)14.13	(-)75.45
02.	Andhra Pradesh	3485.06	8813.85	249.03	223.70	364.15
03.	Bihar	988.00	NA	(-)177.00	NA	NA
04.	Gujarat	4131.50	7430.15	NA	(-)299.03	(-)734.70
05.	Haryana	1903.71	2811.99	104.65	(-)49.70	(-)56.43
06.	Himachal Pradesh	348.75	807.20	NA	(-)62.78	(-)96.31
07.	Jammu & kashmir	NA	NA	NA	NA	NA
08.	Karnataka	5998.85	6498.96	41.59	(-)129.81	6.57
09.	Kerala	...	...	...	...	...
10.	Madhya Pradesh	2476.87	2922.92	48.23	46.32	(-)148.27
11.	Maharashtra	5636.87	12286.52	397.80	148.38	(-)767.74
12.	Orissa	1882.66	1166.65	0.27	11.66	22.01
13.	Punjab	5763.30	3549.00	278.67	(-)317.56	26.00
14.	Rajasthan	1573.33	2017.84	(-)65.08	(-)50.67	49.89
15.	Tamil Nadu	3408.48	8943.64	31.63	(-)988.49	(-)160.38
16.	Uttar Pradesh	5033.94	5091.63	200.00	139.50	(-)325.00
17.	West Bengal	7460.95	NA	(-)1438.89	NA	NA

Source: State Governments.

2.9.2 These corporations form an important segment in all the States except Karnataka and Kerala. They account for from about 20% of the total investment in the public sector in Andhra Pradesh, Bihar, Himachal Pradesh, Maharashtra, Haryana and U.P to as much as about 40% in Gujarat, Jammu and Kashmir, Tamil Nadu and Orissa. The Indeustrial Financial Institutions act as a kind of nodal organisation for the enterprises assisted by them. In this sense also they perform an important role and their rexpertise could be of considerable assistance to State Governments.

2.9.3 Table 2.8 gives performance of these organisations in those States where they have an important position.

Table 2.8
Performance of State Industrial Development and Financial Institutions

(Rs. in Lakhs)

Sl. No.	*States*	*Profit/Loss*		
		1976-77	*1975-76*	*1974-75*
01.	Andhra Pradesh	136.84	110.68	79.59
02.	Bihar	NA	56.44	NA
03.	Gujarata	161.66	169.14	102.41
04.	Haryana	96.15	82.31	51.11
05.	Himachal Pradesh	21.60	18.02	12.95
06.	Jammu & Kashmir	(-)20.22	(-)82.48	(-)27.35
07.	Maharashtra	154.43	84.61	49.23
08.	Orissa	150.35	(-)87.33	94.95
09.	Tamil Nadu	85.03	(-)71.75	(-)38.51
10.	Uttar Pradesh	87.75	111.82	99.40

Source: State Governments.

2.9.4 There has been a steady improvement in their performance.

2.10 Trading and Marketing

2.10.1 This sector is important in the States of Assam, Kerala and Punjab. They are engaged in marketing of local produce like tea, sugar, jute, raw silk, cahsew and handicrafts. The performance of the Trading and Marketing organisation in the three States is given in table 2.9

Table 2.9

Statement showing Comparative Financial Performance

(Rs. in.Lakhs)

Sl. No.	*States*	*Profit/Loss*		
		1976-77	*1975-76*	*1974-75*
1.	Assam	130.38	(-)20.00	35.25
2.	Kerala	(-)53.55	(-)171.96	95.25
3.	Punjab	66.46	102.08	79.73

Source: State Governments

2.10.2 Managerially, there was evidence to show that apart from a few bright spots, the marketing organisations were weak. The inheritance of government culture and the constraints of public accoutnability as much as lack of profesisonal competence have inhibited the performance of these companies and their risk-taking capabilities. These corporations have been assigned the important role of promoting the interests of the weaker sections of society like the growers, craftsmen etc. hence, it is important to professionalise the managements of thes organisaitons and to provide them with the necessary environment to achieve their objectives.

2.11 Contract and Construction Services

2.11.1 Enterprises providing contract and construction services have a relatively important role in Gujarat, Himachal Pradesh and Uttar Pradesh. The performance of these companies in these States has been given in table 2.10.

Table 2.10
Statement showing Comparative Financial Performance

(Rs. in Lakhs)

Sl. No	States	Profit/Loss		
		1976-77	1975-76	1974-75
1.	Gujarat	NA	53.23	45.01
2.	Himachal Pradesh	0.48	1.24	(-)0.45
3.	Uttar Pradesh	7.86	19.71	(-)12.36

Source: State Governments.

2.12 Consumer Goods

2.12.1 Several enterprises are engaged in the manufacture and sale of textiles, sugar, soaps, and oils, machines, breweries, electronics, domestic appliances etc. they form an important group in Assam, Kerala and Uttar Pradesh. The performance of these companies is given in table 2.11.

Table 2.11
Statement showing Comparative Financial Performance

(Rs. in Lakhs)

Sl. No	States	Profit/Loss		
		1976-77	1975-76	1974-75
1.	Assam	(-)348.71	29.64	14.71
2.	Kerala	77.82	(-)50.18	48.29
3.	Uttar Pradesh	(-)225.14	(-)262.97	(-)316.99

Source: State Governments.

2.13 Agro-based Industries

2.13.1 The agro-based industries are significant in Haryana, Himachal Pradesh, Kerala, Maharashtra and Punjab.

2.13.2 The agro-based industries have a crucial role in improving the lot of the rural sector. While from the above statement they seem to have fared will in at least three States, there is much way to go to achieve the full potential of these organisations.

2.14 Minerals & Metals

2.14.1 This sector is important in Andhra Pradesh, Orissa and Rajasthan. The performance of these companies in these States is given in table 2.13.

Table 2.12
Statement showing Comparative Financial Performance
(Rs. in Lakhs)

Sl. No.	States	Profit/Loss		
		1976-77	1975-76	1974-75
1.	Haryana	14.72	(-)60.46	(-)39.27
2.	Himachal Pradesh	2.59	1.29	1.39
3.	Kerala	43.32	78.48	79.21
4.	Maharashtra	14.20	(-)75.47	205.28
5.	Punjab	(-)35.14	(-)118.02	(-)45.68

Source: State Governments.

Table 2.13
Statement showing Comparative Financial Performance
(Rs. in Lakhs)

Sl. No.	States	Profit/Loss		
		1976-77	1975-76	1974-75
1.	Andhra Pradesh	247.99	571.65	323.45
2.	Orissa	NA	276.73	(-)267.20
3.	Rajasthan	21.00	13.94	20.70

Source: State Government

2.15 Engineering Enterprises

2.15.1 This is the major group in Andhra Pradesh, Karnataka, Kerala, Maharashtra and West Bengal. The engineering industries produce a wide range of products from refrigerators and scooters to heavy electricasl and engineering equipments, foundry and forge items etc. The performance of the engineering industries in the States where they are of importance is given in table 2.14.

Table 2.14
Statement showing Comparative Financial Performance

(Rs. in Lakhs)

Sl. No.	*States*	*Profit/Loss*		
		1976-77	*1975-76*	*1974-75*
1.	Andhra Pradesh	61.90	54.80	81.13
2.	Karnatak	493.42	774.81	396.20
3.	Kerala	60.04	29.20	27.74
4.	Maharashtra	57.90	68.71	67.02
5.	West Bengal	279.00	(-)252.90	(-)329.65

Source: State Governments

2.16 Backward Region and Backward Societies Development Enterprises

2.16.1 These enterprises are a recent development. Though numerically significant the investment in these enterprises is small. The States where these corporations have gained importance are Bihar, Haryana, Kerala, Maharashtra and Uttar Pradesh. The management of these organisations requires skills and aptitudes quite different from the others. With their complex relationships with other wings of government they provide in some ways a greater managerial challenge thanother organisations. The evidence was that many of them have not been able to face upto this challenge and in quite a few cases have remained dormant.

2.17 Other Sectors

2.17.1 The other important sectors are development of small industries and tourism.

2.18 The Growth of Public Sector

2.18.1 The pace of growth of the public sector has been increasing over the years. If this growth is studied by decades starting from 1951 the picture that emerges is given in table 2.15.

2.18.2 Overall, the growth was most marked since 1970 in the States whereas in the Centre the major expansion of public seector took place during 1955-1965. The greater availability of Plan fund and institutional finance contributed to this growth. The decade 1961-70 was a period of substantial expansion of the public sector in Andhra Pradesh, Assam, Gujarat, Haryana, Himachal Pradesh, Kerala, Maharashtra, Orissa and Punjab. But, generally the growth was most marked since 1970. In Uttar Pradesh as many as 44 out of 55 enterprises cam into being during this period whereas in Tamil Nadu 34 out of 59 enterprises were set up since 1970.

2.18.3 The large number and the rapid growth of public enterprises have imposed on the State Governments a severe burden of management. Assam, Gujarat and Orissa are the States where the number of public enterprises was relatively highe ven before 1960. In all athe other States, the growth of public sector has been a more recent phenomenon.

2.19 Forms of Organisation

2.19.1 The organisational form in which a Government enterprise comes into being and conducts its activities has been a matter of great interest to students of public sector. The departmental administration has been criticised for its demonstrated rigidities and in efficiencies. The growth of the public sector marks the belief that in order to achieve greater organisational effiectiveness and efficiency, the corporate struture has much to commend itself. It is this belief that has to a great extent accounted for the expansion of government corporaitons in recent years in all developing countries.

Table 2.15
Statement Showing Period of Incorporation of Public Enterprises in the States

Sl. State	Number of enterprises established during			Information available in r/o	Total No. of public enterprises
	1951-1960	1961-1970	1971-1977		
01. Andhra Pradesh	4	4	5	6	19
02. Assam	7	11	11	...	29
03. Bihar	5	4	23	1	33
04. Gujarat	6	9	13	...	28
05. Haryana	1	10	10	...	23
06. Himachal Pradesh	1	4	6	2	11
07. J & K	...	...	...	7	7
08. Karnataka	...	...	...	70	70
09. Kerala	5	18	21	7	51
10. Madhya Pradesh	...	4	6	9	19
11. Maharashtra	...	14	16	3	33
12. Orissa	6	10	12	39	67
13. Punjab	2	11	9	1	23
14. Rajasthan	2	9	3	13	27
15. Tamil Nadu	2	11	34	12	59
16. Uttar Pradesh	4	6	44	1	55
17. West Bengal	6	10	17	1	34
Total	51	135	230	172	588

Source: State Governments.

2.19.2 There is, however, some controversy in regard to the adoption of the corporate form of organisation for governmental activities. It is felt that the use of public funds has to be accompanied by maximum public accoutability for which it is necessary to maintain the departmental form of organisation. Supporters of this school of thought see little justification for setting up government companies, which in their view, dilute accountability and evade constitutional responsibilities.

2.20 Departmental Undertakings

2.20.1 The departmentally managed undertakings is the traditional type of public enterprise in developed as well as under-developed countries. It has been mainly in use ofr railways, posts & telegrphs, ports, harbours, ordnance factories etc. The main characteristic of departmental undertakings are:

(a) The neterprise is financed by appropriation from Government and all or a major share, of its revenue is paid into the treasury.

(b) The enterprise is subject to the budget accounting and audit controls applicable to government departments.

(c) The staff of the enterprise enjoyed the status of civil servants in regard to their recruitment, conditions of service, disciplinary matters etc;and

(d) Departmental undertakings is organised as a major agency of one of the formal departments of Government and is subject to the direct control of the head of the Government department.

2.20.2 The major disadvantges of departmental undertakings is that it turns the organisaation into a typical bureaucracy where initiative and flexibility are seriously undermined. The need to adopt the Governmental system of accounting and other methods of work is not conducive to the speedy or efficient disch arge of industrial and commercial activities.

2.21 The Statutory Corporations

2.21.1 The statutory corporation is, for all practical purposes, a company and cannot be considered in any way comparable to the departmental undertaking in its legal or working aspects. It is established by an act of Parliament or Legislature, which has, therefore, some direct control over its constitution and supervision. The setting up of these corporations is preceded by a debate in the Legislature. The accounts of the company are requiredc to be placed before the House for discussions. These requirements have sometime been felt to be a hindrance to the speed establishment and efficient working of these organisations.

2.22 Company Form

2.22.1 This form of organisation has become the most popular. It expected to achieve a maximum of freedom from governmental and parliamentary interference. This form of organisaiton is, therefore, considered the most suitable for enterprises which have to runm on enterpreneurial risk taking, and relatively informal business methods of maangement. The main objection that has been raised against the company form is that public accountability is given only meagre recognition in its scheme.

2.23 Joint Ventures

2.23.1 This is a variant of the government company. In the central Government such joint ventures have been mainly set up with equity participation by the Government of India and some foreign organisation. In the States, however, the joint venture is the term used for those companies where there is quity participation from both government and the public. The advantages of the joint venture are that it could bring in along with the quity, technological and managerial experitse. In the States it has, as in gujarat, been successful in bringing managerial inputs. More recent joint ventures of the State Governments like that with scoooters (India) Ltd., Indian Drugs and Pharmaceuticals Ltd., Hindustan Lever Ltd., are likely to bring in technological contributions along with financial and managerial participation. The joint ventures have also been set up for promoting egalitarian objectives of the State by inviting public participation in the equity capital. The success of such ventures has, however, been limited and very often the State financial institutions who had underwritten these issues had to take up the shares.

2.24 Industrial and Commercial Cooperatives

2.24.1 The co-operative movement, has in recent years spread into industrial and commercial areas. Many of the co-operatives set up initially to protect and promote producers' and consumers' interest have branched off into direct production and sales of goods and services. Save for some rare shining examples such as The Milk Producers Cooperative of Gujarat and the Indian Farmers' Fertilizer Cooperative, these efforts have not been very successful. The main reasons for the failure appear to be the weakness of mangement and the excessive political pressures working on them.

2.25 Relative Importance of Different Form of Organisations

2.25.1 The statement at Table 2.16 gives the forms in which the public sector is organised in the different States. The most important form is the Corporate organisation whether statutory corporation or company. Out of the 588 organisations for which information has been obtained, 411 are registered under the companies Act and 90 are statuory corporations.

2.25.2 The increasing number of companies registered under the Companies Act indicates the trend towards giving greater autonomy to the public sector organisation and the need for flexibility in the setting up of such organisations without going through procedural requirements of sanction by legislature etc.

2.25.3 The statutory corporations are generally the financial corporations, the road transportation corporations, warehousing corporations, electricity generaiton and distribution organisations and the promotional organisations.

2.25.4 This trend towards greater autonomy has to be accompained by adequate accountability. It has been found in many cases that the mere adoption of a particular form of organisation has not resulted in the objectives for which such a form was selected. The Damodar Valley Corporation is the most eminent example of this. Many organisations were established outside the pale of direct legislative and government control, but inspite of this have inherited bureaucratic characteristics and functioned as extended arms of the administration.

2.25.5 There was some evidence to show that the setting up of public enterprises in the States was hasty and not based on a proper examination of the proposals. In the first instance, State Governments have to be satisfied that the balance of advantage would lie in the State extablishing a public enterprise to take up a particular activity rather than leaving it to private initiative. Having decided that the establishment of a public enterprise was necessary, the msot suitable form of organisaiton has to be selected. The advantages and disadvantages of the different forms and the need for supportive measures to ensure the achievement of the objectives of the enterprise have to be carefully assessed. Environmental factors such as the political and bureaucratic influence, the availability fo managerial talents, local commercial traditions etc., and their likely

Table 2.16
Forms of Public Enterprises in the States

Sl. No.	States	*Departmental Undertakings*	*Statutory Corporations & Boards*	*Cos.registered under Companies Act, 1956*	*Cos, registered under the Co-operative Societies Act*	*Cos.in Joint Sector*	*Data not available*	*Total*
01.	Andhra Pradesh	1	5	12	1	...	...	19
02.	Assam	1	6	18	4	...	...	29
03.	Bihar	...	6	27	...	...	...	33
04.	Gujarat	...	10	15	...	3	...	28
05.	Haryana	4	3	16	...	..	...	23
06.	Himachal Pradesh	...	4	7	...	...	...	11
07.	J & K	...	...	...	...	...	...	7
08.	Karnataka	17	4	49	...	...	7	70
09.	Kerala	...	1	50	1	...	...	51
10.	Madhya Pradesh	...	4	9	...	5	...	19
11.	Maharashtra	2	7	24	...	...	...	33
12.	Orissa	15	4	48	...	...	...	67
13.	Punjab	1	8	14	...	...	...	23
14.	Rajasthan	...	6	9	...	...	12	27
15.	Tamil Nadu	12	7	40	...	...	...	59
16.	Uttar Pradesh	...	7	47	1	...	...	55
17.	West Bengal	...	8	26	...	...	...	34
	Total	53	90	411	7	8	19	588

influence on the working of the enterprise are also relevant in deciding on the setting up of a public enterprise and its organisational form.

CHAPTER 3

A NODAL ORGANISATION: ITS NEED AND ROLE

3.1 An important area of the study by the Group was the need for a nodal organization for the purposes of coordinating, controlling and servicing public enterprises. While public sector organisations are so conceived that they may enjoy a measure of autonomy adequate for efficient and effective operation, the need to ensure that their accountability, functioning and growth ensure that their accountability, functioning and growth are orderly within the frame of a national purpose has been well recognised. It is this realization that has, in most cases resulted in the setting up of a central agency in coordinate, control and service the enterprises on behalf of the Government.

3.2 Coordination

3.2.1 There are many reasons why coordinating among public undertakings is necessary. The number of public enterprises has so increased that without a certain uniformity of approach to common problems, they run the risk of working at cross-purposes. The common ownership of these enterprises calls for a consistent approach to major and similar aspects of management.

3.2.2 Parliamentary control and public accountability provide another justification for a nodal organisation. As Government enterprises, public enterprises are answerable to Legislatures and have to submit themselves to the scrutiny of Legislative Committees on public enterprises. An organisation in Government, which could service the Legislature in respect of public sector enterprises, has, therefore, become inescapable.

3.2.3 Multiple agencies are concerned with public enterprises in respect of investment appraisal, decision on location, wage policy, housing etc. a central agency could reduce the burden of enterprises having to deal with a multiplicity of organisations.

3.2.4 Long term planning in a country pursuing planned economic development has also necessitated coordination. It is essential that the plans of the enterprises are closely aligned to national and State level main objectives.

3.3 Control

3.3.1 The Government's control over the enterprises generally relate to

- appointment of chief executive and Members of the Board;
- approval of capital expenditure above delegated limits;
- approval of upward revision of capital costs;
- approval of revenue budgets where there is a deficit to be made good by Government;
- issue of directives on State policy.

3.3.2 Apart from the formal regulatory powers vested in Government, there is considerable informal control exercised over the public sector enterprises. This is done through the Minister and the official hierarchy, particularly through their powers of appointment and sanctioning of funds. In States where the manning of top posts is dominated by the civil services the influence of civil service hierarchy on enterprise management can be considerable.

3.4 Servicing Functions

3.4.1 Both as a necessity and as a means to greater acceptability, the nodal organisation has, in many cases, consciously striven to become a supporting agency. In these efforts, it has taken on many servicing responsibilities both for the administrative departments in Government and the public enterprises.

3.4.2 There are several such functions that these organisations can play in response to the requirements of the public enterprises and the other government departments and agencies concerned. Their needs would vary from one enterprise to another and from State to State. One important area where assistance from a nodal oroganisation would be welcome by public enterprises is in dealing with various government agencies, both at the State and Central levels. Processing of licenses, advice on and assistance in meeting statutory requirements, organising common facilities for training and management development, trouble shooting, preparation of feasibility reports etc., are some of the areas where a central organisation could be of help to the public enterprises. Such assistance should, however, not undermine the relationship between the enterprises and their administrative departments.

3.4.3 Similarly, the government departments could benefit by the advice and assistance of a specialized body which has intimate and professional knowledge of the working of public enterprises. Such assistance could be of advantage to government in the formulation and examination of common policies affecting the management of public sector. It could function as an information center on various aspects of public sector management and discharge responsibilities relating to evaluation of investment and performance and selection of top management.

3.5 The Bureau of Public Enterprises of the Government of India

3.5.1 The Central Government's experience in this area may be relevant here. Starting from a small organisation known as the Projects Coordination Cell located in the Ministry of Industry, the central agency dealing with public enterprises under the Government of India has grown into a full-fledged organisation called the Bureau of Public Enterprises (BPE). The growth of this organisation ahs been the result of the experience gained and in response to the needs felt by Government and the public sector enterprises. The recommendations of the Administrative Reforms Commission in their report on Public Sector Undertakings (1967) also resulted in a substantial increase in the functions of the BPE. Today, its functions relate mainly to:

- monitoring of performance;
- co-ordination in regard to terms and conditions of service, particularly in order to bring about a desirable rationality in the compensation levels;
- overseeing management development and training;
- evaluation of investment proposals;
- control over expenditure on industrial townships;
- servicing Parliament;
- acting as a catalyst for improving managerial practices;
- providing consultancy services and undertakings trouble-shooting assignments for Government and the public sector enterprises; and
- assisting in the selection of personnel for top management.

3.5.2 The BPE has a staff strength of nearly 300, including the Class IV category. It is organsied in five Divisions viz., Production, Construction, Finance, General Management and Information & Research, each headed by an officer of the status of Joint Secretary to the Government of India. The officer cadre of the BPE is about 80 strong. They are drawn generally from the government specialist and administrative services as well as from the public enterprises. It is located in the Ministry of Finance.

3.6 Views of the State Government on the Nodal Organisation

3.6.1 The State Governments were requested to give their views on the need for a nodal organisation in each State, its size, structure, powers, functions and location. The present position in regard to such nodal agencies in the States was also ascertained.

3.6.2 The States where fairly developed nodal organisations exist are Bihar, Uttar Pradesh and Assam. In Uttar Pradesh and Assam, these organisations are patterned more or less on the BPE. Their functions are similar, though they are smaller in size and less specialised than the BPE.

3.6.3 The Uttar Pradesh Bureau of Public Enterprises is located in the Chief Secretary's Branch. The views expressed by Uttar Pradesh were broadly in favour of a nodal agency, with more or less the same functions as performed by the BPE. The Chief Executives and the officials of the Government were of the view that the organization should not have executive authority lest it should undermine the responsibility of the administrative departments and the management's of the enterprises.

3.6.4 In Assam, there is a full-fledged Department of Public Enterprises headed by a Secretary, which is again under the Chief Secretary's Branch. The Government of Assam was of the view that the nodal organisation should be located directly under the Chief Secretary in order to clothe it with the necessary authority. The staffing of the organisation should be done taking into account the expertise required in the field of Economics, Accounting, Company Law, etc.

3.6.5 The Bihar State Bureau of Public Enterprises is located in the Department of Finance and has fewer functions than the nodal organisations of Uttar Pradesh and Assam. Its functions are limited to:

(i) Coordination of matters of permanent interest;
(ii) Advising Enterprises on organisation pattern, training programmes and personnel policies;
(iii) Acting as a Consultancy Center, Data Bank and Clearing House of information.

3.6.6 The Government of Karnataka, Rajasthan, Gujarat, Tamil Nadu and Punjab have nucleus organisations to coordinate the working of the State public enterprises.

3.6.7 In Karnataka, the Public Undertakings Cell located in the Department of Commerce and Industry acts as the nodal agency for:

(i) Monitoring of performance; and
(ii) Formulation of policies in regard to personnel and management.

3.6.8 There is a Public Enterprises Cell in the Department of Finance in the Government of Punjab which is headed by a Joint Secretary. The functions of the Cell are:

(i) Provide a central point of reference and consultation on important management matters:
(ii) Compile information on terms and conditions of service of officers:
(iii) Advice Enterprises on bringing about rationality in service conditions:
(iv) Assist administrative Departments in evaluation of investment proposals:
(v) Formulate and issue directions in matters of general policies:
(vi) Advice Enterprises in problem areas: and
(vii) Periodical review of working of individual Corporations.

3.6.9 Rajasthan has an Investment Cell in the Department of Finance. This acts as a nodal organisation only for the purpose. Though the Government of Rajasthan does not have a full-fledged nodal organisation at present, they expressed the view that at the same time it is necessary to ensure that the organisation does not impinge on the autonomy of the Public Enterprises or the responsibility of the administrative Department. The favoured location is in the Finance Department. The staff are to be persons with professional knowledge in the area of Marketing, Business Management, Financial Management, Project Management and Project Appraisal.

3.6.10 The Tamil Nadu Government has a Corporation Finance Cell in the Department of Finance with the following functions:

(i) Performance Evaluation;
(ii) Servicing of the Committee of Secretaries;
(iii) Evaluation of common policies in respect of pay scales, accounting and auditing procedures and Management Information Systems;
(iv) Coordinate budgets for the Corporation with the state Budgets; and
(v) Act as a Data Bank on Articles of Association.

3.6.11 The Government of Gujarat has a small Cell known as the Public Sector Enterprises Division in the Finance Department. The functions of this Division are:

(i) Scrutinized proposals relating to establishment of new Undertakings prepared by various administrative departments;
(ii) Scrutinize all proposals involving financial outlay for commitment on the part of the Government.
(iii) Advice administrative Department in dealing with matters relating to Enterprises under their control whenever needed;
(iv) To brief official representatives on the Boards of Directors wherever required;

(v) To scrutinize financial statements and report to Government;

(vi) Examine Agenda Notes and Minutes of the meetings of Boards of Directors and report to Government on important matters; and

(vii) Issue guidelines in matters of common policy.

3.6.12 Some of the Chief Executives of the Corporations in Gujarat have suggested other functions for the nodal organisations. These cover pricing, determination of profits, deciding on the need for stepping up of production capacity, size of the Company and its structure, assisting the Companies in securing long-term and short-term loans, liaison with the Central Government, assisting the Companies in procurement of scarce materials etc.

3.6.13 Andhra Pradesh have also accepted the need for a Central coordinating organization with more or less the same functions as those being performed by the BPE of the Government of India. They are of the view that giving this organization executive powers might erode corporate autonomy and accountability. As for the functions, they consider it necessary to add some additional responsibilities beyond those being performed by the BPE, particularly in the area of costing systems. The organization should be located in the Industries Department.

3.6.14 The States of Madhya Pradesh, Maharashtra, Jammu and Kashmir and Kerala do not have any nodal organisation. The Kerala Government have stated that it proposes to set up such an organsiation shortly. The Government of Maharashtra is not in favour of setting up a nodal organsiation with the functions envisaged for it as they think that these should be primarily performed by the enterprises themselves. A small cell, however, could be located in the Finance Department to be headed by a senior officer and staffed by functional experts.

3.6.15 The States of Haryana, Himachal pradesh, Orissa and West Bengal have not reported on this matter.

3.6.16 In the discussions that the Group had, two schools of though clearly emerged. There was some apprehension about the role of a nodal oroganisation acquiring too dominant a position. It was felt that such an organsiation could impinge on and undermine the autonomy of the public enterprises. It was put forth that it would be better to have a small nodal organisation with limited functions. The important responsibilities of such a nodal organisation should be performed in an informal manner so that they are need based and flexible without being a formal external imposition and introducing undesirable rigidities.

3.6.17 On the other hand, there was the belief that a strong, central organisation was necessary. Protagonists of this view saw the need for centralizing many policy making and regulatory responsibilities in the nodal organisation. To discharge its responsibilities, it would be necessary to arm the organisation with adequate powers even if it meant cutting into the jurisdiction of other government departments and the autonomy of the enterprises.

3.6.18 The need for ensuring that the enterprises function with as much autonomy as is required for efficient and effective performance cannot be overstated. At the same time the public enterprises cannot escape the responsibility devolving on them through common government ownership. A balance has, therefore to be struck between autonomy and coordination and control. There could be different models of the nodal organisation ranging from the expansive set-up of the Bureau of Public Enterprises of the Government of India to the small organisation if normal methods of working as in Gujarat. The exact form has no doubt to be decided taking into account the requirements of each State in relation to the stage and state of the Public sector evolving under it, the general political and other environmental factors etc.

3.7 Recommendations

3.7.1 After considering all aspects of the matter, the Group would recommend that it would be desirable for the State Governments to set-up nodal organisatios with the following basic functions and features:

(a) It should avoid duplicating functions performed elsewhere. If some of its rightful functions are being done elsewhere, these should be transferred to the nodal organisation. The core functions of such an orgnaisation would be:

(1) Investment Appraisal: The organisation should provide professional expertise in commercial and socio-economic appraisal (which is generally not being done now in most Finance Departments who also may not have the requisite expertise). The nodal organisation should service an inter-departmental investment Clearance Committee;

(2) Performance Appraisal: A critical performance appraisal done by an independent expert body can be of great value. Such evaluation should cover not only financial results but also utilization of capacity, materials, managerial and other scarce resources and provide a reliable assessment of management's performance. This appraisal should form the basis of reporting to the Legislature;

(3) Servicing Top Management selections: As for investment appraisal so also for Top Management selections an inter-departmental Committee should be set up comprising the Chief Secretary, the Personnel Secretary, the Secretary of the administrative Department, the Head of the nodal organisation and two senior men from public or private industry. Apart from taking the selections more objective such an organisaiton is likely to reduce the demands on the administrative Departments and the Chief

administrative Departments and the Chief Secretary or timely spotting of talent and ensuring smooth succession. It will also reduce extraneous pressures coming into play;

(4) Relations with the Legislature: Presenting the annual report on the functions of public enterprises and dealing with matters which come under more than one department. This function should not however undermine the role and responsibility of the administrative department concerned with the enterprise. The presenting of the Annual report would also serve the useful purpose of compelling the enterprises to complete their accounts in time;

(5) In most of the states, there will be need for actively promoting management training in critical areas. The paucity of managers make it necessary for the State Governments to pay particular attention to the development of managerial resources. This responsibility should be undertaken by the nodal organisation. While the methods by which it would discharge this responsibility may vary, broadly, these could be the following:

- Imparting training in critical areas. The Standing Group found that some of the critical areas where accounts and audit with special reference to cost accountancy and internal audit ;materials management, personnel and industrial relations; and marketing. The training in these areas could be imparted by the nodal organisation in collaboration with national and local institutes of management training. The nodal organisation should have adequate budget for that purpose.
- Manpower Planning for the public sector-This is a very important activity which should be pursued in a co-ordinated manner. The nodal organisation would be best placed to do it;

(6) The nodal organisation should serve as a center for information on various aspects of public enterprise management and performance. Much of the data in regard to the enterprises of the State would become available to the organisation in discharge of its functions. This has to be supplemented by information on the experience of other States and the Center, as well as of other countries. This way there would be a closer relationship between the States and the Center, which could be of mutual benefit;

(7) There are other service functions which the nodal organisation could perform. These have to be decided depending upon the actual needs of the public sector enterprises. The nodal organisation could, for example, help in the preparation of feasibility reports and project proposals, installation of appropriate information systems for performance review and control, trouble shooting assignments etc.

(b) The location of the nodal organisation should be so decided as to achieve maximum acceptance and effectiveness. It will have to take into account the functions of the nodal organisation. As a rule, it may be desirable not to place it under any one department, which administers some enterprise of its own. It may be preferable to locate the nodal organisation under the Chief Secretary's Branch. It could also be located in a department where the functions will not be fragmented;

(c) The staffing of the nodal organisation should ensure the required professional expertise in business management, personnel management and industrial relations, organisational development and financial management. It need not have production and other technical and engineering staff. These disciplines have become so specialised that it would be best to depend on outside experts. For this, the organisation should have a list of Consultants, drawn-up on an All-India basis, whose services could be indented on as and when required.

CHAPTER 4

PERSONNEL POLICY

4.1 The personnel policy of State Government enterprises has to be seen in their historical perspective. For the manning of these ventures the State Governments had to depend largely on their own cadres, particularly at the middle and higher levels. The rapid growth of these enterprises and the paucity of managers increased this dependence. It is also true that many of the State Government enterprises have a much many of the State Government enterprises have a much closer relationship with the State administration. Their functions and role as important instruments for implementing social and economic policies such as improving the lot of weaker sections of society, providing necessities like transport, power, essential commodities etc., bring them close to the administration. In such situations dependence on the administrative cadres could be natural and even advantageous. In this respect some of the important enterprises of the State Government differ from those under the Central Government and this is an important factor to be taken into account while discussing personnel policy.

4.2 However, the overwhelming evidence available from the States is that no clear and well defined policies for the development of managerial resources in the public sector have been evolved. At the technical level, the enterprises have gone outside the Government cadres. In the employment of such technical personnel a pragmatic approach has been adopted in their recruitment and pay policies and there are quite a few cases where the pay and other terms of service of senior technical personnel were fixed without reference to the pay of the Chief executives or the general pattern of compensation in the enterprises. At the middle and lower levels most of the staff are recruited by the enterprises themselves. These levels constitute the basic internal resources of the enterprises as the top levels are generally manned by deputationists. At these lower an middle levels the pay structure in the majority of the State enterprises correspond to the government pay scales.

4.3 Personnel management in the public sector has to be viewed in terms of the long-term objectives as well as the short-term requirements. The policy for the junior and middle levels well have to be largely implemented by the enterprises themselves. At the top levels greater Government intervention would be necessary and desirable.

4.4 Difficulties in the Way of Managerial Self-reliance

4.4.1 The State Government Enterprises suffer from certain serious difficulties which come in the way of developing adequate internal managerial resources. Firstly, their size and operations are small allowing not much scope for autonomous growth. In the absence of such possibilities of expansion, these enterprises fail to offer reasonable career prospects.

4.4.2 Secondly, the location of these enterprises has also acted as a major disability in developing managerial cadres. Less developed States like Assam and its north-eastern neighbourhood. Orissa, Bihar, Jammu & Kashmir etc., do not attract the proper type of talent required for the running of enterprises due to locational disadvantages.

4.4.3 Thirdly, the remuneration level of the State enterprises is often inadequate attract and retain talent. Many of the State enterprises adopted the pay scales of the State Governments for their employees. Understandably, this has come in the way of attracting the requisite talent.

4.4.4 Fourthly, there is a shortage of local managerial resources in many States. This is true of all States except

Gujarat, Maharashtra, West Bengal, Tamil Nadu and to some extent of Karanataka.

4.4.5 Fifthly, the environmental factors existing in the States might have inhibited proper talents from joining the State enterprises. The higher echelons of management are mainly filled in by deputationists from the administrative culture being carried over to the enterprises. In some States excessive administrative and political influence may be coming in the ay of healthy functioning of the enterprises.

4.5 The requirements of a long-term personnel policy

4.5.1 Serious attention has to be paid to improve the quantity and quality of managerial resources available for the running of State enterprises. The Group would make the following recommendations in this regard:

(1) Selection procedures at the induction and middle level maangement have to be considerably strengthened. These form the core of the managerial cadre from which the future top managers will have to come. It is necessary to ensure that proper talent coming out of the Institutes of management, Institutes of Technology etc, are attracted to the public enterprises. For this purpose, the State Government (or a group of enterprises) may be well advised to encourage campus recruitment and promotion policies and rules which would ensure the objective of strengthening the managerial cadres and pave the way for a healthy organisational growth. They should formulate and execute suitable career development programmes.

(2) There is need to have a close look at the scales of pay and other items of compensation paid to the managerial cadres in particular. It is to be remembered that in order to ensure that the State enterprises which have been set up to achieve important socio-economic objective sand at considerable cost do not suffer from poor managerial

resources due to the adoption of any short sighted compensation policy:

(3) Along with the restructuring of the pay scales and selection procedures the delegation of powers appointment should also be suitable revised. It was seen that in many States the enterprises had very little powers in regard to ap1pointments and had to seek approval for all appointments to posts carrying a pay of Rs. 1,000 and above. This is an unsatisfactory situation and the delegation of powers of appointment should be made taking into account the overall requirements of all the public enterprises as well as the individual needs of the enterprises. Generally, only the top level appointments should require prior Government approval:

(4) There is need for providing reasonable career prospects. The scope for constituting a loose managerial poof or deployment in the various enterprises should be examined. What is required is that there is mobility among managers at the middle and senior levels. For this, the terms of appointment at the middle and senior levels may provide for such transfers without loss of service benefits. A suitable machinery should also be devised to arrange for such inter-enterprise movements which would improve career prospects.

(5) The State enterprises have not so far drawn upon the managerial cadres of the Central Government enterprises. There is good scope for such deputation of the managers of the Central Government Companies to the State Government enterprises. The services of the Bureau of Public Enterprises of the Government of India could be enlisted for this purpose.

4.6 Top Management Policy

4.6.1 The Group gave particular attention to the requirements of top management. Almost universally, it is true that the State government enterprises depended upon officers of the State civil service cadres for their top managerial personnel.

4.6.2 The Group sought the views of the State governments in regard to this policy. The Government of Assan did not think it desirable or even possible at this stage ot do away with the policy of appointing Chief Executives and top managers of public enterprises from the State civil services. Bihar was also of the view that for the present, dependence on the civil services was unavoidable though it was prepared ot agree that in the long term this may not be appropriate. Even advanced States like Maharashtra and Gujarat where there is relatively no paucity of managerial resources, expressed the view that public enterprises will have to depend to a great extent on deputationists from the civil services for heading the organisations.

4.6.3 The evidence collected by the Group will indicate that for some time to come, at least, dependence on government deputationists to man top posts in public enterprises will have to continue. As stated earlier, the interface that some of these enterprises have with Government is one of the important reasons for the need to have greater governmental and public direction particularly in the promotional and service enterprises. Secondly, there is a real shortage of internal resources in the public enterprises for heading these organisations. The reasons for this inadequacy of internal resources have been mentioned earlier. Apart from these factors the disadvantages of the State public enterprises due to their smallness of size, unfavourable location etc., were inhibiting development of internal resoruces. The steps that should be taken to overcome the shortage of internal resources have been discussed in previous paragraphs.

4.5.4 The long-term objective has, no doubt, to be a well planned effort to develop internal self-sufficiency in managerial resources in the public enterprises. The need to depend on State civil service cadres during the interim period poses certain important issues in regard to the management of civil service cadres for discharging this responsibility. With the growing demand of the public sector, it is likely that severed strains would be imposed on these cadres if this has not happened already. To prevent such a situation developing, it will be necessary to augment recruitment to the civil services taking into account the prospective requirements of public enterprises. This would be particularly important in those States where the shortage of managerial personnel is acute, at present, and is likely to continue for a longer time than elsewhere. Such augmentation to civil service cadres should be based on reliable manpower assessments so that the long term objective of developing internal self-sufficiency is not jeopardized.

4.6.5 The selection and training of civil service personnel to man senior managerial positions have also to be reviewed. The requirements of industrial and commercial management are often different from those of Government. Quick decision making, capacity to take risks, familiarity with all aspects of management of Finance Materials, personnel and Industrial Relations etc., are required.

4.6.6 The requirement of training may be first discussed. At present there is very little of management training in the curriculum of the civil services' training. No doubt the Lal Bahadur Shastri National Academy of Administration. The Indian Institute of Public Administration etc., have in recent years made good efforts to fill this gap by incorporating into the executive development programmes of the civil services appropriate management training inputs, but there is a long way to go to make the training imparted to the civil services more oriented towards industrial and commercial management.

4.6.7 The State government should immediately enlist the support of the Management Training Institutions in the country to provide the civil services with this training. Preferably, such training could be organized in groups rather than by deputaiton of individual officers to programmes run by the different institutions. The pay-off from group training may be more than what can be obtained from training of individual officers. In order to organise suitable training programmes some identification of the training needs will have to be done. This is an area where the nodal organisation could play a part. In addition, the Department of Personnel would also have to take a greater initiative in this matter. Such identification of training needs could also help in organising tailor-made programmes for groups of civil servants who are and are likely to shoulder public sector responsibilities.

4.7 Development of Internal Resources

4.7.1 It is necessary to consider the future demands that would arise for the proper management of the public enterprises in the area of top management personnel. Some lessons learnt from the experience of the Central Govenrment would be relevant. In the early stages, the Central Government depend on its own cadre , like the State Governments at present to man the top level posts in the enterprises. This continued till late in the 1960s when the policy was changed on the recommendations of the Administrative Reforms Commission (ARC) made in their Report on Public Sector Undertakings (1967).

4.7.2 The ARC strongly favoured steps for making public enterprises self-reliant in top managerial resources. The policy of Government deputationists has serious disadvantages. Deputationists from Government may not have the right type of professional and entrepreneurial approach which is so necessary for success in the business world. The needs of managing industrial and commercial enterprises require experience, knowledge and skills, which are different from those needed in Government. Reasonable continuity of tenure and loyalty to and substantial interest in the organization are also necessary. The induction of "outsiders" jeopardize career prospects and morale of those permanently employed in the orgnaisation. Deputationists belonging to permanent civil service cadres could also undermine accountability if the system of appraisal is weak.

4.7.3 The Government of India, therefore, decided to reduce dependence of the enterprises on deputationists by requiring them to exercise an option either to be permanently absorbed in the enterprises or to revert to their parent cadres within 2/3 years. This policy has reduced the number of deputationists from Government services manning top posts in the public enterprises of the Central Government.

4.7.4 Along with this policy the Central Government also offered incentives for its officers to seek a permanent career in the public enterprises. These incentives include the grant of pay *plus* pension earned in Government service, as well as carry forward of other service benefits. These incentives have induced mainly Government officers to go over to the public enterprises and thereby strengthen the managerial resources of the enterprises at the top level.

4.7.5 The argument which weighed with the ARC in recommending a reduction of deputationists from Government have their own relevance from a long term point of view for the State enterprises also. While for good reasons it may not be possible for the State Governments to adopt the policy of the Central Government in its entirely, a determined effort has to be made to develop top managers from within the public enterprises' system. The induction of quality materials at eh lower and middle levels and their careful development, no doubt, provide the answer to this question. In the short term, however, certain steps could be taken to ensure that the dependence on deputationists and the ill-effects of such policy are reduced.

4.7.6 At the middle and lower levels, the induction of Government officers should. To the extent possible, be resorted to only where strong grounds exist. In these cases, the period of deputation should be restricted to 2 or 3 years. Suitable incentives should be given to Government officers to get themselves absorbed in the enterprises on the expiry of this period.

4.7.7 At the higher levels also the selection of Government officers for posts in public enteprises should be made after a careful evaluation of their capabilities and aptitudes with reference tot he requirements of the organisation. Their terms of appointment should also reflect the requirements of the organisation and the officer. In other words, the tenure of such appointments and level should provide for a reasonable period of deputation which would be necessary to fulfil the objectives of the organisation. Developments in his own cadre should not be allowed to affect the tenure and reasonable commitment of the deputationist.

4.8 Selection Procedure for Top Posts

4.8.1 Quite apart from the long-term requirements there is an urgent need to improve the selection procedure for top posts in public enterprises. In most of the States, there is no well defined machinery or distinct procedure for the selection of personnel for top posts in the enterprises. The general practice is for the concerned administrative Department of Personnel and the Chief Secretary. This practice is in vogue in Assam, A.P., Bihar., Haryana, M.P., Karnataka, Kerala, Maharashtra, Punjab, Rajasthan, Tamil

Nadu and J & K. In U.P., the "panel system" has been evolved whereby the administrative department prepares a panel, in consultation with the Appointments Department for the final decision of the Minster who is in administrative charge of the enterprise. Bihar proposes to go in for a similar system.

4.8.2 In reforming selection procedure also the experience of the Government of India could be useful to the states. In the earlier days, the Government of India followed an empanelling procedure for selection to top posts. The system was introduced in 1965 whereby a Committee of Secretaries under the Chairmanship of the cabinet Secretary was constituted for drawing up panels of suitable persons both from Government and private sector. A general advertisement was put out soliciting applications from the private sector. Similar invitations were circulated to the Government services. The suitability of applicants from Government service was considered on the basis of their confidential reports whereas private sector applicants were invited to meet the Selection Committee for assessing their suitability. In 1968, some minor changes were effected in the constitution of the Empanelment Committee. Some senior chief executives were also included as members of the committee. It was further decided that the suitability of applicants from both Government services and the private sector should be assessed on the basis of a personal interview.

4.8.3 The major change in policy came in August 1974 with the constitution of the Public Enterprises Selection Board (PESB). As at present constituted the Board has five Members with a Member of the Planning Commission as its Chairman, two Secretaries of the important public sector Ministries, and two senior chief executives of public sector enterprises. The Director General of the Bureau of Public Enterprises is a permanent invitee.

4.8.4 The responsibilities of the Board were mainly two. Firstly, the Board had to advise Government on all appointments to the posts of:

(a) Part-time Chairman;
(b) Chairman and Managing Director/Managing Director;
(c) All full-time Directors.

Secondly, the board had the responsibility of overseeing management development efforts and organisational structures of the enterprises so as to improve top management efficiency.

4.8.5 The PESB was expected to make selection procedures more scientific. Certain steps had to be take to ensure this. Firstly, selection has to be made with clear idea of the requirements of the job. For this, it would be necessary to analyse the description of the job, drawn up with information available on the past performance of the company and its future needs. In the case of top posts it has to be remembered that the job requirements for different posts vary and do not fall into the 'standard' patterns applicable to Government posts. The requirements could vary not only from post to post but in the case of the same post from time to time. Unless the selections are made after careful assessment of these requirements, they are not likely to be satisfactory.

4.8.6 Similarly, the qualities of the candidates have to be assessed in a reliable manner with reference to the job requirements. The procedure of going through the confidential record dossiers and assessing on the basis of performance in posts with unrelated requirements may not ensure the best results.

4.8.7 Thirdly, in order to obtain the best person for the job it is necessary to ensure that there is a wide filed of choice. For this purpose, a Data Bank of suitable persons has to be built up for servicing the various selections.

(i) is necessary to constitute a machinery in the State Governments for spotting of talent particularly for the top management posts in the public enterprises. The sources from which talent have to be drawn would be the State Government enterprises, those from the civil service who have had an exposure to public sector management, managers of the Central Government enterprises and private sector. The availability of a ready reserve of such officers would help in the timely filling up of critical vacancies in the public enterprises by suitable persons. The reserve should be formed after careful evaluation of their suitability on the basis of their record by an expert body. This would result in better deployment of resources.

(ii) A permanent committee comprising of the Chief Secretary, the Secretary of the Adminsitrative Department of the enterprise, where the vacancy has arisen, another senior Secretary and one or two senior men from public and private sector industry should be constituted for screening the names for inclusion in the reserve list and for selecting the best persons for holding top vacancies in the public enterprises. Such selections should be done by this committee on the basis of job requirement of each post.

(iii) If it is necessary to continue for some time to depend on the civl services for providing top management talent, particularly in the promotional and other enterprises having an inter-face with government, it is necessary that a system should be evolved for spotting managerial talent among the civil servants and providing for their training and development. For this purpose, it may be necessary that civil servants are exposed to industrial management in the middle level posts after they have completed five or six years of service and suitable development programmes built into their cadre management.

(iv) The tenure of civil servants deputed to public enterprises should be long enough as to provide an adequate opportunity for performance and accountability. The interests of the organisation should be taken into account while deciding the tenure. The tenure rules should not be applied rigidly and the selection body should specify the exact tenure for which the government officers would be available to the organization.

(v) The nodal organization would be the appropriate body to service the selection machinery. Without adequate organisational support, the difficult process of selection and maintenance of track records cannot be fulfilled.

(vi) The remuneration policy for appointees to top posts in public enterprises should be decided with reference to responsibilities. In the case of officers deputed from the government services, while there may be need to have some relation to their pay in government, it would be necessary to offer some incentive for taking on public sector responsibilities. For outsiders there should be greater flexibility in pay scales, which should be decided in accordance with the requirements and qualifications of the post as well as the general compensation levels for similar posts elsewhere.

CHAPTER 5

WAGE POLICY

5.1 One of the important areas where the need for a common approach ahs been felt is in the matter of Wage Policy. Various issues are involved in this. Though wage matters are generally determined on the basis of industry/region considerations, it has been the experience that considerable variations have occurred which have caused problems. The right of public enterprises to decide on the wages of its employees taking into account industry and regional matters cannot be disputed. The argument that companies may have to use the wage structure as an incentive for motivating employees for higher productivity cannot also be denied.

5.2 There are, however, certain considerations for over all policy which cannot be ignored. "Capacity to pay" cannot be accepted as the sole or even important criterion for deciding compensation. This is not a guiding principle even in private industry. In the public sector where profits are often the result of public policy., e.g., monopoly rights, pricing etc, it is even more difficult to justify the capacity of individual enterprise to pay as an important criterion for deciding on wage levels. There is the further consideration of rationality which is necessary even on grounds of equity. Government companies cannot practice anomalous or discriminatory wage policy amongst themselves. They have to ensure that equal pay is given for the same job. The size of the public sector causes repercussions on other sector of the State and national economy.

5.3 Admittedly, most of these aspects will be covered when a National Wage Policy is formulated. But in the meantime the public enterprises will have to be endeavor to bring about the desirable rationality in their wage structure to avoid undue distortions within the public sector and the economy as a whole. In many cases the lack of a common approach has adversely affected industrial relations in the public enterprises resulting in a set-back in the company's performance. It is in this context that the Group would like to discuss possible measures for improving wage administration.

5.4 In the Central Government the need for such rationality has been increasingly felt during the last more than 5 years. Though initially this was felt in the context of the difficult economic situation caused by drought and inflation it soon became apparent that there were other good grounds for pursuing such a policy. The Central Government have, therefore, been working towards a policy which would reduce anomalies, distortions and heart-burning by direct involvement in any general wage settlement. Since 1971-72 all proposals involving general revision of wages have to be approved by the Central Government. The Central Government examines the matter in the administrative Ministry, the Ministry of Labour and the Bureau of Public Enterprises. The proposals drawn up as a result of this examination are then approved by Government. Prior to this formal examination the companies are advised to have informal consultation with Government so as to be briefed on the board parameters the enterprises should observe in their discussions with the trade unions.

5.5 It may be too early to assess the working of this policy particularly as it relates to a rather extraordinary period in the area of industrial relations. Nevertheless, it may be safely stated that some progress towards desirable rationality's has been achieved. This has smoothened industrial relations to some extent.

5.6 However, there have been occasions when companies felt that this procedure seriously eroded corporate autonomy and resulted in inevitable delays which such consultations result in causing difficulties to management's in maintaining their credibility and relationship with unions.

5.7 From a review of the replies received from the State Governments, it appears that except for Assam none of the other States has made any conscious and positive attempts to bring about a common approach to wage matters in the public enterprises, with the result, the enterprises are generally allowed to decide matters on a bipartite or tripartite basis and go by the normal requirements of the Industrial Disputes Act. In other words, the Boards of the enterprises are competent to decide on these matters without consultation with the Government.

5.8 Assam has however, adopted the central government policy and made it necessary on the part of the enterprises to obtain prior approval of government for revising wage structures. They have also stated that this requirement has been built into the Articles of Association of most of the enterprises.

5.9 The Government of Uttar Pradesh is considering the need for devising a mechanism for a common approach on wage policies of the enterprises under its control.

5.10 In Maharashtra, the enterprises generally adopt the Government's scales of pay. Where this is not so, the Management's are required to consult the Government.

5.11 Punjab have issued instructions to Government enterprises that they should follow the pay scales of the State Government wherever the duties are the same. This would apply generally only to the non-technical posts.

5.12 The absence of a formal mechanism for consultation with the State Governments need not necessarily mean that there is complete autonomy for the Boards of the Enterprises to decide on wage issues. Many States Governments have brought to the notice of the Group that the presence of Government Directors, particularly the representative of the Finance Department has helped in aligning wage policies with government and national requirements.

Recommendations

5.13 The need to have rationality in the compensation policy of the different sectors of the economy has been widely accepted. This would be a difficult objective to achieve but in the meantime the Government enterprises, both at the Center and in the States, should provide a lead to the progressive formulation and adoption of such a national policy by bringing about a common approach to wage matters in their enterprises. The public enterprises matters in their enterprises. The public enterprises constitute the lead sector of the country's industries. The policies adopted here will have an important bearing on other sectors. The determination of policies is admittedly a very complex one. Many local, industrial and national factors have to be taken into account. This would require centralized policy making and decentralized negotiation and decision. The complexity of the problem does not permit it to be left to an informal approach through part-time government Directors. These Directors may themselves be inadequately aware of all the implications. The Group would recommend the adoption of a suitable mechanism which would make available to the enterprises relevant information in regard to other public enterprises, government policy etc. some prior consultation by the enterprises with government either in the administrative department or the nodal organisation before commencing negotiations with organisation before commencing negotiations with Trade Unions may be useful. If such consultation with Government is needed, it is necessary that the machinery in Government should be appropriately structured so as to provide proper high level and timely guidance. It may also be useful to work timely guidance. It may also be useful to work towards a common date for negotiation of wage matters. This would help for an integrated approach to be taken.

CHAPTER 6

BOARD OF DIRECTORS

6.1 For ensuring the proper functioning of the public enterprises sufficient attention is to be paid to the policy regarding Boards of Directors. The Boards of Directors could be of different types. The general distinction that is drawn is between the Policy Making Board and the Executive Board. In the Indian situation, both at the Center and in the States, we have the pattern of a "mixed board"combining both the executive and policy-making functions with the latter responsibility being shared with Government.

6.2 In the mixed type of Boards having executive and evaluation functions, safeguards have to be provided for ensuring that the evaluation function does not suffer. This is sought to be done by providing external Members and a part-time Chairman who does not form part of the Executive. For such a system to work care has to be given to the selection of the external Members and the part-time Chairman.

6.3 Part-time Chairman

6.3.1 In most of the States the general policy is to have a part-time Chairman. This is true of Assam, Bihar, Haryana, Kerala, Madhya Pradesh, Maharashtra, Punjab, Tamil Nadu and Andhra Pradesh. In the States of Karnataka, Rajasthan, Uttar Pradesh and Jammu & Kashmir, there is a shift towards having more Chairman-cum-Managing Director.

6.3.2 The sources from which part-time Chairmen are drawn to head the State Government enterprises are mainly two-public life and Government. Men from public life are appointed as part-time Chairmen in the States of Assam, Bihar, Karnataka, and Maharashtra. In the other States it appears that the Secretaries to Government are more often appointed as part-time Chairman.

6.3.3 In some States appointment of Ministers and sitting MPs and MLAs as part-time Chairman has been the practice. In the State of Jammu & Kashmir, for example, the Minister of Industry functioned as the part-time Chairman of all the public enterprises in the industries sector. In Karnataka also there have been quite a few cases where sitting and former MPs and MLAs were appointed to the posts of part-time Chairman.

6.3.4 As stated earlier, the part-time Chairman can provide a salutary external influence for evaluation and direction of the Company's affairs. His contribution would of course depend on the qualities and experience that he can bring to bear to his responsibilities. Unless he is able to keep cordial relations with the Managing Director it could result in conflict.

6.3.5 The undesirable aspects of a policy of appointing Ministers and sitting Members of Legislatures as part-time Chairman was forcefully brought out by the Krishna Menon Committee on Public Enterprises. The arguments put forth by the Committee have considerable force. They are reproduced below:-

Members of Parliament on Boards

(1) A more difficult question to decide arises in the matter of Members of Parliament or Legislative Assemblies, and whether they should be Members of Boards of Management. The overwhelming weight of considerations must be against it. Such membership even if it carries no emoluments carries much power and patronage. The member of Parliament concerned is apart of the organ of public control and is the exponent of public criticism in Parliament. As a Director and part of a concern's administration he is responsible for the very conduct and affairs which parliament, and therefore, he ,is called upon to examine, criticize and judge. Having specialized and inside knowledge, he can use it in Parliament and elsewhere, when he has disagreements with his colleagues on the Board and whishes to take a line apart from the team

of which he is a Member. His colleagues who are not Members of Parliament like himself cannot reply. They are "officials"-employed in State Undertakings. His Parliamentary colleagues are also at a disadvantage because he purports to speak from expert and inside knowledge. The Minster finds himself in a very embarrassing position when the matter is debated in the House.

(2) There is also the further consideration-for whom does he speak? (1) If he speaks for the industry in Parliament he takes the place of the Minister; (2) if he speaks for the Board as Managing Director or Chairman, being one himself, then he has greater facilities which other MPs do not have; (3) if he turns critic, he places every one including the industry in an adverse position.

(3) It will be understood that such a Member of Parliament, who is not a member of Government, cannot take over the functions and duties of a Minister. He cannot be a critic for the reasons stated above. Thus, he can neither defend nor criticize, for as Chairman or a Director of the Company concerned he has access to information which others do not have and which he should not use. Therefore, if a Member of Parliament is Chairman or even a Director, he would disqualify himself for participation in discussions in regard to the concern he is associated with, and there would be severed limitations in regard to his participation in debates on similar concerns or State concerns as a whole. On the other hand, he cannot be obliged to sit in Parliament unconcerned, when the debt is on matters of which he has knowledge. This, in effect, would prevent him from functioning fully as a Member of parliament. If on the other hand, he were to use his position and his knowledge, then he places the concern of which he is an active and responsible part and the Board at a great disadvantage as well as in a position of embarrassment. His colleagues and the concern are not represented in Parliament except the

Minister represents. In the result, therefore, appointment of Members of parliament in Corporations is altogether an unhealthy practice and is difficult to justify.

(Government decision on the above recommendation)

"Members of Parliament should not be appointed to Boards of Directors".

6.3.6 The appointment of Secretaries to Government as apart-time Chairman also has some drawbacks. By his seniority in the official hierarchy and his proximity to the Chief Secretary and the Ministers, he may exert an undue influence on the running of the company without direct responsibility. This might dilute accountability. Secondly, as the head of the department responsible for administering the enterprise he becomes a part of its successes and failures. His evaluation role is thereby undermined.

6.3.7 These considerations point to the need for giving greater thought to the selection of part-time Chairman. Though part-time he has an important role to play providing objective evaluation of executive performance and necessary guidance to the Board and the Chief Executive. The part-time Chairman should bring skills and capabilities which would supplement those of the Managing Director. The role of the part-time Chairman has, therefore, to be assessed as carefully as that of the Chief Executive and his selection decided on the basis of his qualifications from whatever source he may be drawn-government service, public life, industry or professions. The same institutional machinery recommended for the selection of Chief Executives and top personnel should be responsible for the selection of part-time Chairman.

6.4 Other Members of the Board

6.4.1 Apart from the Chairman and the Managing Director there are full-time and part-time Directors on the

Board of Directors of the public enterprises. It was seen that the public enterprises in the States have not as yet gone in for appointment of full-time functional/executive directors as the Central Government enterprises have done. Apart from the chief executive (who could be either the Chairman-cum-Managing Director or the Managing Director), there is generally no other full-time Director on the Board. A few exceptions are some of the larger enterprises like the Electricity Boards and other major manufacturing corporations where generally the finance and technical functions are represented on the Board. An important advantage of having full time functional/ executive director is that they provide a ready source for succession at the top. The other advantage is that the chief executive could divest himself of day to day matters by delegating these to the other full-time Directors and thereby concentrate on the bigger issues of long term policy, external relations, evaluation etc. the size of the operation would determine the need for having full-time Directors. It would be useful to have them in the larger organizations where responsibilities can be onerous and delegation and functional specialization would be helpful. In the smaller organization which constitute the majority of the State government enterprises there may not be a need for appointing full-time functional/executive directors. Then there are part-time Directors who are to be considered. Generally, these directors are drawn from the Government services, industry, representatives of labour and other important interests. As stated earlier the Board of Directors have an important role to play in regard to the evaluation of the performance of the executive and the drawing up of long term policies and strategies. To do this it is necessary that care is taken to appoint to the Board only those who can make a useful contribution. This requirement holds good equally for these drawn from the Government services and other sources. Extraneous influence should not be allowed to dominate the selection of part-time directors of public enterprises.

6.4.2 It is also necessary to see that the composition of the Board of Directors is well balanced. The general practice is to have excessive representation from the government departments. Government directors should be limited to two or three.

6.4.3 The size of the Board is also important. Unduly large Boards comprising heterogeneous members can prove dysfunctional. It would be best to have a compact Board of about 10 members in order to achieve greater cohesion and effectiveness.

6.5 Recommendations

(1) It is necessary to ensure that the evaluation responsibility of the Board of Directors is adequately performed. This would require that the Board of Directors have suitable members from outside as Directors.

(2) The appointment of Ministers and sitting Members of Legislatures and Parliament on the Boards of Directors would undermine the evaluation responsibility of the Board of Directors and compromise their position as Members of the Legislature. Hence, as a rule it may be desirable not to saddle Ministers and Members of Legislatures with Directorships of publci enterprises.

(3) The need for a part-time Chairman has to be carefully assessed. If it is necessary to have a part-time Chairman his selection should be made with the same care as that given to the selection of the Managing Director.

(4) In larger enterprises it would be good to have full-time executive/functional directors.

(5) In the composition of the Board of Directors it is necessary to see that excessive representation is not given to the Government departments and that the Board is well-balanced.

(6) Small boards could be more cohesive and effective.

CHAPTER 7

RELATIONSHIP WITH THE LEGISLATURE AND GOVERNMENT

"There is no need to argue that the Government and the Legislatures should possess certain powers of control over public enterprises. This is essential to bring them in line with the requirements of current public policy. The alternatives are either no effective control at all or control by bodies without political responsibility-both of which may be ruled out as harmful and/or impracticable".

The quotation from A.H. Hanson may give the proper perspective for discussion of the subject covered in this chapter.

7.1 Control of Legislature

7.1.1 A public enterprise usually needs approval of the Legislature for its establishment and the exercise of its functions. It may also need finances provided through the legislative processes. As a part of the administrative apparatus, supervised by a Minister who is responsible to the Legislature, it also becomes administratively under its control. The relationship and control over the public enterprises of the Legislature is operated through:

(1) Voting of funds;
(2) Discussion of Annual Reports;
(3) Statutory obligations either under special statutes or under some general legislation like the Company's Act:
(4) Reports of the Comptroller & Auditor General; and
(5) Investigations of the Committee on Public Undertakings and questions in the Legislature.

7.1.2 The formal and informal relationship of the public enterprises with the Legislatures would depend on the political environment, the importance of the public sector in the State's affairs as much as conventions regarding corporate autonomy, quality of management etc. this explains the wide differences that can be observed in the State.

7.1.3 The Group was not able to study in depth the relationship between the Legislature and the public enterprises in the States. The Committee on public undertakings of the State Legislatures generally takes great deal of interest in the working of public enterprises. This interest would have a healthy effect in the evaluation of performance of the enterprises. The Legislature will have to concentrate on general aspects like achievement of the enterprises in terms of the objectives laid down, their overall planning and contribution to State policy and satisfy themselves that the resources invested in these enterprises are put to the best use in this context. In order to discharge this responsibility the Legislatures may have to avoid getting into the details of day to day administration. The practice in some States of appointing sitting Members of Legislature as pat-time Chairman could lead to undermining the main responsibility of the Legislature relating to the evaluation of the performance of the enterprises. The Group wishes to emphasize that a concerted effort should be made to create conditions conducive for a healthy and constructive relationship being built up between the public enterprises and the Legislatures.

7.1.4 The main thrust of any effort to strengthen the relationship between the Legislature and the public enterprises would lie in improving the ability of the enterprises and Government to satisfy the legitimate curiosity and concern of the Legislatures. However, as Hanson pointed out, the dilemma of Parliamentary accountability has to be recognised. While lack of information breeds suspicion, the acquisition of it may lead to excessive interference. Though it is accepted that Legislatures should restrict themselves to policy matters and not interfere in day-to-day affairs the dividing line between the two can often be thin.

7.1.5 It would be safe to conclude that much could be done to provide the legislatures with timely and necessary information. The present systems of annual reporting to the Legislatures is far from satisfactory. Very often, it consists merely of the submission of the audited accounts containing perhaps an analysis of commercial profitability. Even this is not done, as very often there is considerable delay in the finalisation of the accounts. Public enterprises have important socio-economic objectives. Lack of information on the achievement of these objectives is often the cause of excessive interference by the Legislature on minor matters. The utility of Annual Reports should be increased by making them more informative in respect of a critical assessment of the performance measured against the objectives set for them not only in terms of profits but also other indices such as utilization of resources, regional development, development of skills etc. The nodal organisation could provide a useful agency for making such an assessment for reporting to the Legislature.

7.1.6 Steps should be taken to improve the communication between the legislatures and the public enterprises. The information gap is often considerable. Appropriate systems could be built up for maintaining such information in the administrative departments and the nodal organisation to meet the legitimate requirements of the members of the legislatures.

7.2 Relationship of Public Enterprises with Government

7.2.1 The relationship between public enterprises and government is governed by:

(1) The power of appointment of chief executive and other members of the Board;
(2) Authority to sanction investment beyond delegated limits;
(3) Call for returns and information to conduct performance reviews;
(4) Approval of plans and budgets;
(5) Approval of the revenue budget if there is a loss which is to be made good from budgetary sources;
(6) Appointment of auditors;
(7) Power to issue such directives or instructions that Government may consider necessary; and
(8) In a few cases power to approve the terms and conditions of service of employees.

7.2.2 Apart from the formal powers indicated above the government can exercise considerable informal control over the enterprises. The degree of such informal control would, of course, depend upon the capacity of the enterprises to withstand it. Wherever enterprises have been headed by competent people of standing it has been observed that the informal control of government is not excessive. On the other hand, where the Boards of Directors and the chief executives are weak the government can assume almost a strangle hold on the enterprises. Another form in which informal control is exercised is through the hierarchy of civil service. When the chief executives belong to the civil service their *inter-se* position with the Secretaries to Government would have considerable influence on the relationship between the government and the enterprises.

7.2.3 Greater clarity of objectives would go a long way is establishing a mutually beneficial relationship between the public enterprises and its supervisory agencies. Unfortunately, this is a weak area in the public sector system. A determined effort should be made both by government and the public enterprises to evolve mutually accepted organisational plans giving in clear mutually accepted organisational plans strategies to achieve them. Such an exercise would enable clarify the boundary roles and keep them to the minimal as well as provide for a more objective yardstick to measure performance.

7.2.4 Another form by which the relationship between the enterprises and the government could be improved is by having a suitable consultative machinery. In most States such a machinery is non-existent. Government will stand to greatly benefit by prior consultation with the enterprises before formulating general policies which effect them. This is a function which could be performed by the nodal organisation.

7.2.5 The other measures discussed elsewhere for improving the exercise of government powers in regard to appointment and appraisal of investments would also help in putting the relationship between the legislature and public enterprises on a better footing.

7.3 Recommendations

(1) It is necessary for the public enterprises to furnish to the legislature and government more information so that they may be better informed of the critical areas of the functioning of public enterprises:

(2) A critical assessment of the performance of the enterprises not only in terms of financial results but also in terms of utilisation of resources achievement of socio-economic objectives etc., should be made available to the government and legislature;

(3) Greater clarity of objectives would put the relationship between public enterprises and their supervisory bodies on a more purposeful and helpful footing;

(4) A suitable machinery should be evolved by government to consult with the public enterprises before framing important policies affecting them.

CHAPTER 8

SOME ASPECTS OF FINANCIAL MANGEMENT AND PERFORMANCE APPRAISAL

8.1 Financial management is, of course, too wide an area to be covered by the Standing Group. Nevertheless, considering its importance, it was thought necessary to broadly examine at least some of the more important aspects like: 1. Investment Appraisal, 2. Performance Appraisal, 3. Costing and Audit and 4. Management Information Systems.

8.2 Investment Appraisal

8.2.1 Few decisions determine the eventual success or failure of a public enterprises than that relating to creation of a public enterprise through an investment. It is the quality of this decision that proves the entrepreneurial capability and the success of the venture. Alas this is also perhaps the weakest area in public sector management.

8.2.2 Investment proposals are appraised on the basis of a feasibility report. This is generally drawn up for the State Governments by professional consultants or the financial institutions. The Group did not have adequate information to comment on the quality of these feasibility reports except to say that it would not be worng to presume that their quality was uneven.

8.2.3 Investment appraisal is generally done by the finance department and the project authorities. Where the project is financed by the State financial institutions, these also appraise investment proposals.

8.2.4 The areas in which improvement is to be effected are preparation of feasibility reports and appraisal techniques. The common experience is that the feasibility reports prove unreliable in many ways particularly with regard to the estimation of costs and time and assessment of demand and benefits. While costs are often under-estimated, demand and benefits are assessed optimistically. Many of the project agencies may not themselves have the expertise required for preparation of reliable feasibility reports. The data base for such reports could also be inadequate.

8.2.5 In regard to appraising agencies there is perhaps a lack of professionalism in the evaluation of public sector investment proposals. The project authorities, the administrative departments, financial institutions and the finance department are the main appraising agencies. While the capability to appraise has to be strengthened in all these agencies it requires to be particularly improved in the finance departments of the State Governments. This is the department which gives the final clearance and strengthening of evaluation at this level could have a healthy effect on the whole process. The staff of the finance department has to be professionalised in order to take a managerial and entrepreneurial approach towards investment in the public sector. It may not be always possible to obtain such experienced personnel from the regular government services. Professional emn will therefore have to be inducted into the finance department. This department should have at least one senior officer at the level immediately below the Secretary of the Department with professional finance background. Expertise other than finance would often be needed to evaluate proposals. It may not be necessary or even desirable to provide for such expertise within Government. It will be best to draw upon the resources available in the public enterprises themselves (both of the State and Central

Governments) and other professional bodies. State institutions like the Finance Corporation, Industrial Development Corporations, Investment Corporations etc, could be strengthened professionally and used to a greater extent by Government for the purpose of evaluating public sector investment proposals. The State Governments would greatly benefit by the advice of such independent second tire institutions which are closer to the real operating situations.

8.2.6 Another way in which investment decisions could be improved is by involving the operating level fully in the decision making process from the beginning. Far too often this does not happen. Investment decisions, particularly in the case of new enterprises are often taken without the association of the managers who will be primarily responsible for implementing the project. Apart from denying the benefit of their experience this could undermine accountability and subsequent evaluation of the project.

8.3 Public Investment Board of the Government of India

8.3.1 The Government of India have taken some steps to improve its investment appraisal system for the public sector. It has set-up the Public Investment Board under the Chairmanship of Secretary (Department of Expenditure), Ministry of Finance. Other members of the Board are Secretary to the Prime Minister, the Secretary (Planning Commission), Secretary (Economic Affairs), D.G., B.P.F. (Permanent Invitee) and the Secretary of the administrative Ministry. This Board examines proposals from overall techno-economic considerations and plan priorities. The association of the Coordinating Secretaries (Planning Commission, Prime Minister's Secretariat, Industrial Development, Economic Affairs) helps in getting quick approval at the highest level.

8.3.2 The experience of the PIB set-up in September 1972 as per the Government of India Resolution given in Appendix VII has been on the whole, satisfactory. It has led to a more purposeful evaluation of proposals, better appreciation of the real cost-benefit aspects of such proposals and a closer integration of individual proposals with overall development programmes. It has also helped in improving the quality of the feasibility reports which is of considerable importance and the homework done by the project authorities.

8.3.3 Except in Assam and Uttar Pradesh, in none of the other State Governments are there organisations similar to the Public Investment Board of the Government of India. The Bihar Government propose to established Public Investment Board on the pattern of the Central Government. Even the U.P. Investment Board has come into being recently. It may not be necessary for the State Governments to go infor a similar organisation but strengthening of the institutional arrangement for evaluating investment proposals is called for. The Standing Group would suggest that a Committee to be called the Public Sector Investment Clearance Committee should be constituted. The Committee should be headed by the Chief Secretary himself or by an eminent finance or industrialist. In addition, the Finance Secretary and the Secretary of the sponsoring department should be associated with the Committee. It would be a good practice if the Committee invites the chief executive or the chief executive-designate of the project to participate in the meeting of the Committee when their proposals come up for consideration. Apart from these 4 members, the Committee would benefit by the association of one or two other members from outside who have mature experience and intimate knowledge of industry and finance. This Committee should be the final body to recommend to Government on all investment decisions beyond a certain limit.

8.4 Performance Appraisal

8.4.1 There is no denying that performance can be significantly improved through more precise, measurement. Evaluation techniques and practices, therefore, assume importance in any systematic effort to improve public sector management.

8.4.2 In the public sector performance evaluation is done at two levels. At the Corporate Level this is the main responsibility of the Board of Directors. Then there is the evaluation done by supervisory agencies-the administrative department and the State Legislature.

8.4.3 The multiplicity of assessing authorities make a dispassionate evaluation difficult. An even more complicating factor is the diverse objectives of public enterprises.

8.4.4 Monitoring of performance at the different levels will, obviously, have to be done by different yardsticks. It requires a certain amount of understanding of the exact responsibility of the different supervisory agencies. While this is accepted there is no gain saying the fact that very often the Board of Directors, the administrative departments, the Finance department and the Legislature are not quite sure what would fall within their supervisory purview in regard to the public enterprises. This is not surprising. Even in countries like the United Kingdom with a longer history of nationalised industry and more advanced management systems than ours, the position is not quite satisfactory.

8.4.5 Often, the dividing line that is drawn between the enterprise and its supervisory agencies in the matter of evaluation is that while matters relating to day-to-day administration would fall within the purview of the former the supervisory agencies will be concerned with overall aspects of policy and performance, achievements of objectives and targets etc. The dividing line however, is often very thin creating complications. There is no easy solution and the supervisory bodies will have to acquire greater understanding of the issues involved in order to perform their role purposefully and to the good of the enterprises.

8.4.6 Broadly, it may be stated that the Legislatures are concerned with the performance of the enterprise with reference to the objectives for which it was set up its contribution to the national good and conformity with State policies.

8.4.7 The Government will be involved in the achievement of long-term and short-term targets: profits and contribution to general revenues and self-financing: utilisation of resources in men, machines and materials; performance of the Board of Directors and the Chief Executives; performance of the company with reference to the general economic conditions and the other relevant sectors of the economy etc.

8.4.8 The Board of Directors should be concerned with the performance of the Executives in regard to the general operations of the enterprise and its day-to-day management. It should also assess the performance of the Chief Executive and other senior members of the management team. It should evaluate the performance of the company with reference to the targets set for it jointly by itself and Government and with reference to the utilisation of the resources at its command and in comparison to other comparable units.

In keeping with the above broad boundary lines in regard to the responsibilities of supervisory agencies suitable reporting systems will have to be evolved. The discussion in the next part of this chapter will also be relevant.

8.5 Costing and Internal Audit Arrangements

8.5.1 Costing and internal audit have by now received universal acceptance as necessary inputs in efficient management of business enterprises whether in private or public sector. On the other hand, there is widespread scarcity of qualified men willing to serve State enterprises in these areas. In some States, it was noticed that these skills were just not available adequately while in some States it was seen the size or scale of operations of some of the smaller enterprises resulted in qualified men being not attracted to them. The Group took note of this phenomenon in their deliberations. It was recognised that certain State enterprises need give higher priorities to procuring these skills than other enterprises and that smaller enterprises may not find it possible or justifiable to obtain professionals in these areas on exclusive basis

8.5.2 The spectrum of activities carried on by the State Enterprises is indeed wide and varied. At one end stand road transportation and electricity generation and distribution while at the other end stand zonal or community development. The importance and urgency of setting up adequate costing and internal audit arrangements differ, therefore from enterprise to enterprise. The road transportation corporations and electricity boards which have now been set-up by almost all the States need to be adequately served by both the Cost Accountants and Internal Auditors. This assumes importance not only for the top management of these enterprises but also for those who provide bulk of the funds for these corporations viz., the State Governments and more often than not other lending agencies also. The scale of operations of these enterprises and the amount of funds invested in them make it incumbent that the evaluation of performance of these enterprises should be done in depth. Inter-enterprise comparisons of efficiency indicators are not only possible in these enterprises but are also taken note of by the provider of funds to these enterprises. The same holds good for major manufacturing enterprises like textile mills or cement factories which some of the State Governments have set up in public sector. Although a reduced emphasis on costing input would be understandable in case of industrial development and financial corporations, the overriding necessity of internal audit arrangements in these financial or predominantly financial entities has to be noted. As these enterprises borrow funds in turn from Central Financial Institutions, there is the added necessity towards providing internal audit as management input.

8.5.3 Outside these categories of enterprises, the paucity and cost of skills in these areas make it obligatory that other enterprises consider other devices to obtain these inputs. Internal audit services, is suitable cases, where the work-load so warrants may have to be obtained on payment from, outside professional experts. It would be, however, much better if the nodal agency maintains under its own umbrella or otherwise a small group, who could provide these inputs to smaller enterprises. In their formative period, it might be advisable for smaller enterprises to share the pool of qualified people than to make separate arrangements internally within each enterprise through men not so well qualified.

8.5.4 The State nodal agencies may have to assess the long-term requirements of State enterprises in these areas and make training arrangements. In this task the assistance of the Central Bureau or other professional bodies would be possible and be of undoubtedly great help.

8.5.5 The Group apprehends that non-provision of these inputs have handicapped identification of locations where resources are under-utilised or losses are incurred. The benefits from supplying these inputs in their opinion, would be more than commensurate with the cost of their supply.

8.6 Management Information System for Performance Review and Control

8.6.1 Some method of periodical reporting by the enterprises to Government existed in most of the States. The form, content and periodicity of these reports varied. Apart from the formal systems the informal links in communication between Government and public enterprises are important.

8.6.2 In Assam, periodical reporting to Government has been recently introduced. The Government may also call for special reports. While some companies of Andhra Pradesh send reports to Government periodically, others do not. The system seems to have been determined in accordance with the changing demands of the departments concerned. The Bihar Government's Bureau of Public Enterprises has devised certain questionnaires, which are required to be sent by the enterprises to the administrative Departments and the Bureau. In Haryana, while monthly and quarterly reports regarding allocations, capital expenditure and physical targets/achievements are prepared for the Board of Directors, these are submitted to Government have three monthly reports for allocation of funds. Madhya Pradesh is in the process of introducing a reporting system. Karnataka has a periodical reporting system. Maharashtra and Rajasthan have a quarterly reporting system. The Tamil Nadu Government has introduced a quarterly information report for a few companies, which they would be extending to others. In Uttar Pradesh a comprehensive quarterly monitoring system is in vogue.

8.6.3 Kerala and Rajasthan are the two States who have replied that no reporting system ahs been instituted so far.

8.6.4 The considerable delay that frequently occurs in the finalisation of accounts, however, gives rise to serious doubts about the extent to which operational data are available and in fact are being used for performance review and control. In some States it was seen that the accounts of important companies had not been finalised for three to four years.

8.6.5 Information systems for the purpose of performance review and control has to be linked with predetermined targets. In most cases, as stated earlier such targets are absent. Every enterprise should be made to develop a perspective plan, even though it may not be quite sophisticated. This could be done on the basis of the initial feasibility report. The corporate plan should have a reasonable perspective for ensuring long term requirements and accountability. The general practice of setting annual targets without taking into account the long term needs would encourage a short-sighted approach. Target-setting should be done jointly by the Government and the management with Government ensuring that the goals have enough "stretch" in them.

8.6.6 The multiple objectives of public enterprises pose a problem in laying down targets. In public enterprises financial aspects have to be seen along with non financial indicators of performance. The non-financial indicators could be: capacity utilisation, productivity, cost reduction, materials management, introduction of better management methods and sound organisational development.

The use of social cost-benefit criteria should be encouraged, but these may be restricted to those projects which have marked externalities. The use of these criteria for all projects has not served a useful purpose. The information requirements for the use of this and other appraisal techniques such as the Discounted Cash Flow have to be built into the general information system.

8.6.7 The data requirements for the operation of a sound management information system are many. Dependence on mere accounts data would not be enough. The data needs of the different supervisory authorities not being the same it has also to be ensured that appropriate information goes to the different sources. Suitable training of staff and redesigning of information systems would be required to enable the enterprises and the Government to perform their responsibilities better. There is great urgency to have this done soon.

8.6.8 The mere introduction of a reporting system is by itself no guarantee of its proper use. The use to which much of the data obtained from the enterprises by the administrative department, finance department, etc., are put to for the purpose of performance evaluation is often uncertain. The administrative department and more particularly the finance department should be properly familiarized with the utilisation of such data.

8.6.9 An important link in the information system is provided by the government directors. In particular, the representative of the finance department and the administrative department have a key role to play here. Through them the formal and informal information systems could work better between the enterprises and the government. The representatives of these two departments should be particularly briefed in regard to the responsibilities to the Boards to which they are appointed and to the government. They should be well-prepared on all matters coming before the Board and obtain necessary guidance from government where ever necessary.

8.6.10 The onerous responsibility cast on the government representatives would necessitate a limitation on the number of director ships held by them. They would, particularly apply to the representative of the finance department. It is not uncommon to find the Secretary of the financed permanent himself on the Boards of as many as 15 to 20 enterprises. This is clearly an unsatisfactory arrangement and he cannot do justice to the work of either the company or Government. Some limitations has, therefore, to be placed on the number of directorships that a government officer can hold. In the Government of India the limit is three to four directorships. If the financial department has to be represented on the Boards of all public enterprises, it would be necessary to draw on more officials. Officers of the department at the joint Secretary and the Deputy Secretary level may also be nominated depending on the size and importance of the enterprise. Finance Department could also explore the possibility of nominating as its representative officers of other departments and organisations like the State Financial institutions who would, no doubt, be fully briefed before attending the Board meeting on government policies and requirements.

8.6.11 The government representatives on the Board if they are to play their role properly, any require familiarity with the working of the public enterprises. The Group has suggested in an earlier chapter that there should be some exposure of civil servants to public sector management in the early years of their service. They should be made aware of the use of the data for evaluation of performance in areas such as productivity, cost, finance, personnel etc. it would be a good idea if the government directors are required to submit their own reports on the important aspects of the functioning of the enterprises to Government after every Board meeting.

8.6.12 It will be appropriate to conclude this chapter by reminding supervisory authorities of the two requirements for satisfactory performance of their responsibility: supervisory authority has to control less in order to control better ;supervisory authority should ensure that operative management be more exposed to market discipline in the matte or funds, prices procurements, etc.

8.7 Recommendations

(1) Professional accounting and financial management expertise in finance departments should be considerably strengthened. As such expertise may not be available from the regular government cadres. It may be necessary to induct into the departmnet professional men at the senior level from outside the regular services.

(2) The State financial institutions may also be strengthened and used for appraisal of investment, preparation of feasibility reports etc., more than what is being done at present. The professional cadres of these institutions should be suitably built-up

(3) A Public Sector Investment Clearance Committee may be formed as discussed in para 8.3.3

(4) The responsibility of different supervisory agencies in regard to evaluation of performance in public enterprises should be more clearly defined with regard to the Board of Directors, adminsitrative department, finance department and Legislature by which are there main evaluating agencies.

(5) Suitably staff for costing and internal audit should be obtained by the State Governments. The enterprises which have stronger cadres in these areas should help the weaker enterprises.

(6) The Industrial Development and Finance Corporations have to develop their internal audit departments so as to provide this expertise as a management input to themselves and also to their clients.

(7) To overcome the acute shortage of qualified internal audit personnel in most of the States, it may be necessary in the short-term to form a pool of such resources for their optimum deployment among the different enterprises. This responsibility could be undertaken by the nodal agency.

(8) The long-term needs in the area of costing and internal audit should be assessed by the nodal agency and suitable steps taken to meet them with the assistance, if necessary, of the Central Bureau of Public Enterprises and other professional bodies.

(9) State Governments should make a determined effort to prepare their accounts and operational data in time.

(10) Enterprises should be asked to prepare long term plans and objectives which will serve a useful base for measuring performance.

(11) The information system should cater for a total performance and management audit which would require data on financial aspects as well as such important non-financial indicators as capacity utilisaiton, productivity, cost reduction, materials management, and organisational development.

(12) The information system for different supervisory agencies should be designed with reference to their respective responsibilities.

(13) The administrative department and finance department should be trained properly in the use of operational data for evaluation purposes.

(14) In view of the importance of the informal information system, steps should be taken to improve the participation of government directors from the administrative and finance department on the boards of public enterprises.

CHAPTER 9

SCOPE FOR ASSISTANCE FROM CENTRAL GOVERNMENT

9.1 The Government of India's experience of public sector management has been both long and varied. There are about 180 odd enterprises differing widely in size, technology and nature of business, location etc., under it.

Over the years, it has accumulated experience and built up institutions that it could usefully share with the States whenever they require such assistance. Such help could be best channelised through the Bureau of Public Enterprises (B.P.E.) of the Government of India.

9.2 The main areas in which the B.P.E. could respond to the request of the States are discussed below.

9.3 Assistance in Providing Senior Managerial Personnel

9.3.1 One of the major difficulties faced by the State enterprises in many States is in finding suitable senior personnel. Here, the B.P.E. could help in two ways. Firstly, the B.P.E., is the secretariat of the Public Enterprises Selection Board, which advises the Government of India on all top appointments in its enterprises. For this purpose, it has built up a Personnel Data Band of more than 4000 senior personnel drawing Rs.1,800 and more from the Central government enterprises, the government services and private sector. The facility of drawing on the Data Bank should be extended to the State enterprises.

9.3.2 Secondly, the B.P.E. could arrange for the deputation of managers of the Central government enterprises. The services of the senior managers of the Central government enterprises should be made available tot he State enterprises when needed, on deputation basis.

9.3.3 This type of help would be particularly necessary to the less developed states where the problem of finding suitable talent is acute. The B.P.E. should actively assist in finding suitable managerial resources for the North-eastern States where the dearth is more.

9.4 Management Development and Training

9.4.1 In the area of management development and training, the B.P.E. acts as a catalyst for improving practices and resources of the central government enterprises. While it may not be possible for the B.P.E. to extend such assistance in a large-scale, it could do so on a selective basis.

9.4.2 Training facilities are inadequate in a large number of States. The central government enterprises have good facilities. Most of the large manufacturing enterprises have training institutions for apprentices, supervisors and junior level managers. About twenty-six of the large enterprises have full-fledged management training institutions catering for middle and senior level managers. These institutions are spread over the country and location-wise also they are well-placed. There is good scope and need for making available these facilities to the State enterprises. The B.P.E.'s services could be enlisted for the purpose of identifying the training needs of the State enterprises, which could be met by these institutions. If necessary, these institutions of the central government enterprises should be expanded to cater for the State enterprises also.

9.4.3 Another facility that the bigger central government enterprises can provide is opportunities for on the job training. This could be made available in the technological disciplines for the engineering industries as well as in such areas as the accounts and audit departments, materials management and purchase procedures, materials management and purchase procedures etc. Here again, the B.P.E. should pay special head to the requirements of the North-Eastern region.

9.5 Setting-up of Nodal Organisaiton

9.5.1 The Standing Group has recommended the establishment of nodal organisations in the States to deal with their public enterprises. The advice and assistance of the central government's B.P.E. could be sought in setting-up such organizations.

9.6 Data Bank of Public Enterprises

9.6.1 The Bureau of Public Enterprises acts as a clearing house of information for the Central Government companies and their administrative Ministries. This role could be extended to the State governments and their enterprises also. New and even established enterprises often require assistance in matters such as drafting of Articles of Association and formulation of policies in areas which have marked external effects such as wages, industrial relations, service conditions, financing etc.

9.6.2 The Standing Group would recommend that the B.P.E. undertakes this responsibility for the State Governments and their enterprises. In particular, it should build information regarding the State enterprises. There is a real gap in this area. Information on the management practices of the State Government's enterprises and the Central Government's enterprises would be of common interest to all concerned. Particularly, information on innovative ideas and significant achievements of the public enterprises in the State should be collected by the B.P.E. for dissemination among the state and central governments and their enterprises.

9.7 Investment Appraisal

9.7.1 It may take some time for the States to have adequate facilities for evaluation of project proposals involving high technology and large investments. Though at present most of the States (barring a few like Gujarat, karnataka, Kerala, Maharashtra, Tamil Naud and West Bengal) do not have much capital and technology intensive industries, ere long they may be expected to venture into such investments. The B.P.E. has considerable experience of appraising such investments both from the technical and financial angles. Its Production, Construction and Finance Divisions provide advisory services to the Finance Ministry of the Government of India. This expertise could be made use of by these States which need it for investments of say Rs. 2 crores and more.

9.8 Other Advisory Services

9.8.1 The B.P.E. could extend its help in troubleshooting work and providing other advice. For this purpose, it could enlist the services of the Managers of the big central government enterprise who have direct operational experience, where necessary.

9.9 Promotion of Joint Ventures

9.9.1 Some of the big central government enterprises are collaborating with the State governments in setting-up joint industrial ventures. Such efforts make available capital and managerial and technical expertise to the States. The major examples are the collaboration efforts with the State governments of the central government enterprises such as the Indian Drugs and Pharmaceuticals and the Scooters (India) Ltd. There could be more scope for such collaboration. The B.P.E. could act as a catalyst in bringing together the central government enterprises and the States in such mutually beneficial ventures.

CHAPTER 10

SPECIAL PROBLEMS OF THE NORTH-EASTERN REGION

10.1 The Group visited the two States of Assam and Meghalaya and had detailed discussions with the Chief Secretaries, Secretaries to the Government dealing with public enterprise, the Chief Executives of the public enterprises and also the Secretary of the North-Eastern Council. The Chairman of the Group met the Governor of the North-Eastern Council to have the benefit of the Governor's deep knowledge and insight into the development needs of the region and the special problems facing the Government tin implementing programs for economic and social advancement. The Group also had the benefit of consultation with Shri M.L. Kampani, Additional Secretary in the Ministry of Home Affairs, Government of India and Shri D.K. Bhattacharya, Chief Secretary, Uttar Pradesh, both of whom had been deeply involved in the administration of the North-Eastern Region. The problems of management of public enterprises of this region differ very considerably from the rest of the country. It, therefore, deserves special consideration.

10.2 Natural Resources

10.2.1 The North-East India comprising of the States of Assan, Manipur, Meghalaya, Nagaland and Tripura and the Union Territories of Arunachal Pradesh and Mizoram has chain of hills and difficult terrain except for the plains of Assam and Tripura. The region has a high rainfall and the plains areas are visited by devasting floods almost as an annual feature.

10.2.2 The region is rich in f rest produce mainly timber, bamboo and cane. Plantation crops like rice, tea, coffee, jute and rubber are important. Coffee and rubber are new crops, which are being tried out mainly in Assam and Tripura. Silk is one of the traditional industries of the region. The region is fairly well endowed in energy resources. It has considerable untapped hydro-electric power potential. In addition, one of the most important natural resources of the region is oil and gas.

10.3 Problems of Development

10.3.1 Owning to the predominantly agricultural background of the region, the infrastructure of industrialization has not developed. The private sector had established oil, tea and timber industries. Some of the country's oldest units in these industries are located in the

State. As a result. The management expertise in sectors relating to oil, tea and timber is indeed well developed in the region as compared to other parts of the country. Unfortunately, however, this has not gone together with the development of local talent for management of these industries and the growth of adequate skilled labour. Most of the higher jobs in these traditional industries were manned by persons from outside the region.

10.3.2 Apart from the lack of industrial tradition and a managerial class the region is handicapped by difficult terrain except for the plains of Assam and Tripura. Communications within the region and with the rest of the country are mainly by rail, road and rivers. These get disrupted during the monsoons. Rail communications is as yet inadequate. Some of the constituent units of the region do not have any rail head within their own territory. Road communication is difficult due to hilly terrain and has not been fully developed to provide the necessary infrastructure for utilisation of local resources.

10.3.3 While the transport and communication problems within this region handicap utilisaiton of resources, there is the other problem of the need ot have long distribution pipelines for the produce of the region in order to serve the markets which are all in other parts of the country. Enterpreneurship and risk taking capabilities of the local population are not developed which has resulted in slow and hesitant growth of industries with in the region. Even though the region is well endowed with hydro-electric and oil and gas, these are yet to be fully developed and harnessed for the growth of local industries. Scare financial resources have been a major problem for stepping up investment in the public and private sector. Private capital has not been forthcoming and even the investments in the traditional industries have dwindled. The need for Government intervention has, therefore, become greater.

10.4 Growth of Public Enterprises

10.4.1 The growth of public enterprises of the region has been slow and inadequate. Till the beginning of the era of planned economic development, the region had no worth while industries other than oil, tea, timber and silk. With the intervention of the Government in planned economic development, various programmes were drawn up to build up the infrastructure industries like transport, power etc. As elsewhere in the country, the public sector started with utilities like electricity, road transportation and procurement and distribution of food grains. With the division of the region into Assam, nagaland, Meghalaya and Mizoram, the State Electricity Board and also the State Road Transport Corporation of the composite State of Assam were divided to form the first public sector units in the newly formed States. Manipur and Tripura, which were union Terriories a few years ago, have also formed their public sector enterprises for essential utilities like electricity and road transportation.

10.4.2 Private eneterpreneurship has not helped the region in industrialisation. In many cases, the primary objective has been to make quick profits and leave the units made sick thereby to be catered for the State Governments. As a result, the Governments have been saddled with many uneconomic units, started by private enterprise.

10.4.3 All the States have now entered other manufacturing and marketing industries. Production and marketing of handloom fabrics and handicrafts have gained importance for employment and well-being of a large number of people, particularly those belonging largest constituent unit, has 29 public enterprises in existence at present. The States have attempted to industrialise the region by encouraging industrial and marketing co-operatives. Such co-operatives are almost fully backed by Government which contribute about 90 per cent of the capital. The weakness of the co-operative movement has made these ventures heavily dependant on Government financial and managerial support. The State Governments had encouraged the private sector to set-up units with Government financial and other assistance. Many of these did not grow due to poor management and become sick quite early. They had to be taken over by the State Government.

10.5 Development Measures taken by Government

10.5.1 The State Governments have taken various measures to overcome the obstacles in the area of faster economic development of the region. Special attention has been given to train persons from the region in business management. The Government of Assam have introduced courses in Tea Technology, Petroleum Technology, etc in its universities; a Regional Forest Training Institute has also been established at Barnihat for training personnel for exploitation of forest resources. The North-Eastern Council has set-up a Committee in May, 1976 to go into the entire matter of formulating a suitable strategy for meeting the training needs both for Government personnel and for entrepreneurial and managerial development. This committee had considered the question of training facilities for business management and the advisability of setting up of management training difficulties in getting the requisite qualified faculty would be considerable and as such, it may be preferable to extend necessary help to the Gauhati University which was contemplating to start a two-year post-graduate course in business management. There is also a proposal to set-up the Administrative Staff College at Gauhati which would cater for all the States and Union Territories of the region as it may not be viable to have separate institutions. The Small Industry Extension Training Institute of the Government of India has decided to set-up a branch at Gauhati. This institute could play a useful role in developing entrepreneurship and middle managerial cadres.

10.5.2 The paucity of financial resources should be made good by greater intervention by the banking system and financial institutions. Non-availability of credit facilities has hampered the growth of industries. The nationalised banks of the region may be asked to adopt a "development approach" towards banking in the region. The step taken by the Industrial Development Bank of India to set-up a consultancy agency in the region is a welcome move.

10.5.3 Marketing is another critical area. There is hardly any marketing organisation worth the name in the region either in the agricultural sector or in the industrial sector. Poor marketing facilities could weaken industrial and commercial enterprises from the very inception. Realising the importance of the marketing, the North-Eastern Council has set-up a North-Eastern Region Handloom and Handicrafts Development Corporation. It is also considering setting up an Agricultural Marketing Corporation, Special care has to be devoted to the development of marketing facilities and expertise for the promotion and healthy growth of public enterprises in the region.

10.5.4 In the context of the special conditions prevailing in the region, the Standing Group would make the following recommmendations:

10.6 Recommendations

(1) The region will benefit by adopting a co-ordinate and common approach towards the development of public enterprises. This is particularly necessary in the area of power development, transportation, finance, taxation and industrial policy in general so that there is no unnecessary duplication of efforts

by setting up similar units in more than one constituent unit if it would be better to concentrate on one enterprise with larger capacity.

(2) In keeping with the above policy, it may be worthwhile examining the scope for having a single nodal agency for public enterprises of the region with suitable representation from the constituent units. This nodal organsiation should play an active role in identifying suitable projects for the region based on local raw materials and resources. The organisaiton should build up a shelf of such project profiles. In this exercise, it should seek the assistance of the Industrial Development Corporation, financing institutions, Central Government agencies like the Bureau of Public Enterprises, Directorate General of Technical Development, the central public enterprises etc.

(3) The development of infrastructure should receive special attention so that individual public enterprise units are not over-burdened with problems of power, transport, land etc, and can thus, concentrate their efforts on the quick implementation of projects and other operational activities.

(4) The assistance of the BPE of the Government of India should be sought and made available for preparation of feasibility reports and more importantly in exploring the possibilities of Central Government enterprises taking up joint ventures in the region which would provide technical, managerial and financial inputs from outside.

(5) The BPE should also assists the governments of the region and their enterprises in locating suitable managerial talent for senior, critical positions. It may be that due to locational disadvantages senior talent may not be easily available. To over-come such difficulties, the BPE should arrange for deputation of senior managerial personnel from the

central government enterprises and other state government enterprises to the enterprises of the region, wherever required for periods of two to three years.

(6) The efforts being taken by the State Governments of the region in developing managerial skills could be usefully supplemented byh other organsiations. The In-house staff colleges of the central government enterprises should provide their facilities for the training of apprentices, middle and senior managerial personnel. There are more than 25 such full-fledged training institutes of the central government enterprises. In addition, organisations like the Indian Institute of Public Administration, the Institutes of Management etc, should adopt a positive role in developing managerial resources of the region.

(7) The nodal organisation(s) of the region concerned with public enterprises should immediately prepares a Manpower Plan. The services of the Institute of Applied Manpower Research, New Delhi may be enlisted for this purpose, if necessary. In particular, the Plan should identify training needs in critical areas such as costing, finance, accountancy and marketing. The nodal organisation(s) should co-ordinate in the identification of training facilities and organise suitable training programmes.

(8) The Department of Personnel and Administrative Reforms of the Govt. of India may consider the special requirements of the North-Eastern region for training of civil servants with 10 to 20 years of seniority and also technical personnel of the state Governments for manning the public enterprises of the region. In the recruitment to the all-India services for the region, the special requirements of the public enterprises should be taken into account.

BIBILOGRAPHY

A review of public enterprises in Kerala, Thiruvanthapuram, Govt. Press, 1998.

Akbar Ali Khan, *Financial Management of SRTCs in India,* New Delhi, Anmol Publications, 1990.

Andhra Pradesh Public Enterprises, "Andhra Pradesh public enterprises Report on performance 1997-98".

Andhra Pradesh Public Enterprises, "Andhra Pradesh Public Enterprises Report on Performance 1998-99".

Andhra Pradesh State Public Enterprises: Performance 1988-89, Hyderabad, Department of Public Enterprises, 1989.

Andhra Pradesh State Public Enterprises: Performance 1991-92, Hyderabad, Department of Public Enterprises, 1992.

Andhra Pradesh State Public Enterprises: Performance during 1985-86, Hyderabad, PENB, 1986.

Central Institute of Road Transport, "Review of the Performance of State Transport Undertakings", 1982-83, Pune.

Central Institute of Road Transport, "State Transport Undertakings in India; a study of performance, problems and prospects", Pune, 1985.

Central Institute of Road Transport, *Proceedings of the Workshop on Capital Financing in State Transport Undertakings*, Pune, 1982.

Devendra Babu, M., "State level public sector reforms - status and case studies", *Journal of IPE,* 23(1 &2), 2000.

El-Namaki, Mss., "Restructuring of state-owned enterprises: cross country analysis is and conceptual frame", *Journal of IPE*, 22(3&4), July-Sept; Oct-Dec. 1999.

Gandhar, R.V. and Yadagiri, M., "Disinvestment in Andhra Pradesh", *Journal of Public Enterprise*, 25(1), Jan-June, 2002.

Karnataka, Bureau of Public Enterprises, "Public enterprises survey 1998-99".

Maharashtra, "Performance of state public enterprises 1996-97", Mumbai, Government Press, 1998.

Mishra, R.K. and Navin, B., *Restructuring state level public enterprises*, Anmol Publications, New Delhi, 2003.

Mishra, R.K. and Navin, B., *Restructuring public enterprises in India - Privatisation and Disinvestment*, New Delhi, Mittal Publications, 2002.

Mishra, R.K. and Navin, B., *Restructuring state level public enterprises*, Anmol Publications, New Delhi, 2002.

Mishra, R.K., "Memorandum of Understanding for Central and SLPEs", Hyderabad, *IPE*, 2003.

Mishra, R.K., "Safety net National Renewable fund: and SLPES in India a case study of Hyderabad Allwyn Ltd.", *International Journal of Public Enterprise*, Dec 1998.

Murty, S.S. (Ed.), *Investment and Financing in State Transport Undertakings*, (Seminar Papers). Hyderabad, Osmania University Press.

Nandagopal, R. and Vudali, Mohan, V. K., "Internal Audit in SLPEs of Andhra Pradesh", Hyderabad, 1991.

Performance of state public enterprises - 1994-95. Mumbai, Government Press, 1996.

Performance of state public enterprises - 1995-96. Mumbai, Government Press, 1998.

Rajasthan, Bureau of Public Enterprises, "Public enterprises profile 1997-98". State enterprises department. Jaipur, BPE, 1999.

Rao, K.L.K (Ed.). *State, Public Enterprises and the Market place*, Ljubljana, 1988.

Report, "Financial contribution requirement ofSLPEs in India 1993", Hyderabad, *IPE*, 1993.

Roy, R.C., *State Public Enterprise in India*. New Delhi, Uppal Publishing House, 1985.

Ruet, Joel, "Entreprisation of the state electricity boards", *Journal of Public Enterprise*, 25(1&2),Jan-June 2002.

Sankar, T.L, Mishra, R K and Nandagopal, R., "Role and relevance of state level public enterprises in the 1990".

Sankar, T.L., Nandagopal, R. and Mishra,R.K., *Management of state level public enterprises in India*. Jaipur, Printwell, 1992.

Saygili S. and Taymaze, E., "Privatisation ownership and technical efficiency: A study of the Turkish cement industry", *Journal of Public Enterprise*, 25(1&2) Jan-June 2002.

Sharma, Atul, "Public Enterprise reforms in India: Restructuring and Privatisation", *Journal of Public Enterprise*, 25(1&2).

Sujatha Rao, T., "Annotated Bibliography on Public Enterprise in India, Hyderabad", *IPE*, 1994.

Weltenhhall, R., "On the centrality of state level enterprises in the Austration enterprise experience, *Journal of IPE*, 23(1 &2), Jan-Mar; April-June 2000 : 9-10.

INDEX

❑❑❑